FROM THE ORDNANCE SURVEY MAP OF ENFIELD, 1920

A section of the 1920 Ordnance Survey Map showing Bush Hill Park and part of Enfield as it was in 1919. Our cottage, on Stuart Low's Royal Nurseries, at the junction of Main Avenue and Lincoln Road, is indicated by an arrow. From where we lived, it would have been possible, if sometimes trespassing, to walk through the orchards opposite us, cross over Southbury Road, and wend one's way through brickfields, farms, nurseries and orchards for many miles before coming to a built-up area. Most of that shown on the map was developed by 1959. The Cambridge Arterial Road, to become the A 10, cut the Nurseries in two in 1920. Our cottage and the Nurseries were demolished in 1959.

Sid's Family Robinson

Sid Robinson

Sid's Family Robinson

The Story of an Early Twentieth Century
Enfield Working-Class Boy

Written and compiled in his eighty second
year by the man who had been
the boy

"OUR LOT"

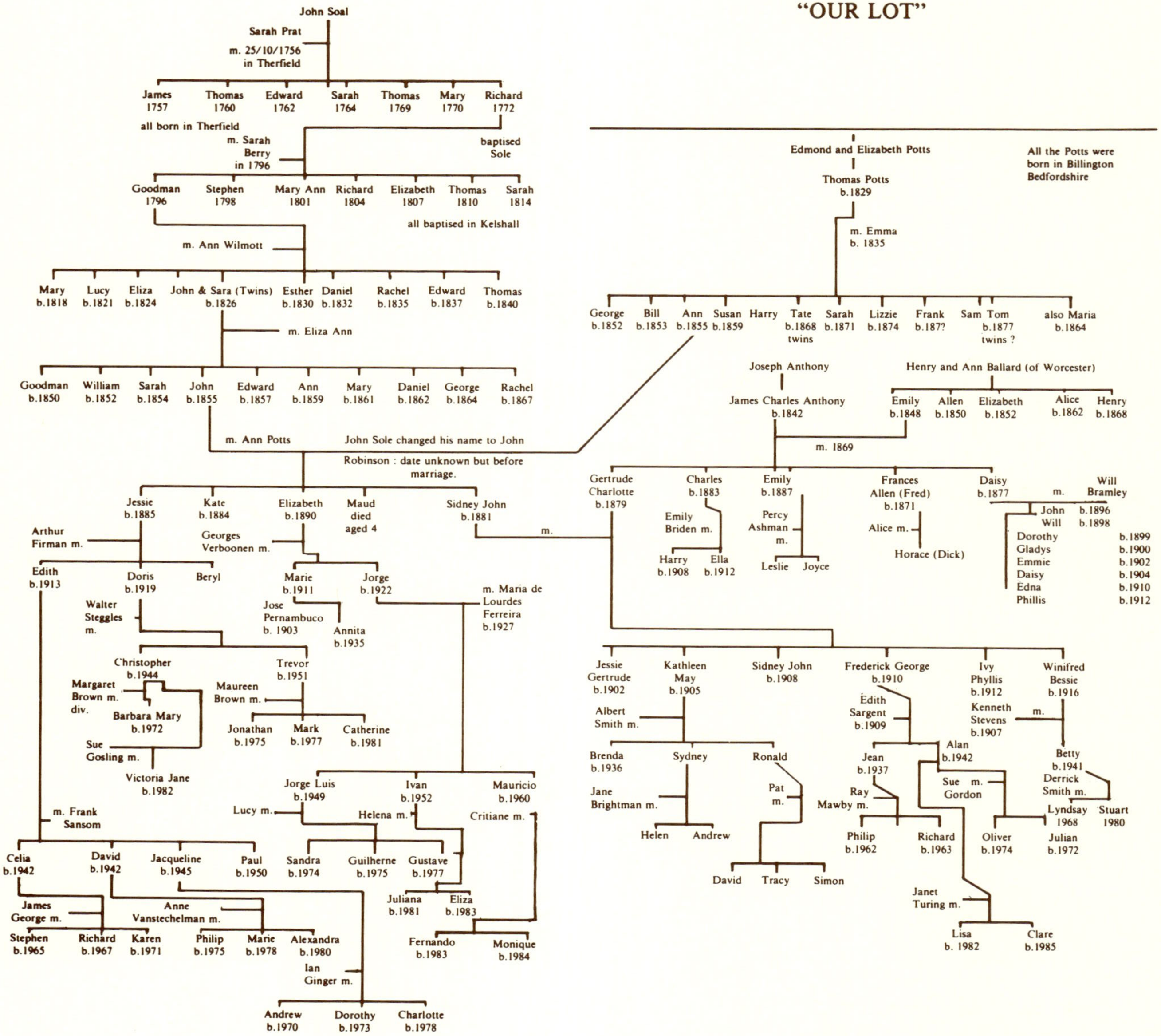

John Soal
Sarah Prat
m. 25/10/1756
in Therfield

James 1757
Thomas 1760
Edward 1762
Sarah 1764
Thomas 1769
Mary 1770
Richard 1772

all born in Therfield

baptised Sole

m. Sarah Berry in 1796

Goodman 1796
Stephen 1798
Mary Ann 1801
Richard 1804
Elizabeth 1807
Thomas 1810
Sarah 1814

all baptised in Kelshall

m. Ann Wilmott

Mary b.1818
Lucy b.1821
Eliza b.1824
John & Sara (Twins) b.1826
Esther b.1830
Daniel b.1832
Rachel b.1835
Edward b.1837
Thomas b.1840

m. Eliza Ann

Goodman b.1850
William b.1852
Sarah b.1854
John b.1855
Edward b.1857
Ann b.1859
Mary b.1861
Daniel b.1862
George b.1864
Rachel b.1867

m. Ann Potts

John Sole changed his name to John Robinson : date unknown but before marriage.

Jessie b.1885
Kate b.1884
Elizabeth b.1890
Maud died aged 4
Sidney John b.1881

Arthur Firman m.
Georges Verboonen m.

Edith b.1913
Doris b.1919
Beryl
Marie b.1911
Jorge b.1922

m. Maria de Lourdes Ferreira b.1927

Walter Steggles m.
Jose Pernambuco b. 1903
Annita b.1935

Christopher b.1944
Trevor b.1951

Margaret Brown m. div.
Barbara Mary b.1972
Sue Gosling m.
Victoria Jane b.1982

Maureen Brown m.
Jonathan b.1975
Mark b.1977
Catherine b.1981

Jorge Luis b.1949
Ivan b.1952
Mauricio b.1960

Lucy m.
Helena m.
Critiane m.

Sandra b.1974
Guilherne b.1975
Gustave b.1977
Juliana b.1981
Eliza b.1983
Fernando b.1983
Monique b.1984

m. Frank Sansom

Celia b.1942
David b.1942
Jacqueline b.1945
Paul b.1950

James George m.
Stephen b.1965
Richard b.1967
Karen b.1971

Anne Vanstechelman m.
Philip b.1975
Marie b.1978
Alexandra b.1980

Ian Ginger m.
Andrew b.1970
Dorothy b.1973
Charlotte b.1978

Edmond and Elizabeth Potts

All the Potts were born in Billington Bedfordshire

Thomas Potts b.1829

m. Emma b. 1835

George b.1852
Bill b.1853
Ann b.1855
Susan b.1859
Harry
Tate b.1868 twins
Sarah b.1871
Lizzie b.1874
Frank b.187?
Sam
Tom b.1877 twins ?
also Maria b.1864

Joseph Anthony

James Charles Anthony b.1842

Henry and Ann Ballard (of Worcester)

Emily b.1848
Allen b.1850
Elizabeth b.1852
Alice b.1862
Henry b.1868

m. 1869

Gertrude Charlotte b.1879
Charles b.1883
Emily b.1887
Frances Allen (Fred) b.1871
Daisy b.1877

m.

Emily Briden m.
Harry b.1908
Ella b.1912

Percy Ashman m.
Leslie
Joyce

Alice m.
Horace (Dick)

m. Will Bramley
John b.1896
Will b.1898
Dorothy b.1899
Gladys b.1900
Emmie b.1902
Daisy b.1904
Edna b.1910
Phillis b.1912

Jessie Gertrude b.1902
Kathleen May b.1905
Sidney John b.1908
Frederick George b.1910
Ivy Phyllis b.1912
Winifred Bessie b.1916

Albert Smith m.
Brenda b.1936
Sydney
Ronald

Jane Brightman m.
Helen
Andrew

Pat m.
David
Tracy
Simon

Edith Sargent b.1909
Jean b.1937
Alan b.1942

Ray Mawby m.
Philip b.1962
Richard b.1963

Sue m. Gordon
Oliver b.1974

Janet Turing m.
Lisa b. 1982
Clare b.1985

Kenneth Stevens b.1907
m.
Betty b.1941
Derrick Smith m.
Lyndsay 1968
Stuart 1980
Julian b.1972

The boy

Sidney John Robinson

born 1908 in Enfield, Middlesex

one of six children of

Sidney John Robinson
a nursery gardener

born 1881 in Kensington, London
one of five children of

John Robinson formerly Sole
a bricklayer

born 1855 in Kelshall, Herts
one of ten children of

John Sole
a labourer

born 1826 in Kelshall, Herts
one of ten children of

Goodman Sole
a labourer

born 1796 in Kelshall, Herts
one of seven children of

Richard Sole
a labourer

born 1772 in Therfield, Herts
one of seven children of

John Soal (Sole?)

married in Therfield in 1756

ISBN 0 9048 0470 4

Printed in Great Britain
by Middlesex Polytechnic
Bound by Petam Bookbinders in Enfield
Designed by Joe Harounoff

Second Impression
(with some additional illustrations)

CONTENTS

ACKNOWLEDGEMENTS

I owe a debt of gratitude to Valerie Carter, Irene Smith and Denis Amos for kindly reading the early manuscript, commenting on it, and encouraging me. Also to David Pam and Anne Bradford for their support, and to Anne as well for her suggestions, one of which was for the title.

My thanks are extended to Graham Dalling, the local history officer, for reading my story, and for the interest he showed in it. He has been of great help, making available to me information and photographs I could not have found elsewhere.

I am particularly indebted to Olive Sellick, without whose continued encouragement my enthusiasm may have waned and my energy flagged as I, at my age with the lack of experience and facilities, endeavoured to convert what I had written, and the many illustrations with the captions for them, into a form acceptable to a printer, then to find such a printer who would produce the book as I had envisaged it at a price I could afford. She was instrumental, indirectly, for putting me in touch with a printer, after Elizabeth Gilbert (Liz), to whom I am grateful, had typed the final text.

Olive is a retired Enfield school teacher with whom I became acquainted through my friendship with her husband Harry Sellick, a retired Enfield headmaster and a fellow book-collector. Olive and I when young lived in the same area. I often played in that part of our park adjacent to the backyards of the row of houses of Cecil Avenue in one of which Olive resided, and I frequently passed her front door when I took a short cut across the park from our cottage in Lincoln Road, to the Town. In those days however it was most unlikely that we would have spoken, because I was a very ordinary boy with a Cockney accent from a large working class family, whilst Olive was the only child of Charles Watts, a well-known Enfield headmaster and secretary to the National Union of Teachers. As his daughter, she would meet socially the very same teachers with whom I stood in so much awe as a reluctant schoolboy.

Acknowledgement is made for the kind permission granted me to reproduce illustrations or other matter from the publications of the British Journal of Photography, the Daily Telegraph, the Enfield Gazette and Observer, The London Photographic Library, the National Museum of Photography, the Express Newspapers and the Fleetway Publications.

Finally I wish to record my appreciation of the friendly and patient manner the Middlesex Polytechnic has dealt with me during the lengthy setting up of the book with so many varied types of illustrations, some faded and tatty.

AUTHOR'S FOREWORD

The idea of writing something about my forebears and about myself had never occurred to me until, in my very advanced years, I began to feel regret when seeing so much family memorabilia of times long past scattered haphazardly throughout the house, and realising that it eventually would be lost without trace unless I did something with it.

Most of this memorabilia had survived not by design but by accident, having been tucked away in my eldest sister's untidy bedroom, probably forgotten by her and unbeknown to the rest of the family. It surfaced when she died at the age of seventy six. Amongst it were birth and marriage certificates, letters and many photographs, some of the latter of me as a boy, scrounged from various photographers when I had been able to squeeze myself into pictures they were taking, for I had an obsession with being photographed from an early age. I usually managed to pester the photographer to give me a reject print or suchlike.

There were also surviving many of our old school reports, somewhat the worse for wear due to bad storage; mine showing signs of boyish interference in my amateurish attempts to disguise their accurate identity or to "improve" them.

As I began to write this account my interest increased and I was then sorry that I had not asked more from Dad whilst he was still alive, because his memory was still excellent when he died at the age of eighty one. He told me that part of my boyhood had been affected adversely by the War, otherwise it had differed little from his, because the changes taking place in the outside world had by-passed large working class families like ours.

Until I was about seven years of age the cost of living had remained more or less stable since Dad was a boy, and our money was still that used by generations before us. Our pound was a gold coin, called a sovereign, which could be exchanged for twenty silver shillings; each of which in turn could be exchanged for twelve copper pennies. But to children, the most important and most used copper coin was the farthing — four to a penny — the smallest coin in circulation, roughly equal nominally to one tenth of today's penny, the smallest coin in use now. We could buy things for a farthing; and when at the Council School I had mastered the art of multiplying arithmetically I worked out that if I had a sovereign I could exchange it for nine hundred and sixty little farthings, sufficient to enable me to buy some sweets each day for nearly three years. Of course this was beyond my wildest dreams — I had rarely seen a sovereign — let alone possessed one. It must have been worth at least twenty pounds of today's money in spending power.

Looking back, one realises now how little was known of other boys' lives except for the time we spent together in the Council School classroom and playground, and in the streets on weekdays after school. We rarely talked of our families, or of what we did in our homes or at weekends when we were out of sight of each other. Judging however from the little I did know, I feel I am on reasonably safe ground by saying that if I had been as many other boys seemed to have been, I would not be able to write more than a few pages about my boyhood unless it was to describe the conditions of life already well documented by other contemporary autobiographers, because life for most working class boys in our area was so mundane that nothing happened to leave a lasting impression on the memory.

That I am able to recount so much which has left strong impressions is not necessarily to my credit — in fact it could be to the contrary — depending on how and by whom it is viewed. When I started school I must have slowly learned that it was more convenient to be selectively secretive, so, as a result, no one individual knew everything about me. But what I have written in this book is mostly personal; how I lived, felt, thought, acted and reacted in the circumstances in which I found myself.

Whilst this was being written I was fortunate enough to be able to visit my old Council School — a strange experience after seventy years — and also to have access to some surviving old Records, thus enabling me to be more precise and factual in some respects.

This book makes no claim to literary merit, for it has been written as I would have related it orally. I have refrained from reproducing the careless, ungrammatical and rather lewd way we sometimes had of talking, except where recall is reasonably exact and its exclusion would cause loss of effect.

It is difficult to believe that a life is mapped out before it is lived, yet I have to admit that because I was as I was as a boy, it seems I was setting myself on a course, unpredictably and perhaps undeservedly, which was to lead to an exciting, interesting and rewarding life denied to most working class men of my generation.

Firstly,

a glimpse of those who came before me

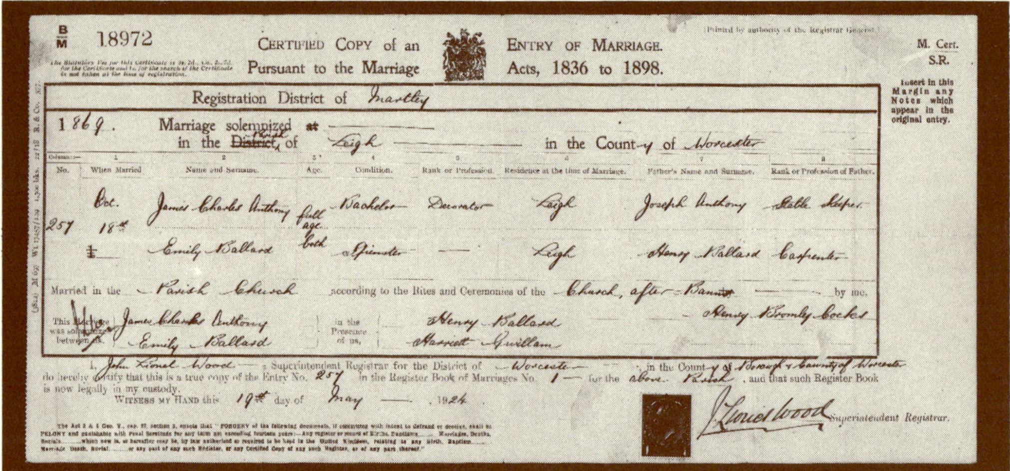

B/M 18972

CERTIFIED COPY of an ENTRY OF MARRIAGE.
Pursuant to the Marriage Acts, 1836 to 1898.

M. Cert. S.R.

Insert in this Margin any Notes which appear in the original entry.

Registration District of Martley

1869. Marriage solemnized in the Parish of Leigh in the County of Worcester

No.	When Married	Name and Surname.	Age.	Condition.	Rank or Profession.	Residence at the time of Marriage.	Father's Name and Surname.	Rank or Profession of Father.
257	Oct. 18th	James Charles Anthony	full age	Bachelor	Decorator	Leigh	Joseph Anthony	Stable Keeper
		Emily Ballard	both	Spinster	—	Leigh	Henry Ballard	Carpenter

Married in the Parish Church according to the Rites and Ceremonies of the Church, after Banns by me, Henry Bromly Cocks

This Marriage was solemnized between us, James Charles Anthony, Emily Ballard — in the Presence of us, Henry Ballard, Harriett Guillam

I, John Lionel Wood, Superintendent Registrar for the District of Worcester in the County of Borough & County of Worcester do hereby certify that this is a true copy of the Entry No. 257 in the Register Book of Marriages No. 1 for the above Parish, and that such Register Book is now legally in my custody.

WITNESS MY HAND this 19th day of May, 1924.

J. Lionel Wood Superintendent Registrar.

The Marriage Certificate of Mum's parents, James Charles Anthony and Emily Ballard, of Worcester, in 1869.

Our grandparents moved about a lot, and grandpa used the assumed name of Wiseman at one time, to escape responsibility for a surety he had given for a rogue who had absconded. Mum's eldest sister has the father's name Wiseman on her birth certificate. They settled in Bush Hill Park in 1891, living at 46 Fourth Avenue, where Grandad is listed as a Bootmaker, but this must have been his son Fred, who was still at home. They remained there until 1903-4, when they had a newsagents at 4, South Street, Ponders End until 1905, then they moved to Hundon. Some time later they went to 126 Northgates, Bury St. Edmunds, as caretakers at an old school, and provided billets for the soldiers in the First World War.

They returned to B.H.P., living in Cross Road until grandad died in 1926, when Grannie lived with Mum's sister Aunt Daisy until she died in 1928. Both grandparents reached the age of eighty.

St. Mark's Sunday School,
BUSH HILL PARK, ENFIELD.

3RD PRIZE.

Awarded to
G. Anthony.

CLERGY,
Charles F. Peploe

Christmas, 1894.

Mum, aged 16, in 1895

Mum, Gertrude Charlotte Anthony, was born in Liverpool in 1879, one of five children to Emily Anthony nee Ballard and James Charles Anthony.

Cousins John and Will Bramley, sons of Mum's sister Daisy, in 1899 at Downs Road, Enfield. Both boys volunteered for the Army in the First World War. John was still alive in 1989, aged ninety three.

Aunt Daisy and six of her children John, Will, Dorothy, Gladys, Emmie, Daisy, in 1912 at Downs Road

(Page 24)

1881. BIRTHS in the District of Kensington Town, in the County of Middlesex.

No.	When and where born.	Name, if any.	Sex	Name and Surname of Father.	Name and Maiden Name of Mother.	Rank or Profession of Father.	Signature, Description, and Residence of Informant.	When Registered.	Signature of Registrar.	Baptismal Name if added after Registration of Birth
147	Thirtieth January 1881 37 Wheatstone Road	Sidney John	Boy	John Robinson	Annie Robinson formerly Potts	Bricklayer	A. Robinson Mother 37 Wheatstone Road	First March 1881	C R Burnes Registrar	

I CERTIFY that the above is a true Copy of an Entry in the Register Book of Births in the Registrar's District of Kensington Town in the Superintendent Registrar's District of Kensington, in the County of Middlesex; AND I FURTHER CERTIFY, that the said Register Book is now lawfully in my custody.

WITNESS my hand, this First day March 1881.

Book No. 149

C R Burnes REGISTRAR.

By the 14 & 15 Vict., c. 99, sect. 14, a Copy of any Book which is of such a Public nature as to be admissible in evidence on its mere production from the proper custody, is made admissible in evidence in any Court of Justice provided it purport to be Signed and Certified as a True Copy by the Officer to whose custody the Original is intrusted.

Sidney John Robinson, our Dad, His birth certificate.

Dad in 1884

Grandad John Robinson with Dad, Sidney John Robinson, in 1883.

Dad in his class at the Carlton Road Board School, near Havistock Hill Station, Kentish Town, in 1887. Dad is 5th from left in second row from top.

Kensworth School
Aug 13 1894

I certify that Sydney Robinson passed the 6th Standard in 3 subjects at the Annual Examination by H. M. Inspector in July 1893

Signed
Fred. Dicking
Head Master

Dad's school certificate. It would seem that this was issued belatedly, in August 1894, possibly at Dad's request, as it refers to examinations passed the previous year. Dad was 13 and half yrs. old when he was then leaving Kensworth with his parents for Bush Hill Park, Enfield.

CERTIFICATE OF BIRTH.

Pursuant to the Acts Anno Sexto et Septimo Gulielmi IV. Regis, Cap. LXXXVI., et Anno Primo Victoriæ Reginæ, Cap XXII.

18*85* BIRTH in the District of KENTISH TOWN in the County of Middlesex.

No.	When & Where Born.	Name, if any.	Sex.	Name and Surname of Father.	Name and Maiden Surname of Mother.	Rank or Profession of Father.	Signature, Description, and Residence of Informant.	When Registered	Signature of Registrar.	Baptismal Name if added after Registration of Birth.
494	*Third October 1885 Cottage Builder's Yard Carlton Road*	*Jessie*	*Girl*	*John Robinson*	*Annie Robinson formerly Potts*	*Cook*	*A Robinson Mother Cottage Builder's Yard Carlton Road Pancras*	*Tenth November 1885*	*G.L. Harris Deputy Registrar*	

I HEREBY CERTIFY the above to be a TRUE COPY of the BIRTH REGISTER, and I further Certify that the said REGISTER BOOK is legally in my custody.

Witness my hand this *10th* day of *November* 188*5* *G.L. Harris Dy.* Registrar.

By the Statute 6 and 7 Will. IV., c. 86, s. 35, it is enacted "That every Registrar, who shall have the keeping for the time being of any Register Book of Births or Deaths, shall at all reasonable times allow searches to be made of any Register Book in his keeping, and shall give a Copy Certified under his Hand of any Entry of the same, on payment of the Fee hereinafter mentioned; (that is to say,) for every search extending over a period of not more than One Year the sum of One Shilling, and Sixpence additional for every additional Year, and the sum of Two Shillings and Sixpence for every single Certificate," in addition to stamp duty 1d.

Aunt Jessie, Dad's second sister, was born in 1885 in the cottage of the builders at 143 Carlton Rd. Kentish Town, where Grandpa was employed as a bricklayer and cook to Walls Bros. Aunt Jess, and her sister Kate, 18 months older, used the yard as a playground, until the family moved to Kensworth in 1891.

Grandad Robinson with Dad's sister Jessie (recovering from measles) aged three in 1888.

Grandad John Robinson with Grandma Anne Robinson (nee Potts), Dad aged ten, his sister Kate aged six, and baby Lizzie, in 1890.

Great Grandad Thomas Potts, a blacksmith, and Grandma Emma, both born in Billington, Bedfordshire in 1829.

Leighton Buzzard Wesleyan Methodist Circuit

George William Potts son of Thomas and Emma of Billington baptised 2nd December 1852 aged 3 months.

Ann Potts daughter of Thomas and Emma of Billington baptised 11th July 1855. born 29th April 1855.

Billington Church of England Baptisms – children of Thomas and Emma Potts, Billington, blacksmith.

1859 Apr 22	Susan.
1864 May 1	Maria.
1868 Dec 25	Katy Jane.
1868 Dec 25	Harry.
1874 Aug 9	Lizzy.
1877 Apr 29	Samuel.
1877 Apr 29	Thomas.

1871 Census Billington

Great Billington

						Where born
Thomas.	Potts	Head	married	42	Blacksmith	Billington, Beds.
Emma	Potts	wife	married	36		Billington, Beds.
William	Potts	son	unmarried	18	Blacksmith	Billington, Beds.
Ann	Potts	dau		15	Scholar	Billington, Beds.
Susan	Potts	dau		12	Scholar	Billington, Beds.
Maria	Potts	dau	unmarried	7	Scholar	Billington, Beds.
Kate	Potts	dau	unmarried	4	Scholar	Billington, Beds.
Harry	Potts	son		2		Billington, Beds.
Sarah	Potts	son		1month		Billington, Beds.

Billington Baptisms

1829 5 Apr Thomas son of Edmund and Elizabeth Potts, blacksmith. ← OUR GREAT GREAT GRANDPARENTS

Grandma Anne Robinson nee Potts born in Billington in 1855.

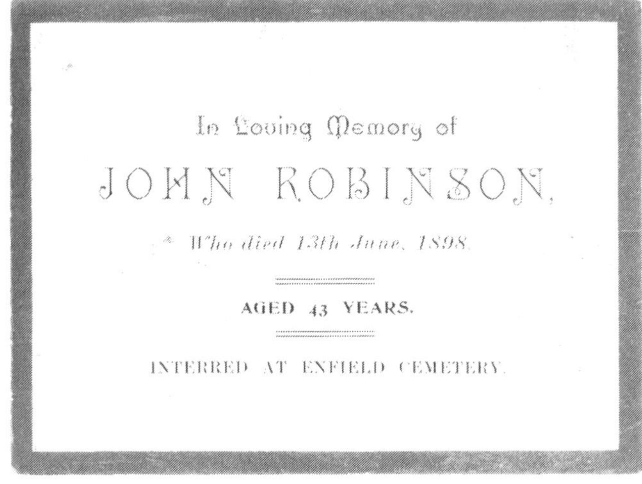

In Loving Memory of

JOHN ROBINSON,

Who died 13th June, 1898.

AGED 43 YEARS.

INTERRED AT ENFIELD CEMETERY.

A Parade of the (Tottenham Det.) of the 1st Vol Btn. The Duke of Cambridge Own, Middx. Regt. Occasion believed to be the Opening of Institution by the Duchess of Argyll, 1899. Dad, sixth from left, front row.

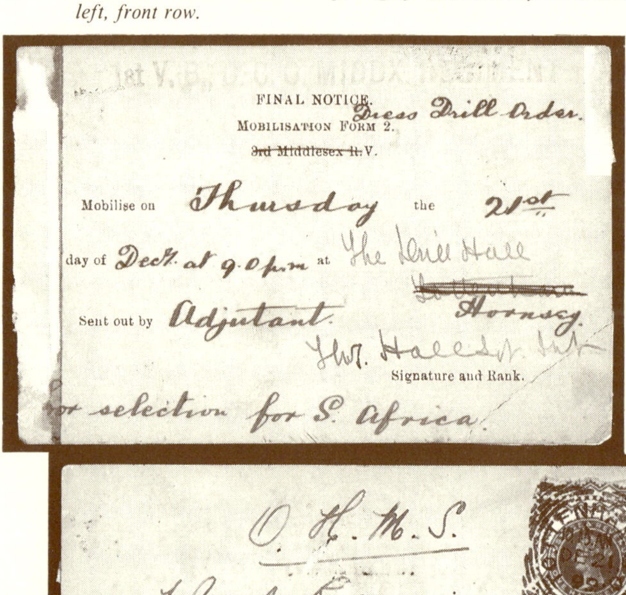

1st V.B., D.C.O. MIDDX. REGIMENT

FINAL NOTICE. Dress Drill Order.

MOBILISATION FORM 2.

~~3rd Middlesex R.V.~~

Mobilise on Thursday the 21st

day of Decr. at 9.0 p.m at The Drill Hall ~~[illegible]~~ Hornsey.

Sent out by Adjutant.

[illegible]

Signature and Rank.

for selection for S. Africa

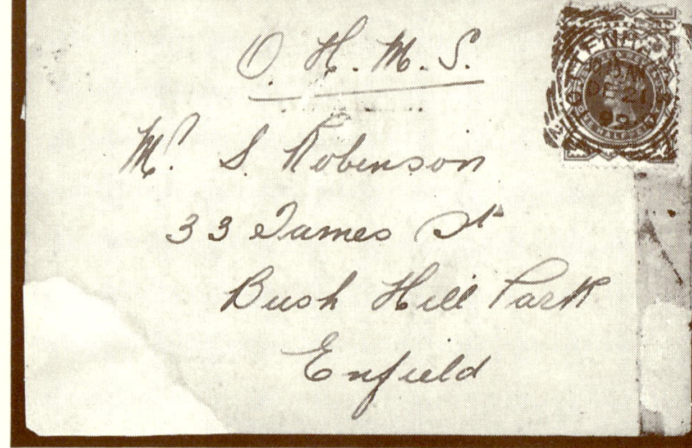

O.H.M.S.

Mr. S. Robinson

33 James St

Bush Hill Park

Enfield

Dad and Mum, Sidney Robinson and Gertrude Anthony, in their courting days, 1901. Photograph taken by Miltom Meyers, Enfield.

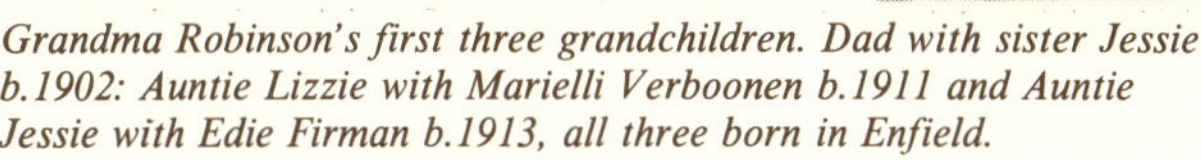

Grandma Robinson's first three grandchildren. Dad with sister Jessie b.1902: Auntie Lizzie with Marielli Verboonen b.1911 and Auntie Jessie with Edie Firman b.1913, all three born in Enfield.

Grandma Anthony and Grandad, Uncle Percy, Aunt Em (Mum's sister), and cousin Leslie 1910

Great Grandma Potts, Grandma Robinson, Dad and our sister Jessie 1903.

The staff and work people at Low's Nurseries Bush Hill Park circa 1900. Dad is last on right in the top row.

Dad with two mates. In the rear is one of the several stoke-holds, with its chimney. Stokers were employed to keep the coal-fired boilers going for the hot-houses, and in the winter to prevent frost in the greenhouses.

Note
During the first twenty years or so of the twentieth century it was rare for a man or boy to be seen out of doors without a hat or cap on his head. Schoolboys in my day wore caps as an essential item of clothing, and during class time kept them under their desks to put on at playtime.

Stuart H. Low has pleasure in asking
you to join him at an
Inaugural Supper of the New Firm of
Stuart Low & Co.
at the Institute, St. Mark's Rd.,
Bush Hill Park, at 8 p.m.,
Tuesday, June 29th, 1909.

Please show this card on entering the Hall.

Dad in Low's Royal Nurseries, c.1902. He is watering the potted plants with a large can which he filled by dipping it into a large tank set into the ground in each greenhouse. In the summer Dad sometimes would spend from 6.30 AM to 5.30 PM doing this. I can recall clearly the strong smell of his wet corduroy breeches as I helped to pull off his high leather boots in the evenings when he came in from the Nursery when I was quite small in Seventh Avenue. I liked to feel useful to Dad. In the Nursery Dad became a specialist in growing, amongst others, cold house plants such as the aspidistra, of which Lows sold thousands. Every self-respecting married couple had one in a fancy pot on a bamboo table in front of the window in the parlour; with the lace curtains so draped that it could be seen by passers-by.

Dad, 3rd. from left, top row,
at Low's, circa 1902.

All the Robinsons gathered together at 17, Poynter Road, Bush Hill Park, in 1905. Dad and Mum, sister Jessie, aged three, Kit the baby, Aunts Kate, Lizzie and Jessie. Grannie Robinson with her foster child, and Will Purdon, Aunt Kate's fianceé, with his sister.

Our Mum

Dad and Mum with baby sister Jessie in 1902. Dad was twenty one - Mum was twenty three. There does not seem to be any sign of poverty apparent in this photograph, which was taken in the Millais Studios, The Market Place, opposite Board School, Bush Hill Park.

CHAPTER 1

If Dad's father had not changed his name sometime before his marriage in the eighteen seventies, Dad would have been called Sid Sole, not Sid Robinson, and so would I, because Grandad was born John Sole, in Kelshall, Hertfordshire in 1855, one of ten children of John and Eliza Sole. He married Anne Potts, one of twelve children of Thomas and Emma Potts of Billington, then in Hertfordshire. Anne had been in the domestic service of the Vicar of Billington before her marriage.

Dad was born in Kentish Town, London in 1881, and attended the Carlton Road Board School in Haverstock Hill whilst his father, a bricklayer, was working for Walls Brothers, Builders, who took part in the construction of the Epping Reservoir. In 1884 the family moved to the cottage belonging to Walls Brothers in Carlton Road, where Dad, and later his younger sisters, used the yard as a playground.

When our Great Grandfather Potts became a tenant farmer in Gaddesden Row, having given up his blacksmith's shop in Billington, Grandad Robinson moved with his family to take over as landlord of the "Sugar Loaf" Inn in Kelshall, Dad continuing his education at the Church of England National School. In 1894 the family came to live in Bush Hill Park, firstly at Fotheringham Road, then at James Street, when Dad had to start work, much to the sorrow of his father who wanted his son to go to a Grammar School, but could not be allowed to do so for lack of money.

Two of Dad's sisters, Kate and Jessie, attended the Church of England School in Cecil Road, Grandad having to pay a penny every week for each of them to do so. Their education finished after they had completed the required number of attendances, at the age of twelve; both girls then leaving to go into domestic service. Dad, sixteen, carried Jessie's belongings in a trunk on his shoulder to her employer's house in Wellington Road where she was going to live-in. Aunty Jessie told her daughter, our cousin Doris, in later life, that as soon as she had unpacked her belongings, she had to do the family weekly wash; then cook a chicken for her employer's dinner.

When Dad was seventeen, his father on his way home from work with Walls Brothers had a heart attack after leaving Bush Hill Park Station, and was carried home to James Street on a barrow, but he died on the way.

Six months later Dad's youngest sister, Lizzie, was sent by Grannie to Dad's place of work, the Gibbons Jam Manufactory opposite Enfield Town Station, with a postcard which had arrived in the morning after Dad had left for work. On it Dad was instructed to parade that evening for selection to go to the Boer War, for he was a very keen part-time soldier. Dad did parade and was selected, but had to claim exemption because he was the sole wage earner, sister Lizzie still attending the Church of England School in Fourth Avenue.

Grannie Robinson had started to take in washing to supplement Dad's poor wages, for he was still only entitled to those for juveniles, but eventually she was persuaded to move from James Street to a more roomy house in Poynter Road where she could take in lodgers.

Dad, for health reasons, left Gibbons and obtained work in the greenhouses at Stuart Low's Nurseries in Lincoln Road, only a few hundred yards from Poynter Road where he lived with his mother and his youngest sister Lizzie. One of the lodgers was Tim Phillips, a foreman at the Nurseries, who was to become a great friend of Dad and Grannie for many years. The other lodger was George Verboonen, a Belgian, who was training in orchids at the Nurseries. At the lodgings he met young Lizzie, a very pretty girl, who, unlike her two older sisters, had stayed at home after leaving school to help Grannie. George Verboonen married Lizzie in 1910 at the Congregational Church in Main Avenue; the second pair to be married at the new Church, and they received a souvenir bible from the Minister. Years later the couple were to go to Brazil where Uncle George had inherited an Orchid Farm from his step-father. Uncle sent out natives into the Amazon jungle to search for orchids and their seeds, for propagation.

Sister Jessie Gertrude was born in 1902

Sister Kathleen May was born in 1905

Photograph taken in 1908

Book, No. 96 **Certificate of Birth.**

190 8. BIRTH in the Sub-District of ENFIELD, in the District of EDMONTON, in the County of MIDDLE

No.	When and where Born.	Name (if any).	Sex.	Name and Surname of Father.	Name and Maiden Surname of Mother.	Rank or Profession of Father.	Signature, Description, and Residence of Informant.	When Registered.
373	Twentysecond September 1908 16 Landseer Road Enfield U.D.	Sydney John	Boy	Sydney John Robinson	Gertrude Charlotte Robinson formerly Anthony	Gardener not (Domestic)	G. C. Robinson Mother 16 Landseer Road Enfield	Thirtieth October 1908

I, William James Matthews, Registrar of Births and Deaths for the Sub-District of Enfield, in the County of Middlesex do hereby Certify that Entry No. 373 in the Register Book of Births, for the said Sub-District, and that such Register Book is now legally in my custody.

Witness my Hand, this 30th day of October 190 8.

An Edwardian baby born into a Victorian environment, and whose enthusiasm for being photographed seemed to have started at a very early age.

After me came brother Frederick George in 1910 then sister Ivy Phyllis in 1912 and finally sister Winifred Bessie in 1916

Whilst Dad had lived in James Street he had frequently seen three young ladies as they talked and laughed on the way to and fro between their home in Fourth Avenue and the Embroidery Factory where they worked. They were three sisters, daughters of James Anthony and Emily nee Ballard, and shared a small house with their parents and their brother Fred, who used the premises as a boot repairers. Their father, who was to be our Grandad Anthony, was called a "Decorator" on his marriage certificate, but he had been a stable boy employed by his future wife's stable-keeper father, and they had eloped. Of the three girls, Daisy was the first to marry — her betrothed being a designer at the Embroidery Factory. She was to have eight children, but a very unfaithful husband. Dad became friendly with one of the other two girls, Gertrude, and began to walk out with her. Dad was courting Mum.

In those days it was understood that a young couple thinking of marrying would save a few pounds for the great occasion and in order to be able to set up home in one of the small terraced houses available for rent near the place of work. The savings were essential as there was no hire purchase nor easy credit in those times. Goods were bought for cash. In any case, it would have been considered most improvident to borrow money. The bride-to-be would leave her place of employment on the eve of her wedding, for it was to be her task to look after the home and care for the man of the house. Children would usually turn up promptly because there was no birth control.

But Mum and Dad must have been unable to save much money, for Mum became pregnant, making a hurried wedding at a Registry Office necessary. She was twenty three years of age and had been earning only low wages on piecework at the Enfield Embroidery Factory. Dad had only just turned twenty one, when he had become eligible for the first time for adult man's wages. Moreover, he had been supporting his widowed mother and younger sister.

Yet the surviving photographs of little family groups taken in the years of the marriage, and the one taken of sisters Jessie and Kitty in the year that I was born, do not reveal any signs of poverty.

My earliest memories before I started school are ones of a cosy home in Seventh Avenue. I can recall sitting on a goat skin rug, alongside Fred, in front of a lovely warm kitchen range fire, with potatoes baking in the oven, whilst Mum sat in Dad's chair, breast-feeding young baby Ivy. I can recall being tucked up in bed, by Mum, clad in grey flannelette combinations buttoned up below the knees, and hearing sister Jessie, aged ten, playing simple melodies on the piano in the front room downstairs — this on a warm summer evening when I was put to bed at seven — the sun still shining through the bedroom window.

A pleasant memory is the sound of the muffin man's bell as he came down the road on a winter's afternoon on Sundays, and how I would beg Dad to give me a penny to run after the man and buy some muffins for tea, toasted on a fork held in front of the fire. On Monday mornings, after the others had gone off to school I would be given my farthing to spend. One Monday, Mum wrapped up carefully in newspaper a small silver coin, a threepenny piece we knew as a "joey", and told me to go across the road to Mrs. Vidal's sweetshop — there to buy myself one farthing's worth of sweets of my choice and to be sure to being back two penny coins in the change, because she had absent-mindedly given the man all her small change when he had delivered the week's supply of coal, and she had left herself without pennies for the gas light meter. I loved going to Vidal's. I got a thrill as I pushed open the door and heard the bell go "clang".

I cannot remember much of those early days before I started school, but memories of some happenings seemed to confirm my suspicions that I was trouble-prone quite early on. A letter has survived which older sister Jessie wrote to Mum and Dad when she was nine and staying with Uncle George and Auntie Lizzie in Low's Orchid Nursery at Crowborough. In the letter Jessie expresses the hope that I had not broken any of her toys, nor had killed any more pichons (pigeons). I recall being spanked for doing something serious to Dad's birds in the garden. This incident I mentioned to Dad when he was old, and asked him what sort of small boy I had been. He said that normally I was a quiet boy, but sometimes unpredictably very disobedient and naughty.

18.8.11 Orchid cottage 18.8.11

Dear Mother and dad
I am having a nice time in the country the little girls next door come in the garden and play with me. There are still some flowers in the garden and I fill Aunty vases with sweet peas And help her

pick the beans and potatoes It is not so hot here As in Bush Hill It is just Right. I am getting a red face I hope sidney his not breaking my toys. And has not killed any more pichons I hope little Fredy is quite well again. give my love to Kitty and

granny Aunty lizzie and uncle George are quite well and send There love to all Love and kisses to you from your loving daughter Jessie

Dad's sister Jess married Arthur Firman at St. Marks Church Bush Hill Park with Aunt Kate in attendance and sisters Jess and Kit as bridesmaids. At this wedding I disgraced myself by running out of the church.
Aunt Jess was a competent, industrious housewife and mother; and her daughters, Edie, Doris and Beryl were a credit to her. Auntie gave Grannie Robinson, and her sister our Aunt Kate her home when they both needed it, Uncle Arthur was a prisoner of war in Germany for four years so she must have had a trying time, pinching and scraping in wartime conditions.

Regarding the pigeons, I had had strict instructions not to interfere in any way with the pigeon cote housing Dad's fantail birds. In the event I had opened it and got inside. A cat had followed me in and I was responsible for the loss of two which the cat caught.

He reminded me, though I did not need reminding because I recalled the incident well, that I had made them ashamed of me at the wedding ceremony of Aunt Jessie and Uncle Arthur at St. Mark's Church. I must have been about four years old at the time. Just at the moment when Auntie was being asked by the Vicar if she would accept Uncle to be her lawful-wedded husband, I had slipped off my seat and run up the aisle out of the Church shouting "I can hear a band". I had a passion for following the Salvation Army, the Boys Brigade or any other musical group in the street.

There was some delay in getting me back into the Church, because Mum first had to pass over to Dad baby Ivy she was holding. Dad was in difficulty with young Fred who was trying to struggle off his lap to join me. I was unrepentant and sulky. Mum and Dad blamed themselves, for, knowing how I was, they should not have put me at the end of the row, but jammed me in between them. Normally it was Jessie's task to keep her eye on me, but that day she was bridesmaid with sister Kitty.

Dad said that several times I had nearly done myself serious injury. One was when Mum was turning out the drawers of a chest on the landing upstairs, and I was being a nuisance. There was a knock at the door, and, as Mum went down to answer it , she told me to keep away from the chest. As soon as she had gone, I could not resist trying to climb up on to the top of it by using the bottom open drawers as steps. The chest toppled over, the full top drawers fell out and I was underneath the lot.

On another morning after Mum had made a basin full of custard, which she thought she had put out of my reach on top of the dresser, I stood on tiptoes and pulled its scalding hot contents on to me, leaving a permanent scar.

Eldest sister Jessie, in later life, told me I had deserved the many spankings I had been given as a small boy.

One day standing in the front porch with Mum, I heard her say to Mrs. Toop next door that she had a couple of "handfuls" and that she would be glad when Sid was off to school. I suppose the other "handful" was young brother Fred. She didn't know that baby Ivy was going to grow likewise.

Little did I know that from the time I had reached my fourth birthday until I was five, Mum had made several requests to the Head Teacher for me to be allowed to start at her Infants' School. Mum was so honest and straightforward that I am wondering if she confessed to the Head Teacher that I was the "handful" she told Mrs. Toop I was, without realising what an unfortunate introduction it might have been to those about to assume complete and undisputed charge of me for several hours each day. It would have been tantamount to a request to cure me of being a "handful".

With brother Fred 1913

Form 12 M. I.

Enfield Education Committee.

School......Bush Hill Pk......

Date of Inspection......19.......11.......13.

Name......Sidney Robinson......

Age......5 2/12......

Weight......2 Stone 9½ lbs

PARENTS' ATTENTION IS DIRECTED TO:

A. ......To breathe......

B. ......through his......

C. ......nose......

D. ......

N.B.—This card should be preserved and shown at the next medical inspection.

Cousin Ella Anthony, a typical Infant School girl of the period.

This photograph shows how thousands of boys from working class homes attended the Infants' School (I among them). The outfit, say before 1915, would have cost roughly:- Vest 2/6d., Shirt 2/3d., Jersey 3/-, Braces 7d., Knickers, Knicker-bockers or breeches 2/8d., Stockings 9d., Garters 2d., Boots with nailed soles 4/-. Total cost 15/11d. (80 pence in today's money)

CHAPTER 2

From an early age I must have been aware of a place called school, for I was born in Landseer Road, only a hundred yards or so from the boys' school playground, and when we moved to our terraced house in Seventh Avenue we were only yards along the pavement from the Infants' School. I could hear the noise of the children at playtime as I messed about in our backyard.

When adults were conversing I always listened, probably having had nothing better to do. One evening I heard Mum say to Dad "He's ready for school — it'll do him good". I knew that they must be talking about me.

I had learned to be wary when hearing people say that something would do me good. Mum always said it when she told me to open my mouth properly to take the teaspoonful of castor oil on Saturday evenings before I was put to bed. Our Aunt Em, visiting us one afternoon, on hearing of something I had done said "He wants a good smacking — it'll do him good". Sister Kitty, normally friendly to me, was upset one day, and shouted at me "You're going to school soon and they'll know how to deal with boys like you and it will do you good". Kitty was eight.

Hitherto school seemed an eternity away, but after hearing both Mum and Kitty I began to believe it was threatening. One morning shortly afterwards, whilst Mum was standing at the front door talking to Mrs. MacKintosh, a lady who always wore a man's cloth cap, I heard the children out in the school playground, so very slowly I sidled out of the front garden and trotted along the pavement to peer through the playground railings. I think what I must have seen through those railings made me tell Mum that I didn't want to go to school after all. But she said all boys had to go — it was the Law.

The morning came when I was got up early, was washed, scrubbed, brushed down and inspected, ordered to be a good boy and then taken down the road through the playground to be handed over to a frightening looking woman in black.

I cannot recall a great deal about my time in the Infants' School, but I do remember not being happy there in spite of being able to learn quickly. I had plenty of spit for my slate, but had difficulty in getting my pencil to write. I complained that it only squeaked, and that my hands were cold. After some time, I cannot recall how long, it seemed that my comportment or behaviour failed to give satisfaction. I was often told to sit up straight and put my hands behind my back like the other children. I was told to stop fidgeting and talking, and scolded frequently for wanting to be excused to go to the W.C. when other children could wait. Attention was called to my mouth which, teacher said, I should not keep open all day long in class. She did not know that my Medical Inspection Card called attention for me to breathe through my nose. Our Aunt Em, always free with her advice on bringing up children, told Mum one day "You want to do something about that boy walking about with his mouth open — he looks daft".

One day in class, probably daydreaming as was my wont, I heard teacher say something quite near me. I looked up and saw a black shelf over which peeped the tip of a nose and some hair. The shelf was teacher's tightly corsetted bosom. Not understanding what she had said, I probably looked puzzled. She then told me to pull myself together. I remained puzzled, because I thought I was all together, otherwise my Mum would have told me. She then called me "Robinson", telling me I was a nuisance. This really upset me, for my name was Sid or Jack, and I had not heard her call any other child by his or her 'other name'. I sulked. Whether it was teacher's attitude which made me become untruthful or if it came naturally to me, I do not know (though I suspect the latter), but when teacher found out, I was one of several boys who often were made to stand up at our desks to receive raps of her ruler on the palms of our hands, the ruler being kept only for that purpose.

During my Infants schooldays, my happiest time was from Friday afternoon until Sunday evening, starting with running out of the playground at the close of classes with a sense of relief

IF THERE IS ANY INFECTIOUS DISEASE IN YOUR HOME YOU CANNOT BE ADMITTED.

THE THROAT HOSPITAL,
GOLDEN SQUARE, W.
(FOR DISEASES OF THE THROAT, NOSE AND EAR.)
Founded by Sir Morell Mackenzie
1863.

26/9 1914

Your Physician, Dr. Sargent
having ordered your admittance as an In-patient of
Hospital, you are requested to present yourself here
Tues day, the 29th inst., at 1-30

If you are unable to come, you are requested to i
me immediately.

A copy of Rules for In-patients is herewith ann

W. HOL
Sec

J. Robinson

1914

de ar dad
when are
you coming
home glad
you are
better

we do miss you
I have to
school
all the week
love from
Siddy
xxxx

A little letter I wrote to Dad when he was in the Throat Hospital. My school teachers didn't think very highly of me, but in my opinion my writing is quite acceptable for a little boy aged just six years.

An Infants' Class at the Bush Hill Park, Seventh Avenue, Council School, in a classroom with desk seats for sixty pupils. Our eldest sister Jessie is seated on the extreme left in the third row from the bottom. I wonder where the slate pencils are?

that there were two whole days before I had to return to that hated place. I looked forward to having my halfpenny next morning to buy my Saturday Comic paper; sitting on a box when the weather was dry outside in the backyard in Seventh Avenue reading it. If the sun was warm enough for me to feel it through my thick jersey and knickerbockers, I would whistle with contentment. The weekends in those early days were a joy, but on Sunday evenings a shadow would come over me as I went to bed thinking of the morrow.

A letter has survived I sent Dad when he was in Golden Square Hospital and I was not quite six. The only piece of news I was able to give him was that I had been to school all the week. Dad would have been amused to read this, for if I was telling the truth he would have known it was only because I had been dragged there by eldest sister and pushed into the playground. Looking at this letter, I am pleasantly surprised how good the writing is for a boy who was always in trouble and who so much hated school.

I had not properly reconciled myself with school by the time my sixth birthday arrived, for on that morning I refused to go. In desperation Jessie took me round to Fourth Avenue to buy me a cheap golliwog as a bribe. Then, telling me Mum would look after it until dinner time, she pushed me through the school gates with instructions to go across to the Infants' playground. She watched until I had done so, for she did not trust me. She knew I was capable of turning about and running home, for which I would have been punished at school.

My reputation was not improved by an incident which occurred some time later, on a very cold day. It was at the end of afternoon classes and we were all gathered in the corridor for prayers, and a hymn, before being allowed in an orderly manner to collect our coats and caps from the cloakroom and make our way home. I was in the back row, well hidden from the head mistress and the teachers, warming myself cosily by leaning against one of the hot radiators — these were still on but shortly to be cut off due to fuel shortage in the Great War.

My mate, Roy Beagles, felt it was his turn so he nudged me with his knee in an attempt to get me away from the radiator. I pushed him and, to my horror, he slid helplessly away from me, for he had freshly studded boots and the wooden floor had recently been highly polished. He banged into several children in front causing cries and rumpus.

There was brief questioning and I was seized and taken out front to stand between the head teacher's desk and the piano. I could not believe what had happened to me — one minute I was quietly minding my own business — the next, standing awaiting my fate in front of the rest of the school. This kind of impetuous behaviour was to get me into plenty of trouble later.

After the hymn had been sung the children went to the cloakroom, then vacated the place, leaving me alone with the teacher who, whilst closing the lid on the piano, looked down at me and said quite pleasantly "You'll get the stick and it'll serve you right".

I then became sullen, which did not help my cause when the head teacher returned. She told me to go home, which I promptly did but told nobody about what had happened. There seemed no point, because when I had complained to Mum that the teacher had started to hit me hard with her ruler, she replied that I should learn to be a good boy.

Next day, in the classroom, Roy and I were called out front. I could not hear what went on, but he obviously was reprimanded by the head teacher. She spoke to teacher then to me. Exactly what she said I cannot recall but it was something like 'You are a naughty boy, children could have been hurt. Your teacher tells me you are bothersome — put your hand out'. She caned me on both hands.

It all happened so quickly that I found myself sitting back at my desk, with my hands squeezed in my armpits, before properly realising what had taken place. It was the first time I had been caned, and after the initial severe pain had abated I felt quite cocky, for all that remained of the caning was a strange tingling sensation on my palms. I had been given the stick and had not cried! Subsequent experiences, however, were to make me realise that my first caning could not have been intended to hurt very much.

No. 33. Vol. 1. PRICE ONE PENNY. September 26, 1914.

THE JOLLY ADVENTURES OF THE BRUIN BOYS—THEY HAVE A MOST EXCITING TRIP!

1. Bobby Bruin and Tiger Tim had saved up their pocket-money, and bought a pair of roller-skates each, and they were having such a fine time. And didn't the other boys wish they had roller-skates, too!

2. But after a while Tim and Bobby hit on a splendid idea. "Fetch some planks, Jumbo," said Tim, "and we'll all be able to skate together. I'll show you." And when they brought the planks, Tim and Bobby tied the skates to them.

3. "Now get some tape, one of you, and we'll be all right," said Tim. And they tied Jumbo's, Willie Ostrich's, Georgie Giraffe's, and the other boys' feet to those planks with the tape. "Now, then, off we go!" cried Joey.

4. And off they went in fine style. Left—right!—left—right! "My word! we are moving!" cried Joey. And so they were, too. But, unluckily, they were moving towards the river. "Look out! Back pedal!" cried Tiger Tim. And they all cried "Stop! We shall be in the water in a second!" Whiz! on they went! "Can't you pull up, you chaps?" cried Georgie Giraffe. But on they went, and although they all tried to pull up, it was no good. "I can see trouble ahead!" cried Jumbo. "So can we!" cried the other boys.

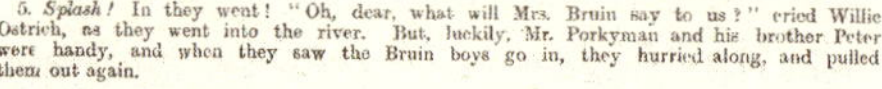

5. *Splash!* In they went! "Oh, dear, what will Mrs. Bruin say to us?" cried Willie Ostrich, as they went into the river. But, luckily, Mr. Porkyman and his brother Peter were handy, and when they saw the Bruin boys go in, they hurried along, and pulled them out again.

6. And in this way they took our Bruin boys back to school again. "Good gracious!" cried Mrs. Bruin, "whatever have you boys been doing now? Run along upstairs at once, and change your clothes! Dear me! did anyone ever have to deal with such boys!"

I had fallen in love with Comics at an early age, but I had to be satisfied with the "The Butterfly" or the "Funny Wonder" which cost one halfpenny. I had my eyes on "The Rainbow" with coloured pictures which always lay so temptingly on the newsagents' counter. During the week of my birthday, the 22nd, September 1914 I managed to get a penny to buy it. From then on I was allowed it sometimes until the Great War started to affect us, when I had to buy only a halfpenny comic.

Although my hatred of school loomed very large in my early boyhood, it did not spoil everything for me. I can recall the pleasure from our limited playthings: our fun with chalk on the pavements, my spinning top, my metal hoop and skimmer, my cigarette cards scrounged from passers-by, and my marbles. I can recall the delicious taste of a teaspoonful of condensed milk sneaked from the tin when Mum's back was turned; the windfall apples, a pennyworth, from Porter's Lodge, shared between four of us, and the anticipatory walk home from the market at closing time on a Saturday evening when Dad had managed to get for a few pence a haddock large enough to share between the seven of us for tea. I can remember the heavenly taste of strawberry jam smeared thinly on bread, something which was to disappear from our table for more than five years. And my scamper across the road to Vidal's sweetshop to spend my Monday farthing on broken toffee, carefully wrapped up in a newspaper cone by the little white bearded shopkeeper — the only sweets until the following Saturday.

Enfield Market Place showing the stall from which Dad bought his cheap haddock just before closing time on a Saturday night, if he could afford it. If we were lucky Dad could get a haddock large enough to share between the eight of us for tea, at a cost of 1/- (5p.). The small boy walking behind the man in the trilby is just my size when the photograph was taken in 1913 - but I wonder what had happened to his cap - boys, like the girls on the right didn't go outdoors without headgear in those days.

Enfield Education Committee.

School Bush Hill Park

Date of Inspection 11-12-14

Name Robinson Sydney

Age 6 1/2

Weight 3st 4lb

PARENTS' ATTENTION IS DIRECTED TO:

A. Slight head

B. infestation

C.

D.

N.B.—This card should be preserved and shown at the next medical inspection.

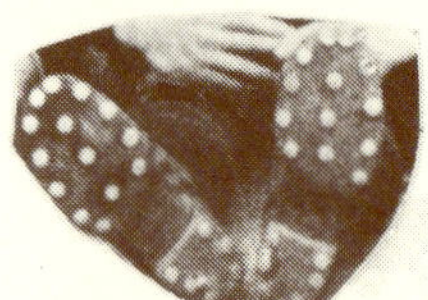

How Dad hoped he would find our boots -

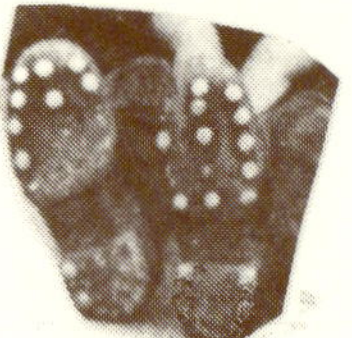

but this is how he often did.

REDUCE YOUR BOOT BILLS ONE HALF BY BLAKEY USING
BLAKEY'S BOOT PROTECTORS
INSIST UPON "BLAKEY'S"

Aged six.

A rare rear view of a Working Class Boy showing the braces, the shaped waist line of the knickerbockers, and the strap and buckle to take in surplus waist. Even in the summer it was rare for a boy to remove his jacket in public.

CHAPTER 3

Dad's wages were about thirty four shillings (£1.70) per week, and on these he had to support himself, Mum and us five children. But because the cost of living was so low before the War, he always managed to dress us smartly on Sundays, so essential in those days of keeping up appearances. Surviving photographs taken of boys in our Council School before say 1916 show most of them smartly dressed and a credit to their working class parents. It was the war that ruined everything for us all. I can remember with pleasure feeling very spruce in my then conventional dark blue knickerbocker suit with long black stockings, highly polished laceup boots and an Eton collar.

For school wear I got a gratifying sense of security in the tough boots Dad bought us. The hobnailed ones costing 3/6 (17p) were fine for the Nursery, greenhouses, backyard, street and school playground, but I had to learn to tread warily on the highly polished floors of the corridor and classroom. It was easier to walk in the boots which had metal heel plates and "Blakeys" hammered in by Dad.

I did not know if I was unusual, but I liked the clatter I made when running along the pavements, especially in the almost unlit streets in the War, and on the many foggy days we experienced in our low lying North London area. Everybody heard me coming. All houses, factories and offices belched forth filthy smoke in those days. Fred and I loved to make sparks by striking the metal heel plates and sole studs of our boots against the kerb. Young Fred excelled at this; he was always better at things practical, but sometimes he paid for this excellence when Dad came to inspect our boots each Saturday dinner time. It was usually I that got the bigger walloping, being the older boy, but on these occasions it could be Fred that did.

When new boots were purchased, the whole family entered the shop to examine the wares. The boots were tried on, laced up and Dad would say in his authoritarian R.S.M. voice "Now tell us where they 'urt yer". I learned to be non-committal because the thick chunks of hard leather were always uncomfortable until broken in. At any rate, the word "comfort" we did not know the meaning of. Ivy became such a tomboy that often at Saturday lunch times Dad would tell her that the next lot of boots bought for her would be exactly like ours. I thought her boots, high up on her calf, were quite strong. It was not rare for girls to be seen in boys' boots. And with these boys' boots how we could slide along the pavements! In frosty weather they were like ice skates and we seemed to have more really wintry periods in those days — also much more wind and rain. The boots were put on immediately upon rising in the morning and kept on until the last moment before going to bed. We had no other footwear, slippers being unknown to us. On Sundays, even if we weren't going anywhere, we wore our boots at all times.

Small boys wore dresses until hygienically ready for trousers, when usually they were first put into short knickers and then finally into knickerbockers or breeches. I was breeched early for reasons made clear to me later. Dad was very keen on corduroy, a cloth favoured by agricultural workers and their boys for its hard wearing quality. There was a very special shop in Edmonton called Fred Wades patronised by Dad, and the trip thereto involved a walk by the family from Bush Hill Park on Saturday afternoon. I can recall clearly walking home along the High Road carrying my brown paper parcel with my first pair of breeches, and then being stood on a kitchen chair whilst Mum and Dad hoisted me into them. They were thick, stiff and smelly. As Mum fastened the last buttons of them below my knees, Dad stood back admiringly saying "There's a smart little soldier". Feeling a thrill in the knowledge that Mum and Dad should be pleased with me, I ran upstairs to look at myself in the mirror in Mum's wardrobe.

Whilst walking, these breeches emitted a whistle as the corduroy rubbed between my legs, and they creaked when sitting down or getting up. They were uncomfortable at first. In those days braces were used to keep up all male nether garments, these being made of thick elasticised webbing over an inch wide and fitted with six stiff leather tabs with slots in them to fasten to

'observing the skill he had in winding on his puttees.'

In the Golden Days.

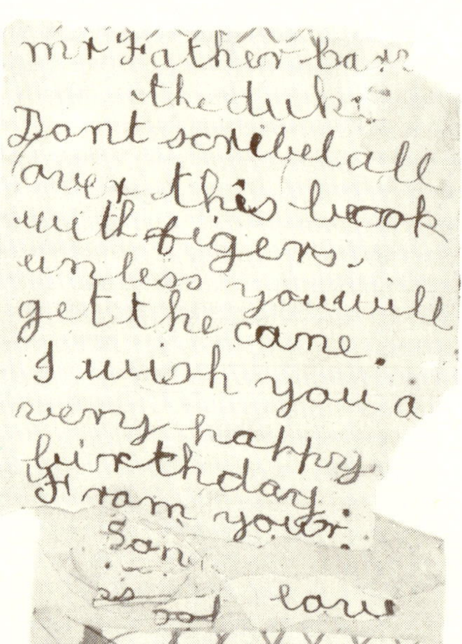

mi Father ba[illegible]
the duke:
Dont scribel all
over this book
with figers.
unless youwill
get the cane.
I wish you a
very happy
birthday
From your
Son
love
X X X X X

My efforts at greetings to Dad on his birthday - I was seven years and four months old. We couldn't afford birthday cards.

'Most of the things in the shops were not for the likes of us.'

buttons on the waistband, the latter being higher at the back of the garment than at the front. If underpants were worn, the tabs were passed through tape loops before they were fastened to the buttons. There were no self-supporting garments in those days, but at the back of the breeches were fitted a strap and buckle to enable any surplus waist to be taken up.

It was the practice amongst working class folk, for economic reasons, to buy clothes at least one size too big for their children because they were intended to be used until completely worn out, or no longer fitted, when they could be passed down to the younger children in the family. Therefore, my first breeches were bought a bit long, requiring them to be considerably braced up, cutting me in the crotch and putting a restriction on my shoulders. After a while I became used to them, finding to my surprise that they gave me a pleasant sense of security when playing in the Nursery, garden, street and especially in the hard-surfaced playground. I certainly felt less cold when sitting on the hard wooden form in the classroom, and I liked to feel the pull of the unyielding corduroy cloth fastened firmly below my knees against the opposing pull of my long stockings tightly gartered above my knees under the breeches. I got so used to them that I did not envy some other boys with bare knees, even in the summer.

This type of garment, or knickerbockers of similar material, I was to wear regularly at the Council School, getting replacements during our shopping trips to Edmonton calling at Wades on Saturday afternoons. I did not discourage Dad, although he would have ignored me if I had tried, but I was embarrassed when he insisted in taking the whole family into the shop, before shouting out in his R.S.M. voice "Give us another pair of your strong corduroy breeches for this lad". This, in front of other customers.

One morning my mate Stan had a scarf around his neck instead of his usual collar and I told him I thought it a good idea. He said I was soppy, it was only because his collars had not come back from the laundry. I asked Mum why she did not send mine to the laundry. She replied that working class boys wore celluloid collars — they looked the same anyway.

I knew we must be working class, because Dad wore a cap when he went to work, and his brass front stud was prominent in his shirt neckband, for he did not wear a collar on weekdays. Some men wore bowler hats and stiff collars all the week, like Mr. Wagstaffe, our Rent Collector. They were not workmen. I suppose we must have been always working class. One Grandad was a bricklayer, the other a "decorator". One great Grandad was a labourer, the other a blacksmith. Our great, great Grandad on Dad's side and his forebears back two hundred and fifty years were labourers.

Dad, since he was seventeen, had been a part-time soldier known as a Volunteer. I was aware when I was quite young how much he enjoyed it. At the time we lived in Seventh Avenue, until we moved to Low's Cottage, I never missed an opportunity of joining him in his bedroom on Thursday evenings and on Sunday mornings to watch him dress for parade, pulling on his tight breeches over his long underpants and observing the skill he had in winding on his puttees from the top of his highly polished boots to just below his knees. If the weather was suitable, I was allowed to march alongside him as far as the level-crossing where he was joined by another Volunteer. I always hoped other boys I knew would see me with my smart Father. I had only one regret which was that Dad did not wear spurs as Bill Toop's father did — but he was in the cavalry and knew all about horses — he drove a horse-pulled removal van at work.

I did not know it then, but these were the golden days before the War began to affect us. Within a short time Dad was to write to Mum whilst she was in Bury St. Edmunds with young Ivy: "I have worked out since the War began that we are having to spend four shillings a week more on coal and food. I am having a job to make ends meet on my thirty four shillings a week. The children, especially the boys, must be made to look after their clothes".

It was not long before we realised that most of the things in the shops were not for the likes of us.

Report of Jessie Robinson

Whitsun - Midsummer 1914

Subject	marks gained	marks possible	position in class	No. in class
Reading	14	20	22	38
Composition	26	40	15	38
Arithmetic	3	4	9	35

Conduct marks Lost 0

General report.- Her attendance pulls her back, but otherwise a good worker.

No of times absent :- 16.

Sister Jessie was eleven years and a half when she wrote all but the General Report and absence note. It shows the standard which an ordinary working-class girl could reach in those much-maligned 'bad' old days. On the occasions when Jessie was absent sister Kit took me unwillingly to school, but she lacked the patience Jessie had, so quite often I got smacked round the head on the way and was sulking before being shoved into the playground.

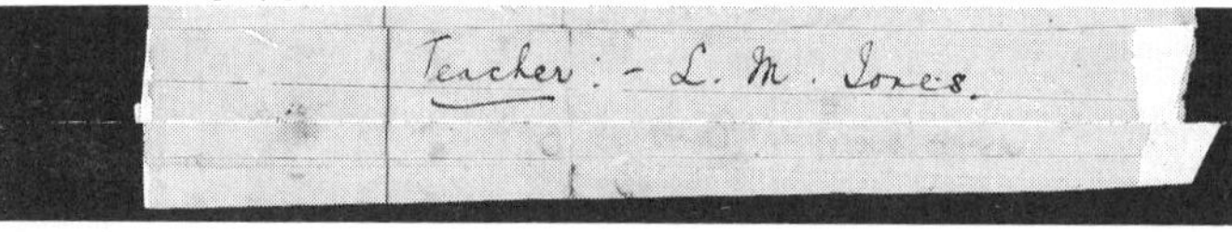
Teacher :- L. M. Jones.

Bush Hill Park, Seventh Avenue Council School, Infants' Department, where all we Robinson children went; Sister Jess in 1906; Kitty in 1909; I in 1913; Fred in 1914; Ivy in 1916 and Winnie in 1921.

The picture shows the state of the unmade road surface.

Sister Jessie at school

CHAPTER 4

From the time young Fred had been promoted to the pushchair, I had had to walk. I cannot recall riding in any vehicle after that until I was many years older except in three special circumstances. One was when I persuaded Bill to let me squeeze into his box on old pram wheels, which he then propelled along the pavement at high speed. Due possibly to his lack of navigational skill he let one wheel run off the kerb into the gutter, tipping me out on to the muddy road. There followed a fierce argument accompanied by bad language in which we were both fluent. Bill would give me no more rides.

Therefore, it was with anticipation that on fine mornings I would watch and listen for Mr. Burch, our milkman, who had a Dairy in Sixth Avenue behind the Salvation Army Hall. This was always on Saturdays after I had read the easy parts of my Comic. I would offer my services to Mr. Burch by collecting the pint-sized galvanised iron cans from his customers' door steps and taking them to him so they could be filled from the brass tap on the large churn at the back of his horse-drawn float. In return he would let me stand on the back step as the horse pulled the vehicle from customer to customer. Unfortunately Mum had told Mr. Burch not to take me too far from home, as I was not to be trusted.

It was on such a fine August morning that I heard the loud sound of metal-shod boots and the clinking of spurs. I ran to the front room window and saw a fine, smart khaki-clad soldier standing at the front door of Billy Toop's house next to us. Almost immediately out came Bill's Dad, equally resplendent. They waved goodbye and left the garden. I ran out to the pavement in time to see them get into step and march up the road, their brasses glittering in the bright sunshine. They had their rifles and kitbags slung over their shoulders. I knew where they were going — off to the War — and I could not take my eyes off them — soldiers fascinated me.

At dinner time, I asked Dad if he was going to go to fight the Germans. Before he could answer, Mum said "Of course not, it'll be over soon".

Correspondence between Mum and Dad has survived which was written in May, 1915 when Mum was ready to return with Ivy from Bury St. Edmunds where she had been caring for her mother, our Grannie Anthony. Dad writes that he ought not to spend 13 shillings (65p) on fare and lose 6 shillings (30p) for a day's pay to go and meet her, these hard times when everything is getting dearer and their responsibilities. He remarks how busy he is, hardly time to breathe. Young Ely in Fourth Avenue and Curly from the Nursery had been killed. Sisters Jessie and Kitty were clearing up whilst Dad wrote his letter. Fred was sitting beside him chattering, Jack (Sid) was drawing and singing the Marsellaise.

Mum always had cut my hair, but when she was in Bury, Dad sent me just across the road from our house in Seventh Avenue to Rhumbke's, the barber, with a note saying that my hair should be cropped short. When I got back home with no hair left except for an inch fringe in front, I told anybody who would listen that I was not going to a barber again because boys had to wait until there were no more grown-ups in the shop, even if they came in after we boys had come in. Some days later I was pleased to see that the barber's shop windows were all smashed. When Dad came in to dinner I asked him why and he told me that since the sinking of the Lusitania there had been rioting and that Rhumbke was a German. There had been lots of bad feeling. The barber disappeared, his shop being taken over by Hooper to open as a newsagents.

Grannie and Grandad Anthony in Bury St. Edmunds were living in a large old school house in Northgates. They let rooms and when the War came they had soldiers billeted on them. In a surviving letter of early 1915 Grannie wrote; "Oh, if this dreadful war was over, what peace and joy would there be all over the earth. We have this time in Bury 20,000 soldiers. Such fine fellows. My heart aches when I think what may be their end..."

Grannie was justified in her heartache. Most of them, the pick of the young men in this country,

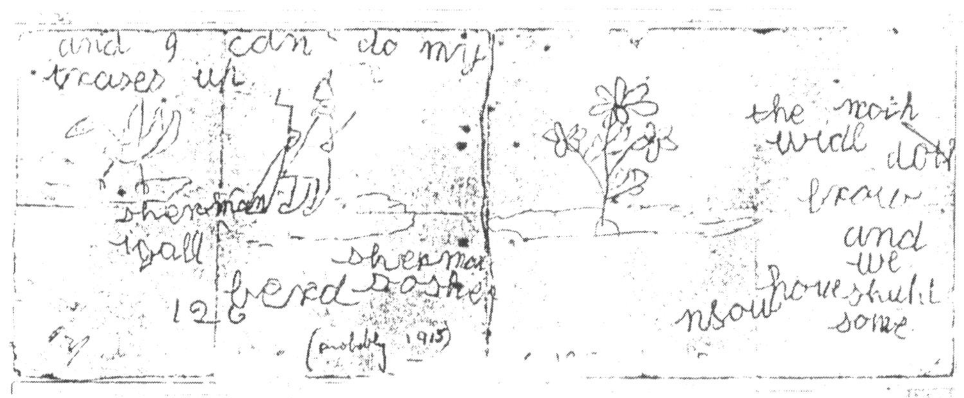

and I can do my
trases up
(probably 1915)
the north
wind doth
blow
and
we
shall have
snow
some

My letter to Mum when she was in Bury St.Edmunds with young Ivy in May 1915. It is in this that I announced a great personal accomplishment, 'I can do my trases (trousers) up'.

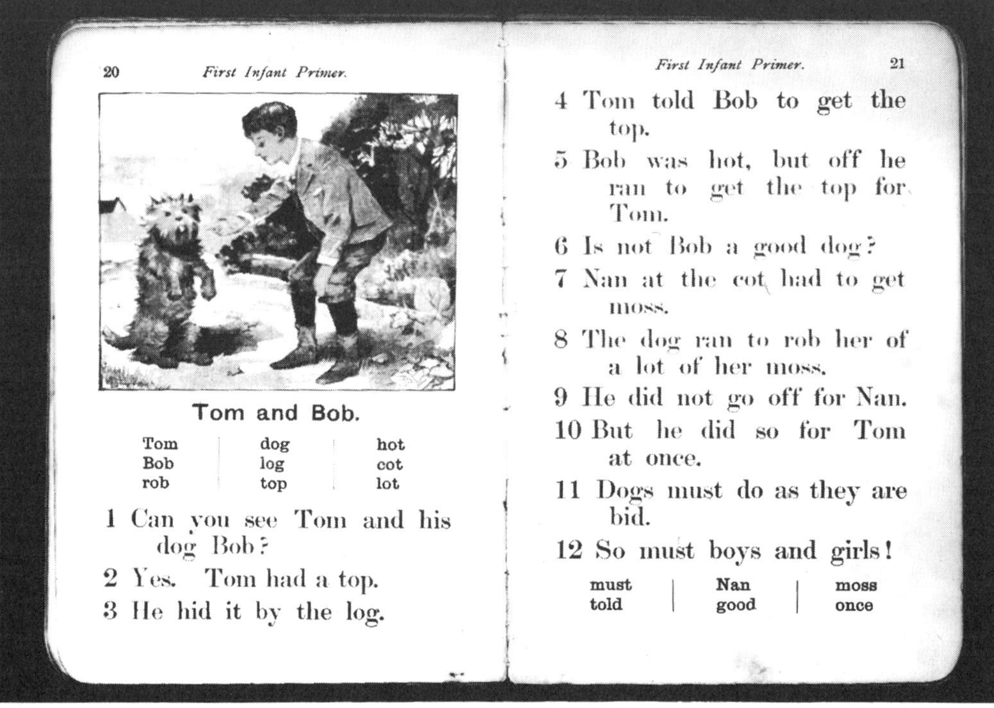

20 *First Infant Primer.*

Tom and Bob.

Tom	dog	hot
Bob	log	cot
rob	top	lot

1 Can you see Tom and his dog Bob?

2 Yes. Tom had a top.

3 He hid it by the log.

First Infant Primer. 21

4 Tom told Bob to get the top.

5 Bob was hot, but off he ran to get the top for Tom.

6 Is not Bob a good dog?

7 Nan at the cot had to get moss.

8 The dog ran to rob her of a lot of her moss.

9 He did not go off for Nan.

10 But he did so for Tom at once.

11 Dogs must do as they are bid.

12 So must boys and girls!

must	Nan	moss
told	good	once

Pages from a First Infant Primer at our School.

must have died in the useless slaughter in the Battle of Loos later in the year. Some may have been gassed with their own gas when a Divisional Commander got it all wrong.

In the summer of that year Grannie and Grandad were to be bombed out of their home in Bury by German aircraft which frequently passed over the town on the way to London. With their very few surviving belongings, they returned to Bush Hill Park to live in one room in Cross Road.

Dad in his letter reported that I had been singing the Marsellaise, the French National Anthem. From the contents of my own little letter, which has also survived, it seemed I had become patriotic. In my letter I had drawn a picture entitled 'Sherman socher' and another 'Sherman Igall'. I am sure at that age I could do better at spelling "German soldier" and "German eagle". I fear that it was just being lazy and slapdash, my usual self if away from strict supervision and the threat of teacher's ruler. In the same letter I was able to report a considerable personal achievement which was "I can do my trasers up". This important news item would have been a considerable relief to Mum, and possibly to my teachers when they got to learn of it, because my trousers, and the fastening up thereof, had presented me with a manual dexterity problem hitherto. In the letter I forgot to tell Mum that there were hundreds of soldiers in the Recreation Ground, our Park, with horses tethered to the railings. I cannot recall what had happened to the sheep which had been grazing there.

The only surviving reference to my stay in the Infants School is a remnant of a Record Slip on which it states that I was showing steady improvement but could do better. My Good Conduct Marks were two out of twelve, and were considered "not satisfactory".

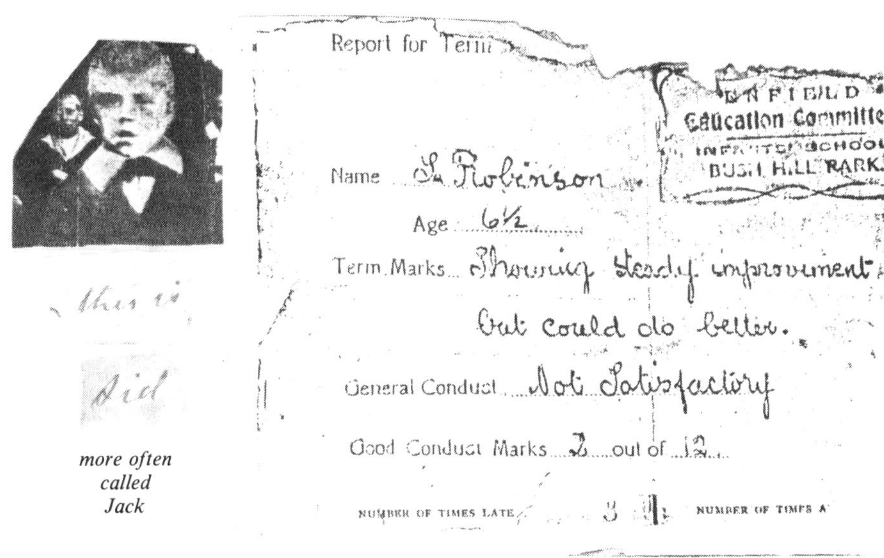

Report for Term

ENFIELD Education Committee INFANTS' SCHOOL BUSH HILL PARK

Name S. Robinson

Age 6½

Term Marks Showing steady improvement but could do better.

General Conduct Not Satisfactory

Good Conduct Marks 2 out of 12

NUMBER OF TIMES LATE 3 NUMBER OF TIMES A

more often called Jack

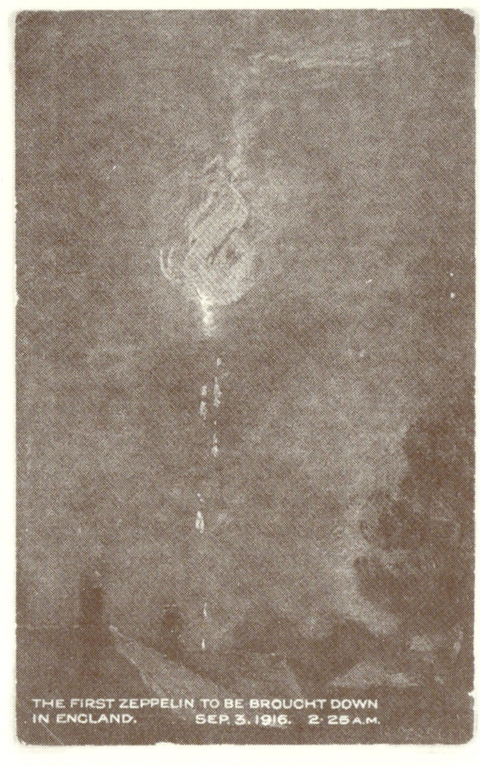

The crowd searching for souvenirs in the field where the Cuffley Zeppelin fell in flames. It was from this field that I claimed I had picked up a piece of wire. That boy on the left looks like me.

'I bent over to let the water run out from under my collar'

CHAPTER 5

When I was promoted from the Infants to the Junior boys, I seemed to have been settling down, but after about nine months teacher started on me because I was lazy. I was glad therefore when classes ended each day and I could get into the streets to play, unmolested by any adult. It was on such an evening that I saw Mr. Hooper, the newsagent, change the news placard outside his shop. I read it, and promptly ran across the road where I shouted through the letter box to Dad "Kitchener drowned", and then resumed my play.

One incident is still vivid in my memory many, many years after the event. It was when Dad came hurriedly into our bedroom in the early hours of the morning, awakening Fred and me to go to our parent's bedroom window in the front of the house to see the German Zeppelin on fire, descending slowly to earth a mile or two away. Next morning when Dad told me it had fallen in a field in Cuffley, I asked him if he would take me to see the wreck. He said he would. Unfortunately, my memory is uncertain about this. I knew so much at the time about the wreckage and the exact spot, that I may have imagined I did go, but I have no recollection of the manner in which we went, because it would have been a long walk. I do know I had a piece of wire I claimed to have picked up on the field, but I was such a fibber in those days. The picture of people hunting for souvenirs shows a boy on the left foreground who could easily have been me, but, given my obsession with being photographed, I would have posed for the photographers as was my wont always.

In our classroom, when we were sitting very quietly, say doing our sums, and, if conditions were just right, we could hear the faint booming of the guns in Flanders. We knew that brave men were being blown to smithereens. Our Dad could be there if he got called up — something that could happen anytime.

The daylight raids by German aeroplanes we called "Taubs" provided excitement. I was delighted one morning to be turned away at the school entrance and told to go straight home because there was an air raid coming. Another time, on a fine summer morning in the garden, I heard some "boomps", then the bugle telling us of a German air raid. I know it had been a Saturday, for I was in my corduroys and it was well past school time. I think it was July because I was looking forward to the summer school holidays. I was sorry it was not on a school day so that I could dodge classes. There were lots of gun fire and I saw a few planes. Later, a boy told me some bombs had been dropped on Chingford.

After Mum had seen the damage done by the German air attacks when she had been in Bury St. Edmunds, she did not like me running out into the open as soon as there was any indication that enemy aeroplanes were approaching. One day I shouted out excitedly "I can see them coming". Sister Kitty came to the scullery door and called out "Mum said you're to come in at once — if you don't I'm to come and fetch you — then you'll get your face washed".

I shouted back angrily "I ain't coming — and it ain't dirty — I washed it yesterday".

Such defiance was unwise in the circumstances, because I had no escape route from where I stood in the backyard; and Kit, aged twelve and a half, fleet of foot and very strong, was able, and willing at that time, to discipline me, aged nearly nine, if so instructed by Mum, who had enough to do keeping an eye on Fred aged seven, Ivy aged five and baby Winnie. Kit knew how much I loathed washing or being washed, and her threat was not an idle one. On this occasion she walked slowly down the garden, passed me, and then suddenly turned to give me a series of violent shoves in the back accompanied by slaps round the head, which propelled me back into the scullery. There, in spite of my struggles, she was able to pick up a flannel from the sink, soak it under the mains tap, and slap it vigorously and carelessly around my face and neck.

She then stood back, saying "So there — that'll teach you". She left me, and I heard her say "I got him Mum". I bent over to try to make the water run back out of my neck beneath my collar, and out of my blocked ears. I was furious, but more so when I was not allowed to go upstairs to look out of

2/6 order enclosed

17 Seventh avenue
Bush Hill Park
Enfield
17th May 1915

Dear Gert
Thanks for your letter, received this morning. I was glad to hear you and Ivy were better, I hope you will soon be able to come home, I did not bargain for you stopping a month but if you feel you must

2

there is no help for it.
Re your information as to the wrecking of German premises, they smashed the windows at the German barbers opposite us the other day, so he has had to clear out there has been a lot of rioting at different places, since the sinking of the Lusitania that has fairly stirred people up, Young Eley of 4th

Dad's letter to Mum when she was in Bury St.Edmunds.

3

Avenue, has been killed in battle, so has young Curly that worked at the nursery. Young Fred is sitting here beside me, chattering all the time, Jack is singing the Marseillaise, and drawing at the same time and the girls are busy clearing up. I have been very busy hardly time to breathe. I do not think I shall

4

be able to come down to fetch you home, because it would cost me 13/ fare and 6/- at least for the loss of a days pay, that is a sovereign gone bang, too much to throw away these times with our responsibilities and everything getting dearer. With love to your father & mother Fred and Allie, and armsfull for yourself and Ivy
I remain your loving husband
Sid

the window when the guns started firing. Next day a boy told me a bomb had fallen in his cousin's school playground in Edmonton. This made me complain bitterly to Kit that if I had looked out of the bedroom window I might have seen the bomb drop. She said that I was starting to be silly.

Before we moved from our terraced house in Seventh Avenue I made my one and only attempt at being self-employed. Opposite was a vacant plot protected by a brick wall. Outside it one morning I laid out neatly a grotto made of little pebbles, little shells, flower heads of dandelions and buttercups, and as a centrepiece a little Union Jack struck into a mouldy potato. I thought it was very pretty. I put down my cap alongside it, as I had seen the disabled soldiers do when they begged. I had not set my targets very high — a halfpenny would do — because although things were much dearer I could still get some toffee with it. I sat down beside my grotto, waiting for passers-by to admire my work and drop something in my cap. I don't know if people that day were hard-hearted or hard-up, but the cap was still empty when along came a big boy. He made fun of me, and I made the mistake of swearing at him, for he promptly kicked my cap into the muddy road. It started to rain, so I recovered my cap, and the little Union Jack, and went back indoors — without any toffee.

A few months later, on a very cold foggy day we moved, by means of a horse and cart, from Seventh Avenue to the Cottage on Low's Nursery. I was thrilled with the large garden all around the cottage, the two large oak trees waiting to be climbed and the very large shed. But the cottage was neglected, cold and very damp, the walls often running with water inside. And this at a time when fuel was scarce.

The Robinson's new home, known as The Cottage, Low's Nurseries. It was situated where the undeveloped end of Lincoln Road, Bush Hill Park, met the undeveloped end of Main Avenue. At this point a lane joined them and led through the nurseries and orchards under the railway bridge to Lincoln Road, Ponders End. It was from Porter's Lodge in one of the orchards that on rare occasions we were able to afford a pennyworth of windfall apples.

Church Street, Enfield, as I knew it when Grannie Robinson took me unwillingly on two occasions to Fergusons, the dentist, after school had ended; for Mum would not let me lose any time off from classes. In the photograph, a cab, probably Welch's, is passing the door of the dentist's surgery, reached by mounting a long flight of wooden stairs.

Report for Half Year ending Oct. 191

Subject	Marks Obtained	Full Marks	Subject	Remarks
Arithmetic	7	11	Oral Work	Very [illegible]
Reading	18	20	Recitation	Fg.
Writing	4	10	Singing	"
Composition	7	10	Drill	"
Spelling	19	20	Drawing	Fair.
Total	55	71		

Conduct Fair.
Regularity Abs. 13 times
Punctuality Exc.

Name S. Robinson
Position in class 25th

Remarks Syd has plenty of brain power, but does not make the best use of it. He is inclined to be lazy, & must work much harder next term.

Head Mistress M. Nye.
Class Teacher M. Matthews.

Name of Child	Amount of Punishment	Mode of Punishment	Reason
Robinson S.	1	on hand	Idleness.
Robinson S.	2	"	

CHAPTER 6

When I took home the Term Report in which teacher had referred to me as Syd, I asked Mum why it had been spelled that way when I was Sid. She told me that there were two ways of spelling it, but I was Sid, as Dad was. Later when a boy told me he knew a girl with my name but it was spelled Sydney, I was glad that teachers did not call me Syd in later Reports. When, much later, an opportunity presented itself, I sneaked upstairs into Mum's bedroom, and, standing on tiptoes on a chair, took down from the top of the cupboard the box in which I thought Mum kept her "treasures". In it I found several Reports, which I interfered with, in a boyish fashion, to erase the "Syd" from one of them and "improve" or disguise other entries. I knew nothing of my Birth Certificate which showed both my and Dad's names as "Sydney"- These entries must have been errors or misunderstandings, because Dad was registered as "Sidney" on his Birth Certificate, and the intention was that I should have the same name as Dad.

These School Reports for the first three years in the Junior Boys, referring to me as Sid or Syd, could give the impression of familiarity or intimacy between teacher and me. I had no such impression. Normally, surnames were used solely in the Juniors, teachers only coupling them with our first or Christian names for special emphasis or effect, which often had an ominous undertone. I expected trouble if teacher called out "Sidney Robinson — come out here". In my fourth year, although I anticipate here, any pretence of familiarity was abandoned on my School Reports.

The Report which shows that I was absent from school thirteen times must have been, apart from one afternoon when I played truant and got severely caned for it, the period when I was suffering from very severe ringworm, and all my hair had been very closely cropped. During that time our Uncle Charlie, a cheerful chap who never seemed to have much work to do, put me on the bar of his bike and cycled several miles with me to see Uncle Fred, a bootmaker, and Aunt Alice. When Aunt saw me, she asked why I was not at school — cousin Dick was. I took off my cap and showed her my head. She asked if a Doctor had seen it as it was a very large place. I said we did not have doctors because they cost a shilling and my Mum was a good doctor. She asked if I had toothache, for my face looked a little swollen — I hastily replied that I hadn't. Aunt told Uncle there was a Clinic open that morning just up the road and there they would know how to treat the ringworm to get it better quickly. I tried to protest, but could not tell them I did not want it to get better that quickly. I did not feel ill and it was nice to be away from school with a proper excuse for once. At any rate, I wanted my hair to get a bit longer before I sat in class again.

Notwithstanding my protests, I shortly found myself standing alongside Uncle in a room where he spoke some minutes to a lady at a table. He then left me, saying I was not to leave the Clinic until he came back. I was sent into a large room where a severe looking nurse was bathing a girl's finger. She told me to take off my cap and sit down, which I did when a boy at the far end of the form made room for me. He was reading a Comic and I marvelled at his relaxed attitude in such a place reeking of disinfectant I always associated with pain. To my horror I found I was sitting within a few feet of a dentist's chair. I had been made to sit in one before on two occasions. The first was when Grannie Robinson told me I was a brave boy, so I climbed up into the chair, prepared to be one. But it was a painful, bloody ordeal and I bit the dentist's hand. The second time, I had toothache and Mum made me promise to be brave and not to upset Grannie this visit. I did try, but I refused to keep still in the chair and, I was told, made it worse for myself because Ferguson, the dentist in Church Street, had to struggle to pull out two difficult teeth. There were no pain-killing devices available for us.

In the clinic, a white-coated man came to the chair, fidgeted about with some tools and then turned to me, asking "Are you first?" I suddenly froze in my seat, overwhelmed with panic, for I suspected that I had sat at the end of the form for those sent for dental treatment. How could I escape? My swollen face was evidence, though I knew that dentists wouldn't be too fussy, for they

A School Clinic somewhat similar to the one Uncle Charlie took me to. I had never heard of such a place, but Ivy tells me there was one at the Southbury Road School which she attended bravely when she had reached the age I was when I was made to go with Uncle Charlie.

Fred
aged seven

Sid
aged nine

'nurse bathed my sore place
and gave me a note for Mum'

liked pulling out teeth, and they got paid for it. Grannie had given Mr. Ferguson a shilling for mine.

There was a temporary reprieve when the boy with the Comic got up and clambered into the chair. I watched with morbid interest the chair being adjusted so that the boy's knees were level with his chin. The dentist, peering into the boy's mouth, took hold of a tool on a long cable, which started to make a buzzing sound, and inserted it into where he had been peering. The boy obviously was feeling discomfort or pain because his hand suddenly tightened its grip on the chair arm and the calves of his legs went taut as his boots pressed down on the footrest. Then, out of the corner of my eye I saw a seat vacated at the far end of the form. I waited for the dentist's back to be turned and I was up like a shot. The boy I had now sat next to said grumpily' "It's my turn next you know". I replied that I didn't care whose turn it was. I kept my face turned away from the dentist. Eventually I was called to the nurse, who bathed my sore place and gave me a note to Mum. I hesitated, uncertain, and then with my back to the dentist, I left.

Uncle was waiting for me. Aunty was pleased I had been a good, brave boy. Mum was even more pleased when I got home. I did not tell that I would have run out of the place if I could have thought up an acceptable excuse for so doing. I never missed the opportunity of posing as a good boy and would never admit to my failings.

The ringworm left a permanent bald patch on my head. I went to the dentist again nine years later. I learned I was the only member of the Robinson family to have gone to a dentist when I was a boy until young Ivy went to the Southbury Road School Clinic, without complaint, later. Ivy is four years my junior and she tells me that when she was bigger she had a tooth brush. I did not have one, and I wonder now if any of my mates had?

Uncle Fred, Mum's brother, Aunt Alice and cousin Dick, standing outside their home at 58 South Street, Ponders End, on the 15th March 1913, when King George V was opening the new reservoir at Chingford. Uncle had been a keen entomologist since a boy, collecting butterflies on the marshes around the River Lea. He made pictures with them which fascinated me. One of these hung in the Prince of Wales public house in South Street. The family moved during the War, but had to move again after being bombed out in the first German air raids on London.

How to keep Sid warm in cold times

SCHOOL SUITS

BOYS' REEFER OVERCOAT.

In Blue Nap.
2/11 3 11 6/11 10/9 14/11 18/11

In Blue Serges,
4/11 6/11 10/9 14/11 18/11

In Red Serge. 4/11 8/11

BUCKINGHAM SUIT.

Jacket, Vest & Knickerbockers,
4/11 7/11 10/9 13/9

In Superior Tweeds and Serges,
16/11 21/6 24/6 26/6

Boys' Tweed or Serge Knickerbockers,
1/11 2/11 3/6 3/11 4/11 6/11

FULLY ILLUSTRATED PRICE LIST FREE ON APPLICATION.

BOYS' FLANNEL KNICKER SUIT.

With Vest complete,
16/11 19/11 23/6 27/6

Jacket and Knickers,
10/9 12/11 15/9

XII

CHAS. BAKER & Co.,

Chas. Baker & Co.'s Price List.

GIRLS'
BUTTONED BOOTS.
Calf Kid 4/11 to 6/11
Glacé Kid 6/6 to 8/6
Ditto Extra high 7/6 to 9/6

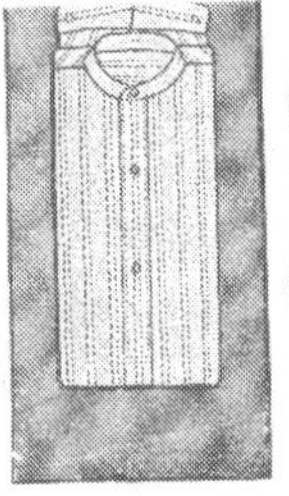

Boys' Flannel Shirts
In neat Fancy Patterns.
1/11 to 2/11, 2/3 to 3/6, 3/3 to 4/11, according to size.

GIRLS'
SCHOOL BOQTS.
Calf Goloshed,
Either Buttoned or Laced
5/6 to 7/6, according to size.

BOYS'
LACED BOOTS.
Small Sizes, 4/11 5/11 6/11
Large Sizes, 5/11 6/11 7/11

BOYS'
HAND-SEWN
BOOTS,
10/6 to 14/6,
according to size.

BOYS' HOSIERY.

To match Knickerbocker Suits, in Black and Navy Blue Cashmere
1/- to 1/4 1/3 to 1/9 1/9 to 2/3

Heavy Knicker or Bicycle Hose, in Black, Navy or Heather
1/6 to 2/4 and 1/11 to 2/8

Boys' Half-Hose—Merino ... -/9½ 1/- 1/6 Worsted 1 6 1/11

Children's Three-quarter Hose ... ... 1/2 to 2/8

The boys wore corduroy knee breeches and jerseys and short coats. Shorts were unknown, and would seem unsuitable for all weathers. Their "uniform" suited the gangling lads, and was adequate protection. The girls wore serge dresses and big coats, and in summer pretty print frocks with pinafores. *Enfield*, 1926,

From Chas. Baker's , Outfitters , Catalogue

BOYS' AND YOUTHS' KNICKERBOCKER DRAWERS.

Nos.	Measurement round Waist—	Small Boys'. 24 in.	Boys'. 26 in.	Youths'. 28 in.	Large Youths'. 30 in.
1.	Stout Unbleached Cotton	2 9	2 10	2 10½	2 11
2.	Brown Balbriggan (English make) (light)	—	2/-	2/1	2/2
3.	**Natural Wool** (stout)	4 10	5/-	5 2	5 5
4.	„ „ „	3 9	3 11½	4 1½	4 3½
5.	„ „ „	—	2 10	2 11	2 11½
6.	„ „ (light)	—	3 6	3 8	3 10
7.	Stout „	3 0½	3 3	3 5	3 7

BOYS' AND YOUTHS' PANTS.

(Extend to the ankle.)

Nos.	Measurement round Waist—	Boys'. 26 in.	Youths'. 28 in.	Large Youths'. 30 in.
1.	Stout Unbleached Cotton	—	3 10	—
2.	Stout White Merino	3 10	4 0½	4/2½
3.	**Natural Wool** (stout)	5 3	5 6	5 8
4.	„ „ „	—	4 3½	4 6
5.	„ „ (light)	—	3 9	3 10

BOYS' KNICKERBOCKER HOSE

STOUT MAKES, FOR HARD WEAR.

Nos.	Sizes— / Length of foot about—	2. 7 in.	3. 7½ in.	4. 8 in.	5. 8½ in.	6. 9 in.	7. 9½ in.
1.	Black Ribbed	1 4½	1/6	1 7	1/8	1 9	1/10
2.	Black Ribbed Extra Stout. Best Quality...	2 0½	2 1½	2 2½	2 3½	2 4½	2/6½
3.	Heather and Dark Steel with Fancy Turnover Tops	—	2/5	2 6½	2 7½	2 8½	2/9½

BOYS' AND YOUTHS' SCHOOL OUTFITS.

BOYS' AND YOUTHS' UNDERSHIRTS.

HALF SLEEVES.

Nos.	Measurement round Chest—	Small Boys'. 24 in.	Boys'. 26 in.	Youths'. 28 in.	Large Youths'. 30 in.
1.	Imitation Gauze	—	1 6½	1 7½	1/8½
2.	Stout White Merino	2 5	2 7	2 9	2 11½
3.	**Natural Wool** (stout)	4 3½	4 6	4 8	4 10
4.	„ „ „	3 5	3 7	3 9	3 11½
5.	„ „ „	—	2 10	2 11	2 11¼
6.	„ „ (light)	—	3 3	3 4	3/5

LONG SLEEVES.

Nos.	Measurement round Chest—	Small Boys'. 24 in.	Boys'. 26 in.	Youths'. 28 in.	Large Youths'. 30 in.
1.	Stout White Merino	2 6	2 8	2 10	3 0½
2.	**Natural Wool** (stout)	—	2 10	2 11	2 11½
3.	„ „ „	3 6	3 8	3 10½	4 0½
4.	„ „ „	4 5	4 7	4 9	4 11

CHAPTER 7

All my years in the Junior Boys were during the Great War when the school central heating had been turned off. I felt the cold so badly that I sat on my hands in the classroom whenever free to do so, in the hope I would be able to hold my pen sufficiently well to avoid reprimand from the teacher, who was able to warm herself standing in front of the miserable coal fire intended to heat the large classroom. Once, I went to school in a tatty jersey because Mum lacked the time to mend my jacket. I sat and shivered, envying other boys in their jackets and collars, and I complained so much that Mum repaired it, having to stay up late to do it. Perhaps she thought I was a bit queer, because I asked her if I could wear my overcoat to Sunday School, even when the weather was warm — I told her that churches were cold places — and I still do. I did not realise that the corduroy Dad found so economical and hard-wearing was close cotton cloth which was a heat conductor, thus making my thighs and knees hot in the summer but cold in the winter. I had no underpants. I doubt if I knew such garments existed for boys until older and saw a high-class boy's outfitters' advertisement which included short and ankle-length cotton or wool underpants. Some boys were lucky!

In the school classroom I always seemed to be sitting below a window which was partially opened even in wintry weather. Looking back, I think I can see why the teacher felt the need for ventilation. It was because she was sharing the room with forty or fifty boys, some of whom must have been somewhat smelly, because by the third year of the Great War conditions for those in large working class families had become so bad and the mothers so harassed, that we became inadequately washed. In addition, our school clothes, made of uncleanable material in those days, were soiled, their replacement impossible due to the high cost and shortage of money to pay for them.

The washing and cleaning facilities in our cottage, and in all the small working class terraced houses in which other boys lived were the most primitive. There were no bathrooms and the only source of hot water was from kettles or pans, placed on the top of the coal-fired kitchen range, in greater demand for many purposes other than for washing boys. There was hanging on a nail in the scullery a tin bath, but it needed a lot of water, and there were now eight of us in the family. I have no recollection of my two older sisters using it, and, to the best of my knowledge I did not bathe from November 1917 until the early 1920's when the coal cellar was converted into a bathroom, with a gas geyser. It was a cold, austere place. I use this opportunity to say that when Dad was persuaded by Mum to try the new bath, he decided against it when, in his own words "I put a match to the gas geyser, and it went 'woof', blowing my bleeding cap orf". He never bathed again as far as I knew. But this is a digression from the teachers' need for ventilation, and our cleanliness.

I can recall one Saturday afternoon after dinner when we were all getting ready to go out for the weekly shopping trip and Mum was struggling to put Fred's newly sponged collar on, whilst I fidgeted about with my back stud, for I always found the fastening of the collar at the back very trying. Dad asked if we had washed.

He could tell from my face that we had not. After Fred and I were sent to the scullery to do so, we hesitated. Dad came out and asked what we were waiting for. I, usually the spokesman, said "We haven't got any warm water". Dad spluttered and angrily asked "What's in the bloody tap? A dose in the Army would do you good". So we did as we usually did. After one another we turned on the cold mains tap, picked up a bit of flannel from the draining board, rubbed it on a chunk of household soap and dabbed it on our faces, rinsing the soap off with our hands from the tap. We tried to dry our faces and hands with the communal towel hanging behind the backdoor, which was usually wetter than our faces. We finished by wiping them with our shirt sleeves. I am sure we were more smelly than when we started.

Fred and I, probably like most working class boys, slept in our flannel vests, shirts — and long

Chimneys belched filty black smoke.

Number 17 Seventh Avenue, where we lived from 1909 to 1917 when we moved to Low's Cottage. Fred, Ivy and Winnie were born here. The ornamental iron railings and front gate had been replaced in this photograph taken in 1959, also concrete had replaced our nice little front garden.

stockings which I kept gartered above my knees to prevent them working down to my ankles in the night, making my legs colder than ever. Sister Ivy went to bed in her underwear, liberty bodice and stockings. These garments were washed only once a fortnight by Mum using the most primitive methods, and were mostly dried in front of the kitchen range in a room where all the cooking was done. The supply of hot water in our home was quite inadequate for all the clothes needing washing.

In the classroom to add to the general smell, a lot of us wore celluloid collars which, after several spongings, gave off an unpleasant odour. Furthermore, the corduroy, so popular for its hard wearing qualities, had a very strong smell considered very disagreeable by many. It is no wonder that the teachers needed some fresh air, though this was in short supply because every factory, office and house chimney belched filthy black smoke and soot which, with the fog, made our clothes, and us, grimy and smelly.

I made my own special contribution to the general smell on at least two occasions, resulting from taking home notes reporting that I had lice in my hair. Each time I feared I would get my head shaved, as some children did. Dad's method, however, though not very successful and used when he was tired and ill-tempered after finishing work for the day, was firstly to tell Mum to cut off what was left of my usually short cropped hair, whilst he had his tea. Then I was told to remove my collar and jacket and go to the scullery, where he clumsily pushed me over the sink. He then poured over my head paraffin from the can used to fill our oil lamps, telling me to keep my "bleeding eyes shut". On each occasion he had to shout out for somebody to bring something to dry my head. If lucky, this could be a bit of Dad's old vest, which I rubbed vigorously on to the paraffined head to try to remove some of the surplus. There were no facilities for washing, rinsing or drying hair in our cottage, though Dad would not have bothered anyway.

Thus stinking of paraffin I would sit in class, sure that the smell emanating from me did not improve my relationship with a teacher I had at that time and equally sure she was delighted to catch me committing any small offence so she could be justified in sending me out of the classroom to stand in the corridor, thus transferring my smell and the responsibility for my punishment to the head teacher.

There was an advantage of the paraffin treatments — I always knew which cap was which when ownership disagreement arose — I just had to sniff mine!

I did not understand why Dad got so angry when I brought these notes from school. Everybody at home knew we had lice, for one of young Ivy's pastimes was to go through my hair with a nit comb. Any nits observed on the comb would end their lives by being squashed with Ivy's thumbnail.

As I had been sent home on two occasions from school, I began to encourage Ivy to comb through my hair as often as she liked, because if I were found to be lousy a third time, I might be sent to the clinic for my head to be shaved. Ivy must have caught the nits off me, because she had to have evil smelling soft soap rubbed into her lovely hair which reached down to her waist. I thought everybody had lice — just as we had bugs in our beds and fleas in our clothes. I was always scratching myself and getting told off in class for fidgeting. No doubt these parasites or their forebears had been resident in our cottage before we moved in. Probably our beds and mattresses, which had been acquired well after the War had started, had earlier owners. Our blankets were certainly never washed — they would have been an impossible task.

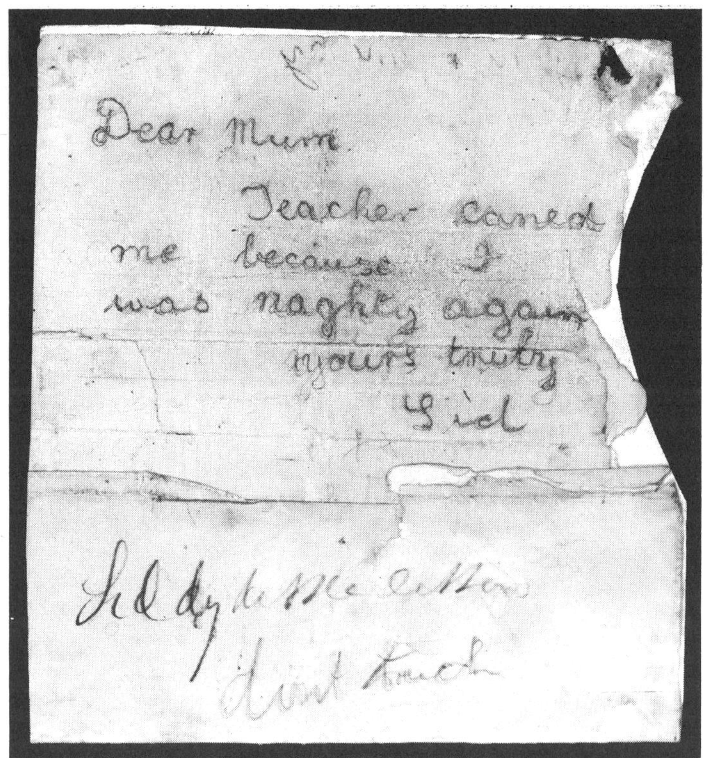

Dear Mum

Teacher caned me because I was naghty again yours truty

Sid

Siddy's little letter

don't touch

If I had lied to Mum I was always sorry afterwards, so although reluctant to tell the whole truth I would leave a little note for her on the mantelshelf before I went to bed trying to put the matter right. The above little note was written because when Mum had asked me that morning if I was in trouble at school, as I seemed more reluctant than usual to go, I had replied angrily that I wasn't. In fact I knew I was going to be. Mum kept this note, putting it away in an envelope on which she had marked 'Siddy's little letter - don't touch'.

'Teacher stabbed her finger at something written in the exercise book'

CHAPTER 8

These living conditions were never queried by any of us, and we expected no miracle to occur to alter them even if we had thought about it, which was unlikely. We knew nothing else — that's how life was. We all grew, and stayed free from disease without the need of a doctor. Young sister Ivy and I were particularly wiry and healthy. I was slowly learning to survive in a manner suitable to my mental and physical make-up, however reprehensible it may seem now, perhaps even to me and certainly to those who have never wanted for the necessities of life. I started to endeavour, not always successfully, to use any subterfuge or untruth to escape retribution for my breaches of the very strict rules of conduct, and I began to develop subconsciously a determination to survive as long as I could. So, in spite of my lapses into uncontrollable foolhardiness and impetuousness, I have been lucky to do so.

As children, we may have been hard-up, cold, under-nourished and very uncomfortable, as well as being strictly disciplined by Dad, but we Robinson children knew that we belonged to our Mum and Dad — that they would not let us down — that our back door was always open for us to run in from school, street or garden. Mum would always be there and Dad would not be far away in the Nursery, except for his time in the Army.

Observing today how molly-coddled children are, yet often unwell, it seems incredible to me that in our day, children, many ill-fed and poorly clothed, spent many hours in the streets in all weathers, including awful London fogs, yet until the dreadful wartime conditions finally started to undermine their health, they were rarely absent from school. We Robinson children were a tough lot. When back in from play, most of us would be given a chunk of white bread thinly smeared with margarine, and a mug of hot water in which some condensed milk had been stirred. Then we would be hustled out of the warm kitchen up the dark, dank stairs to an icy bedroom, which was dimly illuminated by a miniature oil lamp on a shelf. For we boys it would be only a minute or two before we had wrenched off our collars, discarded our waistcoats, jackets, breeches, and had squeezed ourselves under the blankets. Our boots would have been left by the kitchen fire.

In the winter mornings, Fred and I were reluctant to stir ourselves for school. It was only when Mum's voice coming up the stairs reached a strident pitch did we know that immediate action was necessary if we were to get into the playground before the whistle blew. With my eyes still half shut I would reach out for my breeches which I hoped would be found at the foot of my bed; I would tighten up my stockings, adjust the garters, pull on my breeches and tumble down the stairs to the cosy crowded kitchen. We hurried to get ready, trying to do at least two things at once, munching a crust of white Coburg loaf and sipping a mug of cocoa in which we hoped there would be some condensed milk; we fumbled with our collars and studs, fastened up our annoying bootlaces, then quarrelled for our turn in the outside W.C. before finally putting on our waistcoats and jackets. Pulling our caps on to our cropped heads we were up the road; in a panic, to avoid being late.

It was on such a morning, sitting in the classroom feeling relieved I had just managed to squeeze into the playground before the whistle had blown, that teacher stood over me and stabbed her finger at something written in my exercise book, questioning me as to why I had done it. My reply did not satisfy her, so she sent me out to the front. I expected she would get out her ruler — but no — she took me by the arm and escorted me out of the classroom to another, where she talked to a teacher.

I could see by the shaking of heads that things were not going in my favour, this being confirmed by then being escorted to another classroom, where, in front of fifty or so other boys, the head teacher caned me. Back in my classroom I was stood out the front whilst teacher announced that I was untruthful and that I was monitor no longer. Afterwards I sat at my desk and sulked. My only relief was that part of my humiliation, the caning, had not been witnessed by my classmates.

My monitorship had lasted two days. I was more sorry about that than getting the caning,

Bush Hill Pk. Jun. Boys' School

Report for Half Year ending March 191[illegible]

Subject	Marks obtained	Full marks	Subject	Remarks
Arithmetic	13	25	Oral Work	Very Good
Reading	6	10	Recitation	Fair
Writing	4	10	Singing	"
Composition	22	30	Drill	"
Spelling	17	20	Drawing	"
Totals	62	95		

Name – Sid Robinson

Position in class – 35th

Conduct – Fairly good

Regularity – V. Good usually

Punctuality – Exc.

Remarks – Sid has plenty of brain power but is so thoroughly idle that he cannot possibly go into Class 3

Head Mistress M Wye

Class Teacher M. Matthews

On the above Report boyhood erasures and "improvements" have been put right where possible. The "Very Good" for Oral Work remains suspect - it was more likely "Very Fair".

Name of Child	Amount of Punishment	Mode of Punishment	Reason
Robinson S.	2	on hand	Careless Work
Robinson S.	2	hands	Idleness
Robinson, Sydney	2	on hand	Idleness
Robinson S.	3		writing in exercise book without permission and lying
Robinson, Sydney	2 each	on each hand	misbehaviour untruthfulness

because being monitor had made an unimportant boy feel important for once.

On another such wintry morning, not long after classes had started, I was unlucky enough to be sent out to stand in the corridor for some offence or other. I was not allowed to move from there until I had been dealt with by my head teacher or had been called back into the classroom by the teacher if she had relented. However, that morning I had got very cold and my unpredictable bladder required it to be emptied urgently. I did not know what to do, because I dared not re-enter the classroom. But how could I leave my place, cross the corridor, descend several flights of stone stairs and leave the school building, then walk a long way across the playground without being observed or missed? And in my hobnail boots? But soon I had no choice, for I could feel an uncontrollable slight trickle down my thighs.

In the W.C., uncovered and open to the icy wind, I started to wet myself properly whilst undoing my fly buttons. Then, to my utter dismay, I found I was unable to re-fasten myself because of my frozen fingers and the stiff button holes. I panicked and would have run out of the playground home, if I had not feared the consequences. Frustration and fear made me downcast and tearful as I walked quietly as possible back to the school building, up the stairs into the corridor. The head teacher seated at her desk asked me, not unkindly, what I had been up to. I tried to explain, but was completely incoherent, so I pointed at my open fly. She rose and bent down to fasten my buttons, becoming irritated at finding me wet. She said that I ought to be ashamed of myself and "such a big boy too". Tapping my head hard with her knuckles, she told me to go back to my classroom immediately.

As I moved away from her I could not make up my mind what to do. The head teacher did not know I had been sent out of the classroom to be dealt with by her. The teacher did not know that I had gone off to the W.C. without permission. By the time I reached my classroom door there seemed no option left, for the head teacher had followed behind me to deal with one of my older mates, George who was standing outside the door of his classroom next to mine. Timidly, I went in, so overwhelmed by events that I had started to snivel. Teacher looked round from the blackboard on which she was writing. Impetuously I quickly put one of my hands into the other armpit, squeezing it as if I had been caned on it. My ploy worked and I was motioned back to my desk, where I sat, hardly believing my good luck. My cockiness was restored and I am ashamed to have to admit that only a minute or so afterwards I felt even more smug when, judging from the sound coming from almost outside our classroom, I knew that George was getting the stick I had so cleverly evaded. George would not be snivelling. He was a big, courageous, mischievous boy I envied.

When home for dinner, I managed to persuade the rest of the family to let me stand close up to the kitchen range for a short time, so that I could try and get my breeches dry, which were still very damp, though my shirt tail had dried. The unpleasant smell of wet corduroy, so familiar to me, and no doubt to our teachers, was lost in the stench of the boiled cabbage, a staple item for our midday meal in the kitchen. After dinner time, in the playground, I noticed my teacher and the head teacher enter the school building together. My cockiness dissipated and was replaced by a feeling of apprehension, which was fully justified because, on entering the classroom, teacher told me to report to the head teacher at once. When there, she picked up a cane and told me to put my hand out. I did so whilst blurting our "Please Miss, I couldn't help it, could I, I had to go". She hesitated for a moment and then said angrily "You are not being punished for going to W.C., you are being given the stick for being a disobedient and deceitful boy". She then proceeded to do so.

Afterwards she accompanied me back to the classroom, where she talked for a moment with the teacher. I was told to go back to my desk, where I sat frustrated, sullen and in pain. The other boys knew only that I had been in trouble, and they weren't going to learn why from me, even if they had been interested, which was improbable in those days.

To obtain these Certificates from school I must have taken at least a halfpenny each time. I expect I pestered Mum for the money in the hope of getting into teacher's good books for once. Certificates have survived for Fred, Kit and Jessie so it looks as if Mum had to part with pennies she could ill afford. It seems that times became so hard for us in 1917 and 1918 that we obtained no pennies, because no other certificates have survived.

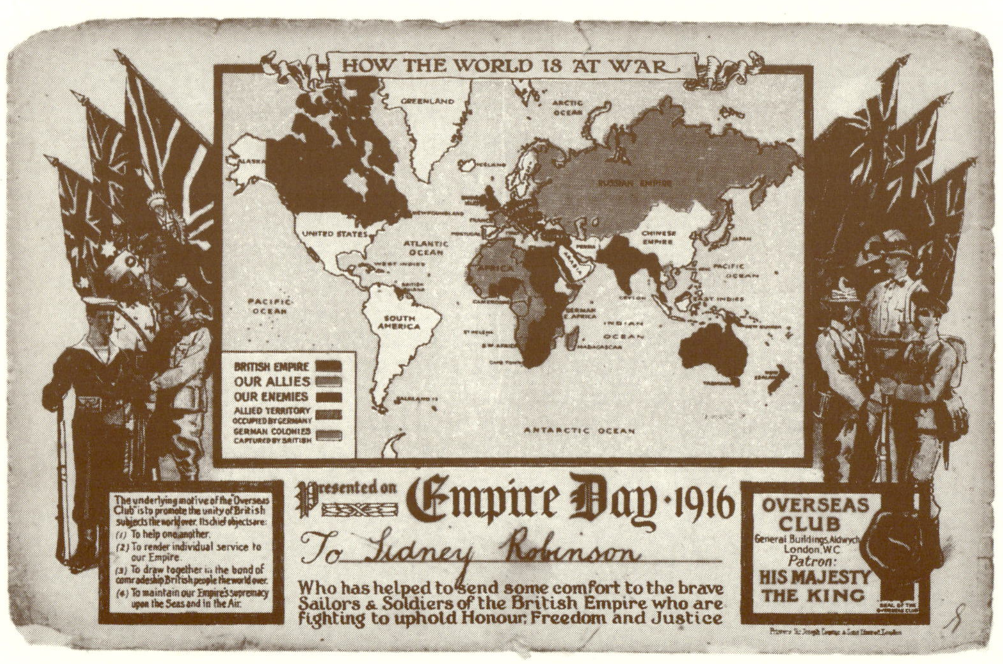

CHAPTER 9

It is likely that experiences such as this started the nervous or anxious feeling about my unpredictable bladder, made worse by the disinclination of teachers to grant permission to "leave the room" or to be "excused", even after pleading urgency, as I often did. It was made clear to me that I was becoming a nuisance, so I adopted the procedure of waiting until the very last minute before the whistle blew in the playground, watching for the emergence of the first teacher on the school steps, to rush off to the W.C. to make sure my bladder was absolutely empty. It was a risky business always, because I never knew the time.

For me in those days, emptying my bladder was not the easy task it is today. There was no zip fastener on the front of the trousers and no coat-type shirt which opened right down the front. I had to undo several buttons, usually with stiff button holes, to make an opening large enough to be able to get my hand inside to grope around and pull out of the way a large amount of shirt and flannel vest which I had tucked down well over my thighs and between my legs. This was a frustrating task at the best of times, but a formidable one when in a hurry, especially with nervous, boyish fingers often cold and numb.

All this had to be restored and buttons refastened before I would rush out of the W.C., hoping that I would be able to join the line of boys being formed, unobserved. Any misjudgement or mishap causing me to try to get into place after the lines had been formed would be interpreted as being late, for which a "hander" was given in the corridor or on the platform, as a penalty.

The satisfactory completion of the precautionary measure of the late visit to the W.C. gave me the necessary confidence to last until the next time I was free. However, should I omit to carry it out, through miscalculation or lateness arriving in the playground, and become aware of the omission once I was seated at my desk, I would start to panic, working myself up until I had an urgent desire to go. If this should occur early on after classes had started, I would not dare to put my hand up to ask to be excused, knowing that I would be ridiculed and refused. I would have to sit in mounting misery and discomfort, unable to concentrate, bringing on me reprimand and threats of "that stick". If I reached a state of emergency and got hot all over, I would blurt out desperately "Miss, I've got to go Miss". If that happened, teacher would reluctantly agree, but tell me to stay outside in the corridor when I returned. This meant that I would have to wait until I had explained myself to the head teacher. In the Senior Boys, though I anticipate here, the teacher could tell me to go, but bring back the stick on my return; this obviously to discourage the other boys from "trying it on".

Although I was a healthy boy I was plagued with other petty troubles. One was a perpetually running nose which needed constant wiping to prevent drips from it smudging the fresh ink in my exercise book. Another was the sudden violent sneezing fit, noisy enough to disturb the class and likely to spray anything within reach before I could locate and pull out the piece of rag, substitute for a handkerchief, which could be in any one of four pockets in my jacket or breeches. My antics were resented by the boy sharing a desk with me, so I tried to remember to keep the rag in a pocket on the far side of him. The jacket pocket was the most advisable, owing to the struggle I would have in fishing it out of a tight breeches pocket; almost an impossible task unless I stood up at my desk, which was asking for trouble. Once, in jerking out the rag which by oversight I had placed in a pocket nearest the boy, I jogged his elbow. Immediately he kicked me under the desk with his heavy boot, causing me to shout out impetuously "You bugger". My explanation to the teacher was not accepted, and my fate was sealed when the boy was able to show how I had spoiled his neat writing. I got the stick. On another occasion, after starting a sneezing fit, I was able to seize only the very small area of the rag with the tips of one finger and thumb at the bottom of the tight pocket of my breeches. I lugged at it hard, and it shot out — so did my set of five stones which bounced down the aisle, making an alarming clatter. I was made to pick them up and give them to the

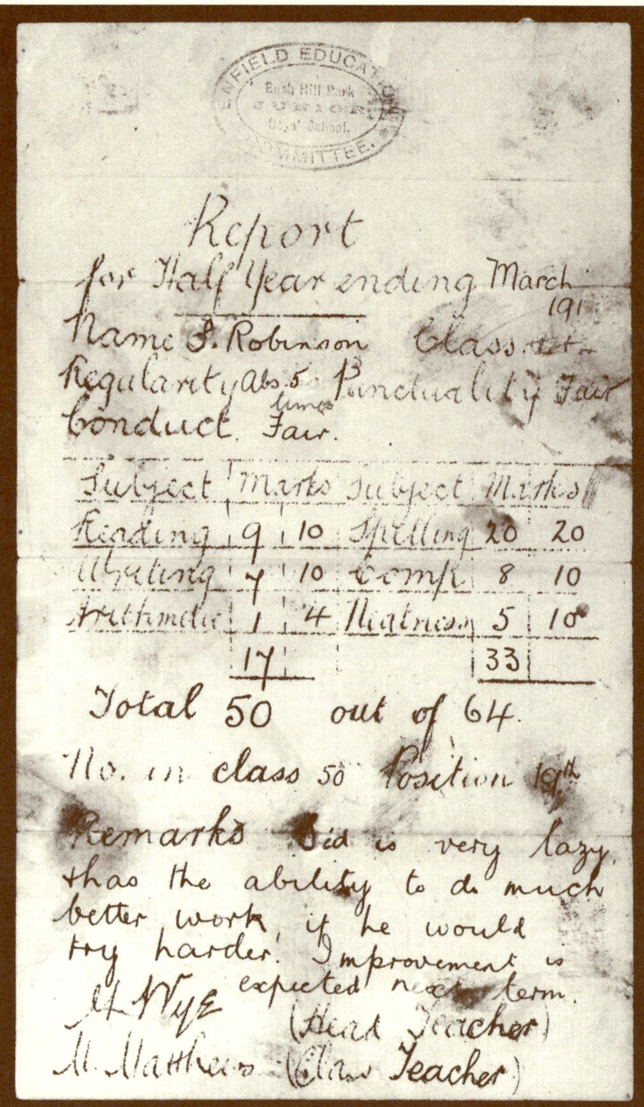

ENFIELD EDUCATION COMMITTEE
Bush Hill Park Junior Boys' School.

Report
for Half Year ending March 191[illegible]

Name S. Robinson Class [illegible]
Regularity Abs. 5 times Punctuality Fair
Conduct Fair.

Subject	Marks		Subject	Marks	
Reading	9	10	Spelling	20	20
Writing	7	10	Comp.	8	10
Arithmetic	1	4	Neatness	5	10
	17			33	

Total 50 out of 64.

No. in class 50 Position 19th

Remarks Sid is very lazy, & has the ability to do much better work, if he would try harder. Improvement is expected next term.

H. Nye (Head Teacher)
M. Matthews (Class Teacher)

Name of Child	Amount of Punishment	Mode of Punishment	Reason
Robinson S. Watts	2 ea	on hands	Continued Idleness
S. Robinson	4	on hands	Truanting
Robinson S	3	on hands	Disobedience & Deceit

teacher, who then gave me the stick.

Sometimes I could not find the rag, so I had no choice but to wipe my face on the sleeve of my coarse tweed jacket on which a hard matted patch had formed. This probably accounted for my permanently sore nose.

These troubles, coupled with my alleged laziness and impetuous acts, about which I was sometimes untruthful, disappointed the teachers who told me I could do well if I only tried. I earned the reputation of being a difficult boy.

Scholastically I did seem to be improving, judging by those School Reports which have survived for that time. I moved from 35th place in a class of fifty boys to 18th and from "thoroughly idle" to "very lazy". Conduct wise however, I slipped from "fairly good" through "fair" to "inclined to be troublesome". It was fortunate for me that Dad had other things on his mind over that period otherwise I would have been in bother at home as well as at school. I had not learned a reliable way then to keep the Reports from Dad but he had troubles of his own, fearing that he would be called up for the Army.

My unpredictable bladder had to be borne in mind at weekends when going out with the family on our shopping trips and for the occasional Sunday afternoon walks. I usually kept the rest of the family waiting whilst going outside to the W.C. in the backyard as a precautionary measure at the last minute, but even then, on cold days, I would be on tenterhooks after being out for a while for fear I would find myself in a place where there was no public convenience. Very often on the way home I would be running ahead of the rest to get round the backyard to the W.C. What bliss when I safely got there! I envied Fred and Ivy who never seemed to want to go.

On Sundays fortunately we went out only on warm, sunny days which suited me, but I was not really at ease because the public lavatories were closed on Sundays. My bladder did not know what day it was so, if caught out, I would have to run off somewhere to a place not too exposed to curious eyes, much to Dad's annoyance. For some reason such behaviour was strongly disapproved of, especially on Sundays. I must have peed in many public places and private alleyways in and around Enfield, nervously and hurriedly. What I would have been like if wearing short knickers with bare knees as some boys did, dared not be imagined — and with no underpants!

In the school lavatories across the playground, in spite of my always ready and copious supply of water, I failed miserably in competition with other boys to see who could shoot the highest or the farthest. My failure in this contest, for which I was well endowed to take part, showed my lack of manual ability or dexterity; for although at school I learned to read, write, and do sums quickly and to draw, I could not use tools other than pen and pencil. Brother Fred, two years my junior, could always beat me at flicking "fag cards", spinning tops, playing at marbles or tip-cat. He could do carpentry. One summer evening when we both were sitting together on a box in the garden, Fred boasted that he had so sharpened his penknife that he could cut anything, and to prove it he very carefully sliced off the ribbed pile of the thick corduroy on the knee of one leg of his breeches, tightly stretched.

When Mum came out to take in some washing, she was shocked. Dad came out and seized hold of Fred, taking him indoors. I do not know how other boys might have behaved in similar circumstances, but I stayed put, being glad it was not I in trouble. I was not the nice boy others thought me to be. They were fooled — the exception being my teachers, who saw through me.

But this time I had not fooled Dad. After a few minutes, he came to the back door and shouted for me. In the privacy of the front room he angrily asked "Where's your bleeding common sense, why did you bloody well not stop him?". The walloping he gave me with his strap on my bare backside was the first and not the last. It ought to have been a warning to me. Dad was well justified in being angry, not appreciating Fred's demonstration of his manual skill — the corduroy breeches were nearly new and had cost nearly eight shillings.

Dad was getting desperate. The cost of living had risen so much that all his wages, including overtime, were required to pay the rent, to buy what food could be afforded if found, and for the

ENFIELD.

Local Tribunal:—Name PUBLIC OFFICES

Address

Certificate No. 1539

This is to certify that:—

Name (*in full*) Sydney John Robinson

Address (*in full*) The Cottage, Lows Nursery, Bush Hill Park, Enfield

Age 36. Where attested Edmonton

Group 40. Number on Group Card 651.

Occupation, profession or business Nursery foreman.

is exempted from being called up for Military Service.

The exemption is* for a period of three months from 7th September 1917, conditional upon following above occupation

The ground on which the exemption is granted is

Certified occupation, and Domestic position

Signature T. W. Scott

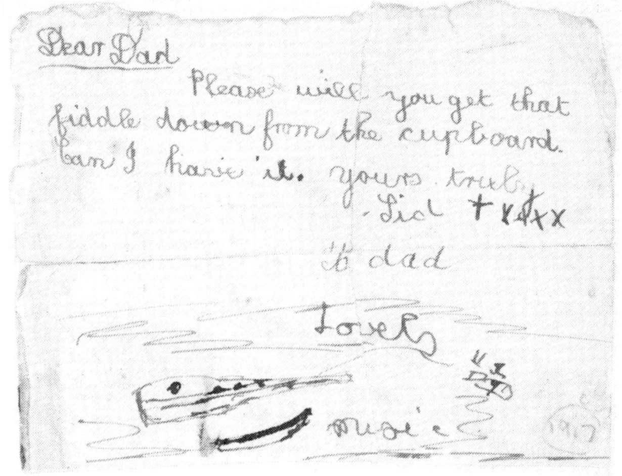

Dear Dad

Please will you get that fiddle down from the cupboard. Can I have it. yours truly

· Sid +xxxx

to dad

Lovely

music

1917

Written on my ninth birthday

coal to keep the kitchen range fire going summer and winter, because we had no gas cooker.

Mum had to stay up late that evening to repair the damage Fred had done. The patch on the knee of his breeches was a reminder, for months to come, of the incident.

People unfamiliar with those times may think we were being harshly treated. I doubt if we had such thoughts. We knew the world was a hostile place. Our two cousins were fighting in France; Uncle Arthur was a prisoner of war in Germany (this was the Uncle at whose wedding I had disgraced myself). The Germans were sinking our ships carrying food which we needed in order not to starve, and dropping bombs on us at random. Some families of soldiers were living almost in poverty with nobody seeming to care. Discharged soldiers with no arms or no legs were not an uncommon sight in our streets; some of them being seen to beg.

Those boys with soldier fathers or brothers liked to wear their Regimental Badges proudly on their jackets. If my Dad was called up, I intended to do the same. I remember one such boy who sat just to the right in front of me. One morning he was absent and stayed away from school for three days. On the fourth he returned with a black band on the arm of his jacket. His Dad had been killed. He had been a mischievous boy, but now he sat quiet and pale faced. Teacher was kind to him. I didn't know teachers could behave like that.

I cannot recall how I felt seeing him thus. I did not understand tragedy, for nobody in our family had died nor had anybody I knew. In fact, although, there were twenty seven of us closely related living in Bush Hill Park, not one died when the dreadful Spanish Influenza swept over Europe to us. Even our three surviving grandparents, who were very hard-up, managed to keep going.

Funerals in our roads and avenues were frequent, and the black-plumed horses drawing the funeral carriages were a common sight as they slowly went past the neighbours' houses in which the Venetian blinds were lowered in respect of the dead. Men and boys would remove their caps as the cortege passed.

To Mum's dismay Dad was called up into the Army sooner than expected and she found herself isolated from her old neighbours and with less money than ever. In retrospect, I do not know how we survived from 1917 to 1919, but the seven of us did, staying healthy. Fred and I slept in a room with three outside walls, with a water cistern fastened to one wall. This iron cistern froze as soon as the first icy weather came, and deprived us water for our W.C. As we were very undernourished it was not surprising that we all got chilblains on our feet as well as on our hands.

In the dreadful winter of 1917 coal became almost unobtainable. Dad previously had tried to burn anthracite from the nursery boiler stokeholds on our kitchen range, but it was no good. Fred and I would trundle our old box on pram wheels to Cowell's the coal merchants in Fourth Avenue, in the hope he would be able to shovel a bit from the floorboards of his front room on which, in ordinary times, there was a small mountain of it. We would come back with some scrapings. I had felt the cold even on cool summer days, now I was frozen both at home and in school.

Due to extreme shortage of money, Mum considered herself lucky if she could earn a shilling or two, by sitting up late after we had been put to bed, trimming with scissors a long length of lace on a reel, for the Enfield Embroidery Company. It was slave labour, but Mum needed the money. When the task was finished I would be given the reel to take back together with a note asking that the half crown (12 n.p.) be wrapped in newspaper and carefully put into my breeches pocket and not into my jacket pockets in which there were holes.

This pocket in my breeches was used also when rumour had it there was a supply of margarine at the Maypole Dairy in Church Street. A shilling would likewise be wrapped and pushed to the bottom of the pocket, then I would be told to run the mile or so to the shop and join the queue. If I was successful, Mum would be pleased. Too often, however, the iron gates at the entrance of the shop would be closed before my turn came, and a notice put up which said "All sold out — no more goods expected today". If this errand was during the dinner hour I would be anxious, not ever knowing the time. Once, when I was back late for afternoon school, I had joined two other boys

The Maypole Dairy - nothing to queue for this time.

Food queue

A potato queue in North London

waiting in the corridor, unaware they had been interviewed by a teacher and told to wait. Suddenly Miss Wye emerged with a cane and had used it on all of us; my vociferous protest being the last of three.

I queued for potatoes, sometimes having to make do with swedes or turnips, which I disliked. Mum gave us boiled rice, but I had difficulty in eating it without milk or sugar. Once, I was sent to Mrs. Curson's the Cornchandlers, to buy some chicken maize which Mum boiled for our weekday dinner, but it was a failure, we hated it. Ivy could eat dog biscuits, but I could not. She filled any holes in her stomach with hip and haws from the hedgerow opposite our cottage. It was a pity we could find no use for the thousands of acorns which dropped off our oak trees. I was sent with an empty jar to Ebenezer Gibbons' shop opposite Enfield Town Station to join a queue in the hope I could buy some rhubarb jam, when a penny or two could be spared. Sometimes, when Mum could find nothing else she would give each of us a mug of hot water with "Oxo", into which we dipped our bread.

Poor old Mum must have often gone without for our sakes. She, and older sister Jessie, did what they could for Christmas in 1917 and 1918, managing to give us, as presents in our stockings, an apple, and orange and a penny bar of chocolate. For dinner we had meat stew, followed by some fruit pudding and custard, eaten in our kitchen decorated with home-made coloured paper chains. Christmas was always a magical time for us even if we had so little.

Hitherto, I had been unaware that children could be given anything by anybody other than by their parents, so I was surprised when Aunt Kate, Dad's sister, called on us, with a small parcel. She told Mum she had visited Uncle George Sole in Therfield, who had been pleased to have news of Dad and his family. He had given Aunt a pair of leather breeches which his youngest son had grown out of, with the thought that they may do for young Sid. I was delighted and persuaded Mum to let me take them upstairs to try on. When back down in the kitchen, protests and tears followed when Mum said they were too small for me, but they would do fine for Fred.

Next morning, when I heard Fred complain about having to put on the breeches intended for me, I became inconsolable, for I would have been thrilled to have gone to school in them; and to have romanced to my mates how I came to be wearing such lovely, country boys' leather breeches. Fred unwillingly went to school thus attired, much to my chagrin and envy.

Ebenezer Gibbons Jam Factory and Confectioners Shop (the supplier of rhubarb and apple jam), facing Enfield Town Railway Station, where Dad worked as a boy until the age of twenty when for reasons of health he started work in the open air at Stuart Low's Royal Nurseries. It was to this shop that Dad's sister, our Aunt Jess, was sent with a postcard for Dad requiring him to report on parade that evening for selection for the Boer War.

2. Wt. W0818/G1359. 1,000,000. 10/18. S.O.,F.Rd. Army Form Z. 18.

CERTIFICATE OF EMPLOYMENT DURING THE WAR.

(To be completed for, and handed to, each soldier.)

soldier is advised to send a copy rather than the original when corresponding with a prospective employer.

is particularly important that an apprentice whose apprenticeship has been interrupted y Military Service should have recorded on this form any employment in a trade similar to his own on which he has been engaged during such Military Service.

gtl. No. M/332548 Rank Pte

rname (ck letters) ROBINSON

ristian Names in full SIDNEY JOHN

R.A.S.C. M.T. Unit MT Depot Sydenham

Regimental Employment.

Nature of.	Period.
(a) Reg duties	From 25-6-18 To 31-1-19
(b)	
(c)	
(d)	

Trade or calling before Enlistment (as shown in A. B. 64).

Nurseryman

ourses of Instruction and Courses in Active Service Army Schools, and certificates, if any.

(a)

CHAPTER 10

It was not until Dad was in the Army did I realise what a strong-armed and strong-willed man he was. Mum was strong-willed, but good natured, so she gave way to Dad. He was often bad-tempered, probably justifiably so. He had chronic indigestion, had large family problems with inadequate means to solve them and had to labour physically long hours. Three of his children of school age were a handful. Ivy and Fred were troublesome in different ways, but were straight-forward, responding to discipline. I was the one who upset him with my devious ways and impetuousness.I became a little scared of him after he had so severely belted me for failing to stop Fred from spoiling his corduroys. Fred told me in later years that he had not feared Dad. This could be because I was the older boy and would have been considered the ringleader in any common acts of misconduct around the home. Moreover, I would not have been given the benefit of the doubt in view of my bad school reports. The result was that I got the most punishment, probably justifiably.

Dad's training as a part-time soldier had taught him what was necessary to give the outward appearance of being smart with the minimum of effort. This knowledge he put into effect with me. I was required to keep my boots highly polished and properly laced; my jacket and breeches buttons all fastened, my stockings unwrinkled and my collar to appear clean. Any other parts of me mattered little, and those that did not show mattered not at all. Only when I was to appear with him in public did he seem to be aware that I had a face, neck and hands.

But in his absence I no longer needed to please him. Unfortunately at the time we had a severe teacher who periodically and unexpectedly would make us stand at our desks before classes started in the mornings whilst she walked up and down the aisles inspecting us. Those who failed to pass the initial test were sent out to the front. I suppose teacher made allowances for our dusty or muddy roads, and the poor facilities for cleaning ourselves in those hard times, but the only excuses acceptable to her were from those boys who had to deliver early morning newspapers. We others were likely to receive "a hander" for having dirty boots, collars, hands, or knees if visible. In spite of last minute vigorous rubbing of my boots up and down my stockinged legs, the surreptious spitting on my hands and the wiping of them down the seat of my breeches I sometimes got the stick. Dad would have been shocked at the state of my boots, but my hands got me into most trouble. Only a Spartan boy, which I was not, would have put his already numbed hands under the mains tap (if it was not frozen up) in the winter of 1917 — the coldest for many years.

Not long before Dad was called up, he sadly discovered that both my school and weekend boots had their soles splitting due to the frequent repair work made necessary because both Fred and I kicked out our studs and Blakeys, requiring Dad to hammer fresh ones in almost every Saturday after dinner. Being very short of money he looked around for some really cheap ones, which he found. They were real clod-hoppers, a pair of country boys' boots of thick unyielding leather, higher up the legs than the usual school boots. They were initially kept for weekend use which was fortunate, because when I first put them on ready for our Saturday outing, I ran into difficulties, finding to my dismay that they lacked the metal hooks around which the laces could be looped easily before tying them round the tops of the boots, finishing with bows in front. These boots had "eyelets" the whole length of the uppers and because they were higher up the legs than usual and made of stiff leather, I found to pull them on and to lace up an almost impossible task for my young fingers. Fortunately, as they were for weekend wear, Dad and Mum were available to help me. I was pleased that they were not for school.

As most children lived only a few minutes walk from the school, no excuse for being late was accepted unless the child brought an explanatory note from his mother. There was certainly no excuse for any of the Robinson children being late — we lived almost across the road from the school. But, whilst Dad was in the Army I was. A contributory factor, though a minor one, was

BUSH HILL PARK SCHOOL.

SENIOR GIRLS' DEPARTMENT.

REPORT. DECEMBER 1917.

NAME, Kittie Robinson CLASS. 1a

SUBJECT.	MARKS. MAXIMUM.	MARKS. OBTAINED.
ARITHMETIC	10	10
READING	10	9
COMPOSITION	10	10
WRITING	10	10
SPELLING	10	7
RECITATION	10	9
HISTORY	10	10
GEOGRAPHY	10	10
DOMESTIC SCIENCE	10	9
DRAWING { Painting	10	9
DRAWING { Pastel	10	4
NEEDLEWORK	10	6
TOTAL	120	103

ATTENDANCE.
REGULARITY. } Excellent.
PUNCTUALITY }

GENERAL CONDUCT.
Excellent.

REMARKS.
Works well ~~on the~~ whole.

NO. OF GIRLS IN CLASS. = 50.

CLASS TEACHER M. U. Smith

POSITION IN CLASS.
8

HEAD TEACHER E. J. Groome

Older sister Kit's School Reports reveal excellence for Attendance, Punctuality and Conduct, coupled with good scholarship during a period in which we were all experiencing considerable hardship. Brother Fred and I however were getting unsatisfactory Reports, and Kit made it obvious to me that in Dad's absence what was needed was a firm strong hand to discipline us, which she was willing to provide (she was nearly thirteen), if so delegated by Mum; but in practice only with occasional and marginal success.

when I had to start to wear my weekend boots because the school boots were beyond repair.

One wintry morning I awoke, opened my eyes just sufficiently to see if it was still dark, and caught a glimpse of a thin layer of ice that had formed during the night on the lower part of the window inside only a few feet from where I lay in bed. My waking thought was to determine if it were a school day. I worked out that it was, so I snuggled down again, confident Mum would make me get up in time. As I turned over in bed I felt the cold air waft over my bare thighs in the gap between my rucked shirt and the tops of my long gartered stockings.

Then I knew what had awakened me. I heard Mum's voice calling up the stairs — "Come on Jack, come on Fred, you'll be late for school". Mum was not prone to exaggeration, and I could tell, even with head under the blankets, that there was urgency in her tone. Reluctantly, I reached out, with my eyes half closed, for my breeches always kept at the foot of my bed, straightened my stockings, adjusted my garters, dragged on my breeches, stuffed the vast amount of surplus flannelette vest and shirt right down over my thighs and between my legs, and then sorted out in semi-darkness my jacket, waistcoat and collar from those of Fred's which we hoped would be on the one chair in our little bedroom. Then we stumbled down the cold dark staircase, avoiding the wet wall on the outer side, and into the steamy, gas lit confusion of the kitchen; a haven from the gloomy hostile world outside.

I was only in there a minute when I realised that I had no braces to keep up my breeches. I asked Mum where they were. She replied that obviously I had not removed them from my Sunday knickerbockers last night, as I had been told to do. I said I did not know where they were and she told me to stop being silly and go upstairs and find them. So in my stockinged feet I went back into the cold and dark of the stairs and my bedroom. Ivy and I were notorious for not properly looking for mislaid things. After creeping about on my hands and knees, even under the bed, I could not find my braces, so went to where Mum kept my Sunday outfit praying that I would find them still on my knickerbockers. My heart sank into my stomach, and I started to wet myself. I shouted down the stairs in desperation. Sister Kit came up, in a bad temper saying "Don't you know that Mum overslept and it is already time for school — I'm not wasting my time up here". She grumbled whilst she looked, and because of something I said, she took the huff and was about to leave me when she pulled back the blanket — there were my braces! I instantly knew what had happened. Last night I had taken them off my knickerbockers, but had been too lazy to put them on my school breeches immediately, leaving them on the top ready for the morning. When dragging my breeches towards me whilst still in bed, the braces had been pulled under the blanket.

Perhaps my sister was a bit upset by my apparent ingratitude of her help, because, as she left me, her parting remark was that big boys got caned for being late and, as I was a big boy I had better hurry up, for it would serve me right. I knew that smaller boys got it as well.

Down in the kitchen again, I found difficulty in getting anybody to give me room to pull on my boots which had been warming by the fire. I felt an urgent need to go to the W.C., so I went out into the cold misty backyard with my boots unlaced. More delay followed, for young Fred was sitting in there. I shouted to him to hurry, whilst marching up and down making as much noise as I could so that he knew I was still waiting. At last I was back in the kitchen. To my surprise Fred was nearly ready for school. Knowing how much he hated clothes and never dressed himself properly, I could see from his tidily laced up boots, his collar in place, and the coveted breeches buttoned up correctly below his knees, that Mum must have dressed him. I was pleased because it could mean she would have time to help me; help I badly neeeded, for my fingers were numbed with the cold.

I started to dress, but was in great difficulty trying to fasten the stiff leather tabs on my braces to the buttons on my breeches, a task I wished I had done the evening before, as I was told to do. I moaned to Mum about them, but she ignored me for she was trying to get the kitchen fire going again. We were short of coal, as of everything else to keep us alive. The many buttons on my breeches and waistcoat took me minutes of effort. Luckily my collar fell into place on the studs.

Young Fred was asked, as he put on his cap, if he had washed. He did not reply, but grabbed a

Try one pair of Hurculaces, and prove for yourself their outstanding value. They are well dyed, solid and strong, and never look shabby in wear.

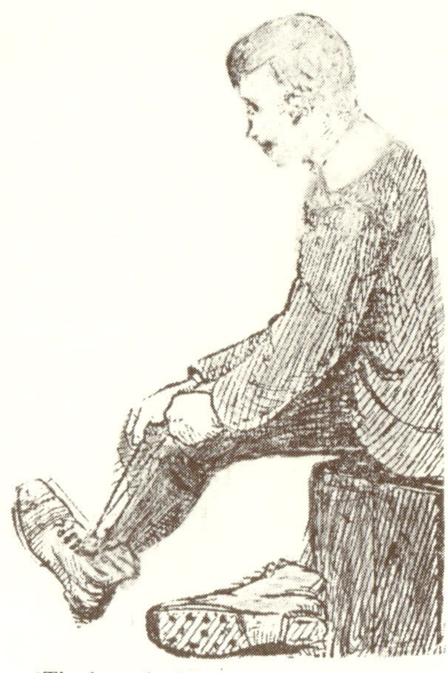

'The laces had to be started off right otherwise one had to begin again.'

The Boy and his Breeches

Every Boy has a knack of wearing out his knickers at least two pairs to one jacket.

What can be in worse taste than odd garments? Our

"Scotian" Tweed Suits

have an extra pair of knickers and are made from tastefully-coloured materials, specially woven to withstand "rough and tumble" wear.

They are designed, cut and tailored *specially for Boys, made doubly strong just where the tension comes*, and have more style than most suits.

Buy a **"Scotian"** Tweed Suit. *You* will effect a real economy and *We* make another friend.

"Rugby" Suit
including extra knickers
Boys 10 to 15 years
29/6

An interesting book, entitled "New Ideas," and patterns of "SCOTIAN" Tweed will be sent **Free** to all "Strand" enquirers.

We pay carriage in the United Kingdom.

THE SCOTCH HOUSE, Ltd.
Corner of Brompton Road
KNIGHTSBRIDGE
LONDON, S.W.

We lived in the days before anything had been invented to enable us to put on our clothes speedily and to get them to stay in place without the need for buttons. There were no zip fasteners, no self supporting pants nor trousers, no elastic waisted underpants, no socks, stockings or tights which stayed up by themselves.

FOSTER

UNDERWAIST
For Boys and Girls,

which supports the underclothing direct from the shoulders, and removes all pressure from the delicate abdomen.

No Cording to Retain Dampness.

Fitted with Foster Pin Tubes, which provide a secure fastening for the Foster Hose Supporter.

With Hose Supporters, **1/6, 2/-, 2/6, 3/-, 3/6.**
Without Hose Supporters, **1/-, 1/6, 2/-, 2/6, 3/-.**

OF ALL PRINCIPAL DEALERS, OR SENT POST FREE ON RECEIPT OF PRICE.

J. H. B. DAWSON, Ltd.,
72, Foster Road,
Parkeston, Essex.

chunk of bread which Kit had got ready for him, and hurried out to school. Of course he hadn't washed — nor had I.

I turned to deal with my boots. Lacing them needed concentration, as well as firm fingers, qualities both missing that morning. The laces had to be evened up both sides of the eyelets and started off right, otherwise I had to start again. But one side of the lace was nearly pulled out altogether. I lugged at the other end and pulled off the metal tag. In spite of spitting on the end and twisting it wet, I could not get it through the eyelet — all I did was fray it. I called Mum for help but she told me to wait until she had dealt with Ivy and had potted baby Winnie. I moaned and said I would get the stick again. I saw Ivy sitting on a chair swinging her legs impatiently with her high, lace-up boots undone. Knowing what a trouble she was when the boots were being done up, I had another go at the lace, but frayed it even more. I gave up, and ate my crust of bread which had been thinly smeared with some margarine I had managed to get from the Maypole Dairy. This together with the condensed milk-flavoured hot water, was the substitute for breakfast.

At last Kit took Ivy off to school; young Win sat contentedly on her pot, and Mum turned to me. She cut off the end of the lace with scissors, and tried to push it through the eyelet, but could not do it with the boot on. She then found I had left the length of the laces unbalanced so they had to be threaded through again. Whilst putting the boot on finally, Mum remarked quite casually that she thought the clock was slow, and that I had better hurry up. Realising there would be no time to nip into the school W.C. as I usually did at the last moment, I had to go back to the outside W.C. On returning to the kitchen to get my cap, my instinct to avoid retribution prompted me to ask Mum for a note to excuse me for being late. It seemed I had upset Mum as well as Kit that morning, for her reply was that I should stop being so bothersome and do as I was told. So, without the note, I hurried from the kitchen, through the scullery, round the garden and into Main Avenue, pulling on my cap as I went.

As I passed the Girls' playground they were filing in orderly fashion into the school building. I increased my speed, knowing I was late. Turning into Seventh Avenue I slowed down and edged forward stealthily, hidden by the Manual Room building. On reaching the school gates, I could just discern through the mist the last few boys of the lines standing to attention waiting for the second whistle. Another boy was standing behind the brick pillar on the other side of the gate so I moved slowly to stand behind the pillar nearest me.

I planned to slip into the playground quickly and slyly join the end of the line of boys in my class as soon as they started to move off, trusting that the poor visibility would hide my action. I never was to learn that I got into more trouble by trying to dodge punishment than owning up; expressing regret for the breach of rules. This time was no exception. Both of we late-comers moved in together at what we considered the opportune moment, but were spotted by a teacher as we became visible to her on getting nearer. The mist had let us down.

We were made to wait until all the boys had entered the building and into the corridor. Then, accompanied by the teacher we went in to stand in front of the assembled boys. At the end of prayers, before the boys were dispersed to their classrooms, we were asked why we were late and why we did not report to the teacher? I was about to answer, when the other boy said "Please Miss our clock was slow". Asked if he had a note from his mother, the answer was "No, Miss I haven't". My excuse was; "I didn't have time to get a note, I didn't want to be any later, please Miss".

We both got "handers", and we both snivelled; for the impact of the stick, spitefully wielded twice on our very cold left hands was torture. At my desk I normally sat on both my hands when free to do so to try to keep them warm, but that morning for an hour or so I sat only on my right; the other I kept gently squeezed into the armpit.

During my last year in the Junior Boys, I had the bad luck to find myself with a teacher I had previously, who didn't like me. I hated her. Within a week or two of the start of the Term I fell foul of her again. She had set us some sums on the blackboard, and told us to get on with them.

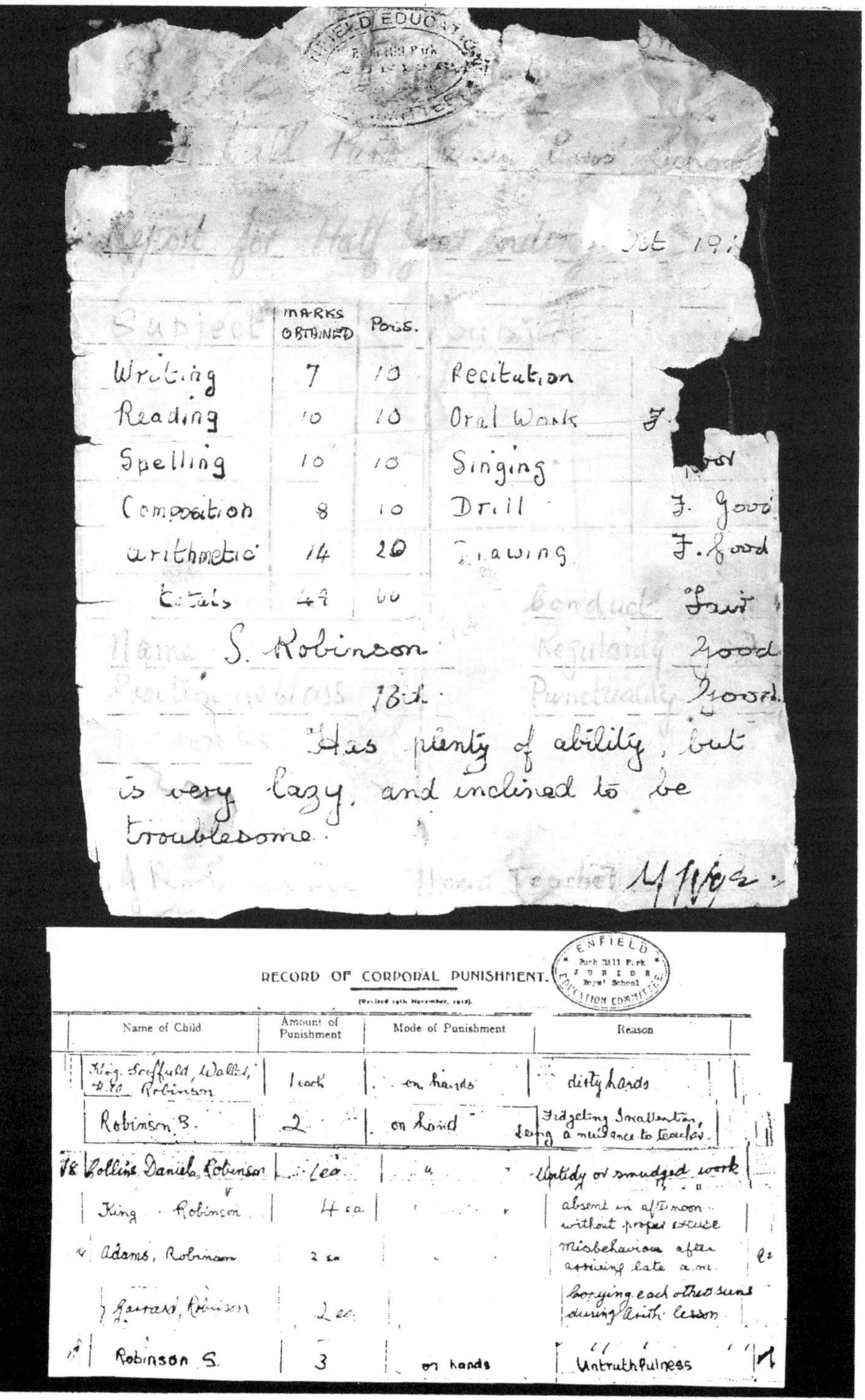

Report for Half Year ending Oct 191

Subject	Marks Obtained	Poss.	Subject	
Writing	7	10	Recitation	
Reading	10	10	Oral Work	F.
Spelling	10	10	Singing	Poor
Composition	8	10	Drill	F. Good
arithmetic	14	20	Drawing	F. Good
totals	49	60	Conduct	Fair

Name S. Robinson — Regularity Good

Position in Class 18th. — Punctuality Good.

Has plenty of ability, but is very lazy, and inclined to be troublesome.

Head Teacher M Wo...

RECORD OF CORPORAL PUNISHMENT.

Name of Child	Amount of Punishment	Mode of Punishment	Reason
King, Scoffield, Wallis, Robinson	1 each	on hands	dirty hands
Robinson S.	2	on hand	Fidgeting, Inattention, being a nuisance to teacher.
Collins, Daniels, Robinson	2 ea.	"	Untidy or smudged work
King, Robinson	4 ea.	"	absent in afternoon without proper excuse
Adams, Robinson	2 ea.	"	Misbehaviour after arriving late a.m.
Garrard, Robinson	2 ea.		copying each other's sums during Arith. lesson
Robinson S.	3	on hands	Untruthfulness

Normally she would prowl up and down the aisles whilst we tried to do them, but on this occasion she was occupied for a while talking to the head teacher. My desk mate and I took advantage of the unsupervised period to help each other with the sums.

Later, teacher collected our work and sat marking it at her desk, whilst we did our writing exercise. Boys who made mistakes were called out front. I became a little anxious when my mate was called, and I saw him appear to bluster, with a red face. I tried to gather my wits, in the hope that I could counter any accusations. But in spite of my glib tongue and protests I was sent off to fetch the cane for us to be punished for cheating.

The corridor was empty and the stick was not on the head teacher's desk, so I went in search, finding it and her in the younger boys' classroom. The head teacher asked me what I wanted. I told her I had been sent for the stick. As I spoke I noticed my brother Fred seated at a desk within ear-shot of us. All I wanted was to disappear as quickly as possible, for I wished Fred to know nothing of me in school. But I panicked when the head teacher said "Now what have you been up to?". In no way was I going to say in Fred's hearing that I had been cheating, so I blurted what came into my head "Please Miss it isn't for me Miss".

Back in my classroom the teacher gave my mate and me two "handers" each. I was then moved to another desk nearer the teacher where I could be more easily observed. At dinner time as we left the building my mate swore at me, complaining that I had got him the stick. I swore back at him angrily, saying that he had got the sums he did wrong, whilst mine were right. I added "You bloody well got me the stick".

Things caught up with me the next day when the head teacher came into our classroom, and I was called out. I was asked why I had lied by saying the cane was not for me. I replied that I didn't know that it was going to be. The head teacher told me I had behaved disgracefully, and that I was a difficult boy. Of course I got severely caned.

From then on I was in trouble. If I had to reply entirely on memory I would have said my last Junior School year was one of frequent punishment, being an unsatisfactory boy in all respects. But it seems that this severe teacher had been successful in one sphere — she had made me apply myself to my lessons. The surviving Report shows me tenth in my class of about forty five boys in the end-of-term tests. Success seems to have eluded her in other ways, for she still classified me as "troublesome". It had not helped when a boy told teacher I had altered something in my exercise book when her back was turned. I denied it without success.

I told Mum I had another teacher who didn't like me, and that she was always giving me the stick. But poor Mum was at her wits' end trying to keep us alive. Moreover she had an additional worry — Dad's employer had intimated that he could not go on indefinitely without a resident caretaker at the Nursery — a job Dad had assumed when we moved to the Cottage. Although time passed and nothing more was heard, it did not stop Mum worrying. She worried more still when somebody from the Nursery told her we were losing the War; that the Germans were marching on Paris. But at last it seemed that the War might end when the American Army joined in an offensive. This it did towards the end of the year, but our hardship was to continue for months.

During Dad's absence in the Army I did things he would not have let me do if he had known. In the dark winter evenings before I went out into the streets, I would prepare my winter warmers. This was an old tin can in which I punched holes with a nail and Dad's hammer. A piece of string or wire fastened through holes in the top of the can served as a handle.

Taking from my small collections of bits and pieces I had hidden in our big shed, scraps of old soiled rag, little bits of wood and some paper, I would set them alight with matches stolen from our mantelpiece, and put them in the tin. Blowing vigorously through the holes, and swinging it through the air by its handle I would get the little fire going. The stink was appalling, and I am sure that my school clothes stank to high heaven.

I was very contrary at times with my mates, especially if they agreed with each other in an argu-

RETURN TO ANY FOOD OFFICE.

RATIONING ORDER, 1918.

If a general mobilization is ordered, every soldier on pass must return immediately to his unit, without waiting for instructions.

PASS CONTAINING LEAVE Serial No.

or DUTY RATION BOOK.

SOLDIER OR SAILOR.

No. .... (Rank) .... Regiment .... (Name) ....

Regt. No. .... has permission to be absent from his quarters from .... to .... for the purpose of proceeding to ....

Is holder proceeding at end of leave or duty on active service or service afloat? ....

Signature and Rank of Officer issuing .... Station LOWESTOFT .... Date ....

N. 9a.

Army Form W. 3276. (Part II.)

Transfer of Payment of Separation Allowance and Allotment of Pay.

NOTIFICATION TO PAYEE.

To Mrs Robinson.

The Cottage, Lines Nursery, Lincoln Rd. Enfield.

You are requested to note that as Pte. (Rank) Robinson (Name)

has been transferred from 19th Q. R. W. S. (Unit)

to A. S. C. M. T. (Unit) (New Regtl. No. M 332548.)

separation allowance and allotment (previously dealt with by Hounslow II)

will in future be dealt with by this office.

Any communication on the subject of this allowance should be addressed to the Regimental Paymaster, Army Pay Office, Cambridge Barracks Woolwich S.E.18.

and reference given to the following number S.S.T.S. Group 2.

Date 17/12/18.

for Regimental Paymaster, A.S.C. M.T.

[2471] 500m 3/13 T1028 G & S 276 Forms/W. 3276/5

ment, against me. At the time of the General Election, in the last year of the War, they chose to be Labour, so I said I was Conservative. To prove it I joined a gang of boys who marched round the Avenues on Election Day chanting:-

Vote, Vote, Vote for Colonel Bowlsie
Chuck Old Hillie out the door
For Bowlsie is the man
That will give us bread and jam
And we won't vote for Hillie anymore.

Who put us up to this I don't recall, but I could be daft enough for anything. Bowles won, and I was cocky. I had failed to tell my mates that my Uncle Charlie, always broke but cheerful, was an active member of the local Conservative Club, and had informed me Bowles was sure to win.

When Dad had been called up he expected that he would join the 1st Battalion of The Middlesex Regiment of which he had been a member as a Volunteer; but he was assigned to the Royal West Surrey Regiment, then based in Lowestoft. I wore the badge of the unit on my school jacket. Later he was transferred to the Royal Army Service Corps, where he worked with horse-drawn waggons, eventually becoming a lorry driver. When he gave me the badge for this Corps I did not use it as I preferred to show my Dad was a real soldier.

He came home on leave for a few days in the autumn of the last year of the War, bringing a large can of bully beef and some plum and apple jam. We hungry Robinsons scoffed the lot in about three days. What a luxury! It looks as if things were falling off the backs of lorries then as they do today.

On the morning Dad was returning to his unit I realised that he was going to Bush Hill Park Station at just the time I should have gone off to school, so I asked him if he would give me a note explaining to the teacher that I would be late because he wanted me to accompany him to the station. He did so; and one of the biggest thrills of my dull life at that time was to march along with him, really proud of my Dad, as we went to the station, passing children on their way to school in the opposite direction. I kept in step with him, sorry again that he was not wearing spurs to provide a musical accompaniment to the sound of our metal-shod boots as they struck the pavements. When I returned I made as much noise as I could crossing the now empty playground and up the stone stairs to the corridor, in the knowledge that for once I could be late and proud of it.

IF FOUND, RETURN TO ANY FOOD OFFICE

LEAVE OR DUTY RATION BOOK Serial No. L 1 No. 134508

SOLDIER OR SAILOR.

1. Holder's Name .... Rank .... Number ....
2. Unit or Ship ....
3. Proceeding from ....
4. Beginning of leave or duty ....
5. End of leave or duty ....
6. Is holder proceeding at end of leave or duty on Active Service Abroad or Service Afloat? ....
7. Signature and Rank of Officer issuing ....
8. Unit or Ship of Officer issuing ....

N. 9 (Revised).

Lieut & Adjutant, M.T. Depot, Sydenham

M.T. DEPOT SYDENHAM

THE ENFIELD GAZETTE AND OBSERVER, FRIDAY, MAY 2, 1919.

Your boy is returning to School this week and he will need a Hard Wearing Suit.

We are offering for this week only!

Boys' Norfolk Suits

23/6

(We have only 200 of these Suits)

Boys' Standard Three piece Suits

as illustration, **35/-**

Size 3.

Boys' Cord Breeches

7/11

all sizes.

The boys wore corduroy knee breeches and jerseys and short coats. Shorts were unknown, and would seem unsuitable for all weathers. Their "uniform" suited the gangling lads, and was adequate protection. The girls wore serge dresses and big coats, and in summer pretty print frocks with pinafores. *Enfield,* 1926,

FRED WADE,

ALL TRAM AND TRAIN FARES

174-176 Fore Street, Upper Edmonton.
467-469 High Road, Tottenham.
399 Lower Edmonton.

The advertisement which prompted Dad to march the whole family to Lower Edmonton on a Saturday afternoon in May 1919 to buy new suits for Fred and me. He spent three pounds of his Army Release pay of twelve pounds: a Norfolk suit for £1.17p., and a Standard suit for £1.75p. & stockings and collars. Dad was earning £2 per week.

CHAPTER 11

When Dad came out of the Army he found Fred and me looking shabby; so on seeing an advertisement in the Enfield Gazette dated May 2nd, for boys' hard wearing suits at Wades of Edmonton, a shop he always used to buy our corduroy breeches, he decided to buy us new outfits for weekend wear. On an early summer Saturday afternoon, after Mum and Dad had been on their feet all week, the family was taken on a route march to the shop, where he used some of his Army Release Pay to buy us the toughest suits, some new stockings and celluloid collars.

Fred and I were each given our brown paper parcel to carry home — a task I performed with great pleasure and anticipation — but not so younger brother Fred who was already tired from playing in the street all morning. Moreover he had no interest in clothes whatsoever, and managed to look untidy however much he was bullied by Dad and cared for by Mum. He held his parcel by the string, swinging it back and forth as he reluctantly dragged himself along. Slowly he trailed farther and farther behind the rest of the family. Eventually he refused to carry it anymore, and put it on the pavement, leaving it yards to the rear before being noticed, much to Dad's anger. The parcel spent the rest of the journey home in young Win's pram which was propelled at times erratically by Ivy, to the danger of passers-by. She was an enthusiastic pusher of prams. Ivy was seven that day. Fred was eight, and had tremendous bursts of energy, but lacked my stamina and determination for things which required no special skill.

These clothes had cost Dad more than a week's wages, so we were constantly warned of the consequences should we not care for them. They were put on each Saturday dinner time when Dad came in from the Nursery; Fred and I then being sent upstairs to get the suits out of Mum's wardrobe. We had to take them into our bedroom, take off our breeches, and remove from them our braces to fasten on to our weekend knickerbockers. When dressed so that we thought we would pass inspection, we went back into the kitchen. If the weather was cold, I would be chilled right through before we started out on our shopping expedition. Whilst we had been upstairs in our gloomy bedroom, Dad would have been inspecting our school boots, to see how many Blakeys or studs we had kicked out during the week. Quite often there would be angry words, a clout or two round our heads, and threats of thrashings. Dad knew of course that we made sparks by kicking or striking the metal studs, Blakeys and metal heelplates against concrete kerbs to make sparks. Ivy only had the odd Blakey or two in her high leather lace-up boots, but she was frequently reprimanded for their state.

Now that Dad was out of the Army we were a little better off, affording meat on Sundays, which Dad cooked on the kitchen range, summer and winter. All eight of us sat down together at the kitchen table, but not before Jess and Kit had been sent to fetch their spare pinafores for Fred and me to put on to protect our waistcoats and knickerbockers; our jackets having been removed.

In those days, even the poorest people tried to have best clothes for weekends. We boys would dress fully on Sundays upon rising in the morning, knickerbockers, waistcoats, celluloid collars, jackets and boots, summer and winter. Ivy wore her best dress and high boots. We never questioned this habit — it was something everybody did.

I chose to go to Sunday school in the afternoons, primarily to show off my smart clothes. I met different boys there from those I went to school or played with in the streets weekdays. The boys I knew at school I rarely saw at weekends — I did not know what they did nor what they wore. Children did not play in the streets then, for there was quite a sharp dividing line for most children when their Dads came home from work on Saturday dinner times.

In my days there was no uniformity of dress for working class Council School boys. Most of us wore what was acquired for us by our parents, and we had no say in the matter, even if we wanted one, which was most unlikely. In the larger shops there was a considerable variety of suits available, but these shops were distant. Dad's priorities were for garments hard wearing, boy resisting,

In the Wade suit which cost 35/-

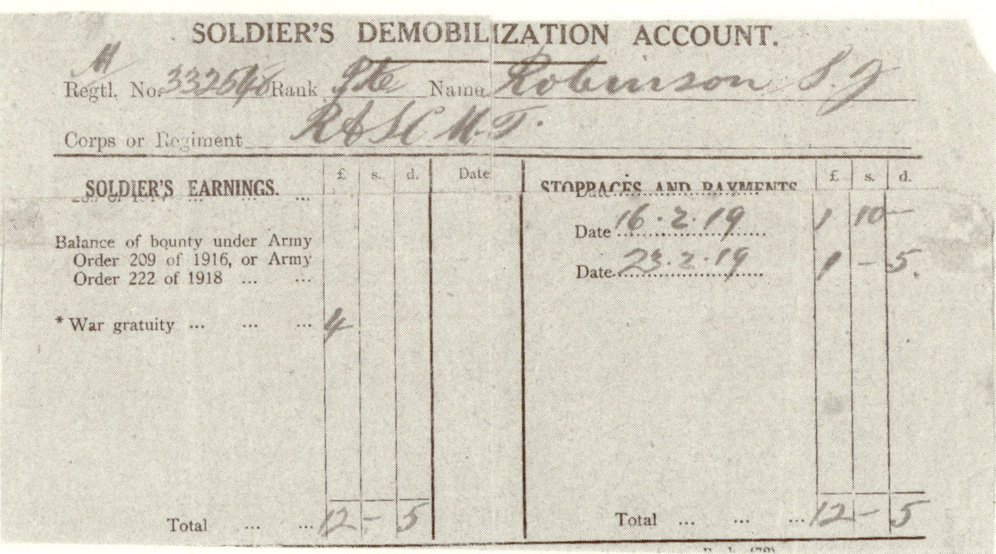

SOLDIER'S DEMOBILIZATION ACCOUNT.

Regtl. No. M 332646 Rank Pte Name Robinson S J

Corps or Regiment R A S C M T.

SOLDIER'S EARNINGS.	£	s.	d.	Date	STOPPAGES AND PAYMENTS	£	s.	d.
Balance of bounty under Army Order 209 of 1916, or Army Order 222 of 1918					Date 16.2.19	1	10	—
* War gratuity	4				Date 23.2.19	1	–	5
Total		12	5		Total		12	5

warm, of a colour which would not show the dirt, and cover for us as a protection from the neck to below the knees. He did not understand the meaning of the word fashion.

For smaller boys at school, a jersey and cord breeches were the cheapest, but bigger boys wore waistcoats and jackets, usually requiring an Eton collar. If money was short, a choker could be worn, but it was taken as a sign of poverty, for this choker was only to hide the neckband and brass stud of the shirt. Collar-attached shirts were not readily available in our area at that time, and the habit of wearing a starched linen or a celluloid collar both by men and boys died hard. Knickerbockers, knickers or breeches were worn with long stockings to above the knees, or to just below when usually they had fancy turn-over tops. Both kinds had to be firmly held in place by elastic garters.

Although things had started to change, it was so that until I was about eight or possibly nine years old, no boy would appear in the Senior Boys without being the object of comment if he showed bare knees, or was in long trousers. This was in spite of the fact that most boys were indifferent to what other boys wore — it was that bare knees were for small boys, and long trousers were for boys leaving school to work, though not always then. If money was scarce it would be permissible to appear in older brothers' cast-off long trousers if cropped to just below the knees. Slowly bigger boys started to appear with small amounts of pale knees showing between the bottoms of the knickers and their turn-over stockings.

The fashion of bare knees was created by Baden Powell for the uniform of his Boy Scouts in the mistaken belief that fresh air circulating around the private parts of young growing males would damper their sexual ardour, and encourage them to expend their energy in manly healthy exercise. I knew only one boy who became a Scout. Before he got his uniform he persuaded his Mum to shorten the legs of a pair of his knickerbockers, then he turned down his long stockings to expose a little of his bare knees.

None of my mates seemed interested in being a Scout. The discipline, the training, the punctuality required, and the drill seemed like an extension of school. Moreover, I disliked the wide-brimmed hat held in place by a chinstrap, the khaki shirt, the fancy garters, the rather baggy blue serge coarse short knickers and the broomstick. I knew I lacked the manual dexterity to tie knots, to light fires by rubbing two sticks together, and to use the broomstick for something. Young Fred would have made a good Scout in some respects, especially the skills required, but he was too lazy for that kind of physical activity, and he certainly would never have passed inspection on parade.

Some of the bigger louts in our roads would call after a uniformed Scout going on parade "Get your knees washed — Brussell Sprout". These louts would not have have dared do it when there were several Scouts going along together.

I have to admit that when I saw a uniformed boy passing by on his way to a Scout meeting, I felt just that little bit disturbed, realising that he had something in him that I lacked.

My contemporary autobiographers refer to short knickers as "shorts". Such a term was unknown in our day. Boys' nether garments could be called knickers, breeches or trousers, but never "shorts". This term was invented in the mid-twenties for boys. When for the first time in history these short knickers began to be advertised for sale, they were described as knickers with "open knees" or "open ended", to distinguish them from the knickerbockers which fastened with buttons or straps and buckles below the knees. Short knickers, often made of coarse tweed or serge, were narrow, and as they ended just at the backs of the knees, they caused soreness, leaving the bare flesh red and chapped in the cold windy weather.

It is strange that boys should have started to be so dressed at a time when living conditions for them were so harsh. Most of us were under-nourished if not underfed, and some of us were with bad circulation, getting chilblains on our hands and feet during the winter. Homes were cold, uncomfortable places unless near the firesides in the kitchens. We walked everywhere, and played in the streets in all weathers. Nowadays, when boys are if anything over-nourished, never need

Boys' suits could be got for 14/6d. in 1914, but the same suit cost 32/6d. in 1919 in Edmonton, and 75/- in the West End. It is no wonder that our Dad got mad with us when we were careless with our clothes. His weekly wages were about 40/- with overtime.

Fred in his Wade suit costing 23/6

*Right-
Cousin Harry Anthony*

The girls' favourite game 'Hopscotch', at which they would play for hours. All it needed was a button, or a small stone or a little bit of broken china, a piece of chalk and a length of pavement.

walk anywhere, and are in over-heated homes and classrooms, they wear long trousers from infancy. Thus is fashion! I wonder what Baden Powell would say if he were to see his beloved young Cubs and his Boy Scouts in long trousers, having forsaken his precious short knickers and bare knees! Moreover, it is impossible to imagine any boy over the age of nine appearing in school thus dressed today. He would not have the courage! Still, I digress.

Our Dad, of course, had no time for fashion, even if he had become aware of any changes. Our Nursery environment was unsuited for bare knees, and anyway, I was always complaining of the cold. The girls were not allowed to wear socks even when young, and in spite of Ivy's frequent requests when fashion started to change, she had to wear long stockings. She had great difficulty in persuading Mum to ask Dad if she could have shoes for Sundays when she was bigger, and it was only with reluctance that Dad agreed. She still wore her high lace-up stout leather boots for school.

Some social historians have recorded that in Dad's and my day, children were dressed as little adults. This was definitely not so. We expected to be dressed as children and were dressed thus until we left the Council School to start work. We were easily identified as such — even at a distance — boys by their tightly fitting jerseys fastened at the shoulder, or their conspicuous white stiff collars over their jackets. And the shape of their legs would not be disguised by adult long trousers. Girls wore long flowing hair or plaited hair down their backs fastened with gay ribbons; and their dresses, often with white pinafores, shorter than those of adult women. Girls wanted to look prettily feminine; boys wanted to look like boys.

Within my circle of relatives and acquaintances I was not at ease with girls, with the exception of my sisters, but these were at different ages to mine, and the gaps were large enough up or down to make us not have much in common. Fred and I had different mates, but we never played with girls, though young Ivy sometimes joined us in our rowdy messing about in the back yard; but she was a tomboy. I must say however that I did admire some girls from afar when they turned up at Sunday School in nice white dresses edged with lace, and in white stockings.

Girls no more wanted to play with us than we with them. The segregation of sexes was also in our schools, but we were able to see each other through the railings separating the playgrounds, before the start of school or during playtimes. Girls were prone to complain that boys shouted rudely at them through the railings; efforts then being made to identify the culprits by their teachers. Quite often even if the boys denied the offence, the girls' word would be accepted and the boys would get the stick. Should the news of this reach the girls there was general jubilation amongst them. Some girls referred to boys as "nasty" but I never knew any really nasty boys. We all could be noisy, boisterous and mischievous, and some of us rude and blasphemous, but not any more nasty than girls could be in different ways.

In our household Mum cared for everything feminine, Dad only being involved when money was wanted, or Ivy's boots needed replacing or repair. Although Ivy's misbehaviour differed from mine, she would have got as many beltings from Dad as I had done if she had been a boy. She may have been luckier though, because by the time she had reached the age I had been when I was in most trouble with Dad, he had started to mellow, he was less hard-up, and was getting weary of rearing children, six of whom had turned up in fourteen years.

Two Typical Elementary School Classroom Scenes

This excellent photograph showing a friend seated in a classroom identical in all respects to that in which I sat is included in my book because there seems to be no photograph taken of children seated in classrooms at our school, and this one serves my purpose admirably. Our school and others built by the Board of Education and the London School Board were intended to last for ever, and judging by what I saw when I visited my old school ninety years after it had been built, mine was going to do just that. The iron railings and gates, stone stairs, doors, hall, floors and the corridors had survived ninety years of use, as well as the glass partitions one of which can be seen on the left in the photograph, and the brown highly-glazed tiles, boy proof, on the walls, in the background. But there was one difference. Our indestructible desks and been replaced by frail furniture which could be pushed about. Our desks had been of thick solid oak planks bolted on to strong cast-iron frames fastened to the floor. We sat on planks roughly eight inches wide. The desks were shared by two boys, and were in rows on a tiered floor to give a better view of all the pupils when teacher was seated at her table. The desks had a small shelf underneath in which we were allowed to place our caps ready to don at playtime or at the end of school. These caps were the only personal property apart from that which could be carried in our pockets to be allowed in the classroom. Small white china inkpots were let into holes in the desks in which we dipped our pens, and care had to be taken not to dip them in too far or to pick up sludge which accumulated at the bottom.
In this photograph can be seen suspended from the ceiling the gas lamps intended to be used on gloomy days, but these were very rarely lit - in fact it was quite an occasion if they were. Out of sight to the left of the photograph was the coal fireplace, conveniently close to the teacher's table to ensure her comfort.
When teacher felt so disposed we were required to sit bolt upright at our desks with our hands clasped behind our backs, as shown in the photograph.

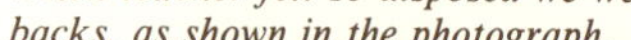

CHAPTER 12

After Dad was discharged from the Army I began to notice that he was very fussy about our appearance when going out with him at weekends. Perhaps it was that whilst he was away he realised how good-looking we all were, and was proud to be seen out with such a fine brood. One Sunday afternoon I really irritated him, when, just as we were going out he saw a wrinkle in my stocking. He made me partly undress, and stand on a kitchen chair, whilst he tied a knot in the offending garter. This cured the wrinkle but left me feeling very uncomfortable, adding to my difficulties next day at school.

In class on Monday, when seated in my desk, the restriction so fretted me under my thick cord knickers on a warm day, that I could not keep still, and I had to be constantly shifting my position and pulling at the garter through my corduroys. This brought reprimand and threats from the teacher. On the way out of the playground at dinner time the boy who sat next to me at the desk asked me if I would look after some money for him until the afternoon. I ought to have said "No", but I pocketed the coins.

My garter troubled me less when I was not seated, and I forgot it for a while. After dinner I did not see the boy in the playground, and to my dismay did not find him sitting next to me when class started. Boys sometimes, though rarely, were absent; but hardly ever absent in the afternoons if they had been present in the mornings. The space left in the otherwise completely occupied class-room made me feel deserted and conspicuous. My garter started to trouble me even more now, and I could not concentrate because of my apprehension when I remembered that the boy had come to school in the morning with a spot of blood on his ear, and on his collar, resulting probably from being hit. Before the end of the afternoon classes I got the cane for fidgeting and inattention. I looked out for the boy on the way home without avail.

The money was burning a hole in my pocket. After tea somebody came into the kitchen and told Dad he was wanted. Soon he came back angrily, seized me by the scruff of the neck, and propelled me to the front door. There he shouted at me "Have you got some money belonging to another boy?" I tried to explain, but he would not listen. I fished out the coins and gave them to him, and he passed them on to the women at the door. It seemed that the boy had stolen some money from his Mother's purse, had spent some, and given the rest to me to keep, because he was being beaten for him to confess. Eventually he had done so. I thought I would get a thrashing, but Dad clouted me saying that I was being more stupid than usual.

Next morning, when brushing off the blanket fluff that had adhered to my stockings in the night, I saw the deep red ring on the flesh above my knee, so I hurried down to Mum, but all she could advise was to try a bootlace intead of the knotted garter. I did so, but it was more uncomfortable. That evening sister Jessie made me a new garter.

The trouble really was Dad for having bought me a pair of thick, ribbed, worsted long stockings especially a size too big, in the hope that I might not push holes in their toes so quickly, but as they were thus large in all respects they had to be very tightly gartered to stay up. I knew why I made holes in the toes — it was because, on the rare occasions I cut my toe-nails, I did so with the very blunt kitchen scissors — a very unsuitable tool in my awkward hands. As a result, my big toe-nails were jagged with sharp points, which soon cut the fibres of the stockings. I had not heard of a nail file.

◁ *Some classrooms in our schools had desks which lacked the front panels. Thus were exposed to view our caps, of assorted colours and patterns of tweed, which we had hastily and untidily shoved on to the ledges underneath the desk tops. Such caps are just discernible in the part photograph shown here of a junior boys' class.*
Copies of these photographs cost six-pence (2 ½p), a sum rarely afforded by working class parents of large families.

Stuart Low's Nursery with our Cottage and our two oak trees in the rear. This photograph was taken in 1959 when the site was being cleared for the erection of office buildings. Everything was unchanged since we had played there as children forty years before, except for the houses at the rear of the cottage in Lincoln Road erected years after we had grown up. These were built where there had been orchards from which I had supplied myself illicitly with apples.

'landed on the backside with a bump'

CHAPTER 13

It was the partial realisation of two of my boyish ambitions that was to bring me trouble early on. One of these was to be able to get up into the oak tree which grew just the other side of the fence in the Nursery from our backyard. I liked climbing trees and I wanted particularly to get up this one because I could thus try to make myself invisible when I so wanted, especially for slightly dishonest reasons.

There was one obstacle for me to overcome — it was the narrow but high piece of fencing just in front of the tree which joined the lane fence to our shed. I thought about it a lot and planned one day to fasten a piece of wood on to it which would serve as a step up to the top and thus clamber on to the tree. The task would require tools, manual dexterity which I feared I lacked, and no interference from anyone.

My other ambition was to get hold of the boys' weekly papers on which I had my covetous eyes when I saw them in small piles, available to wealthier boys, on newsagents' counters. I so keenly wanted to read them but lacked the money. Then, one evening when I was buying a newspaper for Dad, I found I had picked up underneath it a boy's weekly paper from a small pile. I hesitated then succumbed to temptation. I paid for Dad's paper but did not pay for the boys' paper, and left the shop guiltily but trembling with excitement.

I looked round several times on the way home, and when in my backyard I stuffed it up inside my Norfolk jacket. I stood there absolutely thrilled that I had a copy of "The Magnet". I thought how lovely it would be to perfect the operation and supply myself from then onwards with this much desired reading matter.

It was now up to me to find that safe place to read it, and I thought of the oak tree. I went into the kitchen and found Mum alone with young Winnie. Dad had gone back into the Nursery with Mr. Phillips — young Ivy and Kit had gone to Aunt Em's — and young Fred had been allowed to go over to the park to play in the hay. If I had known earlier I would have gone too because haytime was fun. After being detained to turn the handle of the sewing machine for Mum whilst she did a thick hem on the petticoat she was making from Dad's old shirt for Ivy, I took Dad's hammer, pinchers, and the few long nails Dad had, and went to the fence, where after losing or bending all but one of the nails, I managed to fasten a piece of wood to the fence to serve as a step up to the top. It worked, and I clambered up into the tree to read my "Magnet".

So engrossed did I become in it that I did not realise how time had passed, so I hurried to descend before somebody was sent to look for me.

As I transferred myself from the tree to the fence I caught my jacket on a branch, and, in trying to release it, lost my balance. The hammer fell out of my pocket and I tore the knee of my corduroys on one of my bent nails amateurishly banged into the fence. I slid off the fence and landed on my backside with a bump. I went to pick up Dad's tools but could not find the pinchers and I started to panic. I went hot all over when I remembered that I had put them in my jacket pocket and that they must have fallen out as I climbed the tree, dropping over the Nursery side of the fence in the narrow gap between the lane fence and a greenhouse. I ran into the house to return the hammer and to see if Dad was still in the Nursery. Hearing him in the kitchen, I sneaked out again and ran through the Acacia House and into the Nursery.

Fright made me confused, and I found myself pushing through tall thistles and nettles down the wrong alley. It was with difficulty that I found the exact spot, which was covered with brambles. It was so near the side of a greenhouse that it seemed a miracle that the pinchers had not crashed through the glass and as likely as not smashed the plants. I could not have recovered them because on my way, searching for the spot, I found this greenhouse locked. Such a mishap would not only have involved Dad but others in the Nursery, and I shuddered at the thought of what might have happened to me in such an event.

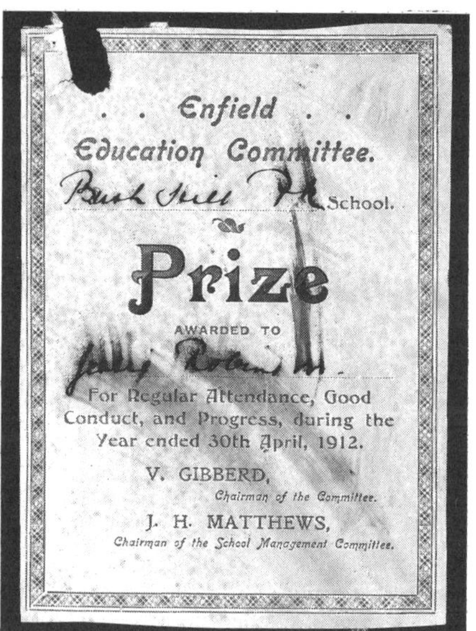

. . Enfield . .

Education Committee.

Bush Hill Pk School.

Prize

AWARDED TO

For Regular Attendance, Good Conduct, and Progress, during the Year ended 30th April, 1912.

V. GIBBERD,
Chairman of the Committee.

J. H. MATTHEWS,
Chairman of the School Management Committee.

The oak tree viewed from our backyard.

R.A.S.C.

Army Form Z. 21.

CERTIFICATE of* ~~Discharge~~ / Transfer to Reserve / ~~Disembodiment~~ / ~~Demobilization~~ on Demobilization.

Regtl. No. M 332548 Rank Private

Names in full Robinson Sidney John
(Surname first)

Unit and Regiment or Corps from which ~~Discharged~~ Transferred to Reserve Class Z — M.T. Dpt Sydenham R.A.S.C.

Enlisted on the 10th Dec 1916

For 19th Queens R.W. Surreys
(Here state Regiment or Corps to which first appointed)

Also served in ....

Only Regiments or Corps in which the Soldier served since August 4th, 1914, are to be stated. If inapplicable, this space is to be ruled through in ink and initialled.

†Medals and Decorations awarded during present engagement — Nil

~~Has~~ Has not served Overseas on Active Service.

Place of Rejoining in case of emergency Osterley Pk. Medical Category B2

Specialist Military qualifications Lorry Driver Year of birth 1881

He is* ~~Discharged~~ / Transferred to Army Reserve / ~~Disembodied~~ / ~~Demobilized~~ Class Z on 2nd March 1919 in consequence of Demobilization.

[signature] Lt Signature and Rank.

Officer i/c R.A.S.C. Records, WOOLWICH DOCKYARD. (Place).

* Strike out whichever is inapplicable. † The word "Nil" to be inserted when necessary.

(20906). Wt. W 8211—P.P. 2329. 3,000m. 1/19. D & S. (E 1256.)

N.B.—Any person finding this Certificate is requested to forward it in an unstamped envelope to the Secretary, War Office, London, S.W. 1.

WARNING.—If this Certificate is lost a duplicate cannot be issued. You should therefore on no account part with it or forward it by post when applying for a situation.

"they were under the brambles somewhere"

I now knew that the pinchers were beneath the brambles in the dirt and dead vegetation. I tried to kick the brambles clear, only getting my breeches and stockings entangled dreadfully. I had to use my hands to free my clothes, and then to clear a gap, scratching and pricking my hands severely. I found the pliers embedded in the muck, and hurried back to the house, putting them away with a sigh of relief to be safe at last.

But my luck did not hold. As I brushed myself down I became appalled when I saw the horrible tear I had made in my fairly new, seven shillings and eleven penny, cord breeches from Wades of Edmonton. I instantly thought of what the man had said when he passed over the parcel to me in Wades "You will have to grow out of them, you'll never wear them out". He didn't bargain for boys like me. But it was what I had done to my nice Norfolk jacket in which I was so pleased to go to school that frightened me most. Dad had told me to take it off after school if I was going to muck about in the garden, and put on my old jersey instead.

I think I must have stood in the scullery some time not knowing what to do, when Mum came out. She told me to go into the kitchen, which I did, standing behind the table away from Dad. Mum examined my damaged breeches, said that it was a bad tear and perhaps it would be easiest to cut off the bottoms. Dad looked up angrily from his newspaper and said "No bloody fear, Gert, you put a patch on them", and ordered me to get my boots off, then my torn breeches, so that Mum could repair them in time for school next morning. As I did so he saw the scratches on my hands and asked what the bloody hell I had been up to. Before I could think of an acceptable untruth, he saw Mum looking at the torn lining of my jacket. He exploded with wrath and, picking up his strap he pushed me into the front room and face downwards on to the sofa. He gave me it with nothing between it and my bare bottom. I did not protest, as I had nothing to say, being completely overwhelmed by the events of the last three hours.

When he left me, I stayed in there in my vest, shirt and stockings. I heard young Fred come from the scullery into the kitchen, and be shouted at for being late as well as dirty. Then I heard sisters Kit and Ivy return.

I was grateful to Mum for not calling me back into the kitchen until the young ones had been given their hot drink, and had been despatched upstairs to bed. When I returned to the kitchen no further mention was made of the incident. Kit made me my hot drink whilst Mum sat repairing my breeches by hand. I was told to get out of the way upstairs to our small bedroom, shared with Fred, who seemed to be asleep already. As I dropped off to sleep I wondered which part of me hurt most, my bottom, or my hands which now seemed to be on fire. I also thought of my precious "Magnet", abandoned in my fright somewhere at the foot of the oak tree.

My troubles were not over. Next morning I had great difficulty in buttoning up my clothes because of the thorns in my fingers. In class that morning I just managed to get by, but in the afternoon, using pen and ink for our writing exercise I could not. I saw two boys sent out to the front, one going off to fetch back the stick, so I knew teacher was in no mood to listen to one of my frequent excuses. She examined my fingers and said it could be that I had thorns in them, but that my hands were so filthy she could not be sure. I had not washed them since the previous morning, and not very well then. Of course I got the stick with the others, but only a "hander". Sister Jessie kindly poked out the worst of the thorns with her sewing needle. The remainder had to work themselves out.

Our Fred

It was quite a come-down when, about to take my place at the table, I was shouted at by Dad.

Main Avenue looking towards the junction with St. Mark's Road and Fourth Avenue. East Crescent, with the footbridge over the G. E. Railway line is at the rear. In the near left is the corner with Millais Road, on which stood Lucombe's pawnbroker shop. The three brass balls hanging in front of the shop can be seen against the background of the roof of the C. of E. school.

CHAPTER 14

On Sundays our kitchen was always in a state of crowded confusion. We were eight in the family, and the four younger ones, including I, were not allowed out to play. Children were not, in those days. These restrictions especially applied to us because we lived in the place where Dad worked, and his employers could be near our back garden unbeknown to us. Unfortunately for Dad's peace of mind our language was not beyond reproach. So we had to amuse ourselves the best we could on Sundays, dolled up in our best clothes.

Usually I went to Sunday School in the afternoons, for two reasons other than from escaping the medley in the kitchen. One, already told, was to show off my Sunday suit and white collar; the other was to play with children I did not meet in the week, outside the Church before Sunday School began. There, if I were lucky I played with a boy who sometimes had toffees in the jacket pockets of his green knickerbocker suit — lucky because he at times gave me some. I loved him for it. People not familiar with those days cannot appreciate what a treat it was to get toffees given to me — I had no sweets except the few I could buy on Mondays and Saturdays with my pocket money — and those did not last long.

Although I found churches cold uncharitable places, and still do, I went with Grannie Robinson some Sunday mornings. Sitting in Church I felt smug and self assured, as smart looking as the others in the congregation, and although I found the Service boring, I liked the part where we left the church. On rising from our seats, Grannie would remind me not to put on my cap until we were outside. At the door the Minister Mr. Gray would shake hands with Grannie, and then with me, addressing me as "young gentleman". On returning home and entering the kitchen, it was quite a come-down, when, about to take my place at the table for dinner, I was shouted at by Dad "Get that bloody jacket off and your pinafore on before you sit".

On the second Sunday after our visit to Wades, Grannie was unwell, so she was not going to Church. I sat trying to solve the puzzle in my weekly Comic for which a prize was offered. To my surprise I was able to do it, and boasted to anybody who would listen, about my success, but I read that all solutions had to be received by Monday morning. I wanted that prize — I had never won anything in my life. So I set about overcoming the formidable obstacles in getting my solution delivered next morning.

In those days there was a collection on Sundays, and the post was absolutely reliable, so all I had to do was to find an envelope and a stamp before asking Dad's permission to go up the road and post the letter. I persuaded my eldest sister to part with an envelope, but there was no stamp. I plucked up enough courage to ask Dad if I could go and find a shop to sell me a stamp, and would he give me the money? Dad was stoking up the kitchen fire ready to cook Sunday dinner. He replied tetchily that it looked like rain, and that he was not going to have my new suit, collar and boots soaked which had cost him more than a week's wages. I told him it was not going to rain — "it hadn't done for weeks and all the roads were covered in dust".

I ought to have known better than to argue with Dad — his job in the Nursery required him to know about the weather. He got angry, but I continued to plead with him. I had nearly given up when he suddenly picked up a coin from the mantelshelf, and tossed it to me, saying that I could go on condition that I came back at the first sign of rain. He also said "You know what the roads will be like if it rains after that long dry spell". I promised.

With my cap on my head I started off. I knew that the only shops likely to be open were the newsagents and some sweetshops. I first tried in Seventh Avenue, and then moved to Main Avenue. Surely Dad could not be right? There was a little drizzle. As I went on to East Crescent the rain began, but not heavily. I started back, but on reaching St. Marks Road I turned right, determined to have one more try. As I reached the railway station the rain was heavy, but I felt a strange sense of elation at defying Dad. Having no luck at any shop I reluctantly turned towards home. The skies

St. Mark's Road viewed from the junction with Fourth Avenue and Main Avenue. It shows the state of the road surfaces when it rained heavily after a long dry period.

A view of Lincoln Road end of Seventh Avenue taken in 1959 before the Avenues were demolished. It shows the original corrugated sheet-iron hut used by the Salvation Army, and the small houses, one of which, out of view, was used by Mr. Vidal as his sweetshop.

seemed to open, and the rain came down in sheets. I ran down Main Avenue, my covered knees already soaking, and the water running down inside my celluloid collar. Within a few yards of home, I slipped on some wet horse manure on the cobbled sloping entrance to the nursery stables, and fell flat on my face.

I was in a sorry bedraggled state when I ran round our backyard to the scullery door. To my dismay I found it locked, requiring me to tap on the kitchen window. I heard Dad shout angrily; but it seemed an eternity before young Ivy came to turn back the key with which she had been playing.

In the scullery I brushed off as much water as I could, and bent over to let the water run out from beneath my collar. It was then I saw the horrid brown stains from the manure on the knees of my tweed knickerbockers.

I gave up hope of escaping a walloping as I entered the kitchen, but I stood behind a chair to try to hide the mess I was in. Dad straightened himself up from the kitchen range, red in the face, and shouted angrily to me "Look at you, you bloody little sod — where's that bleedin' leather?". I looked puzzled, and said "What leather?". He shouted "Letter — not leather — I'll leather you". I gave him the sodden envelope containing my puzzle solution, which he threw into the fire, saying that I was to get upstairs and change into my school clothes, and "Be quick about it". At that moment I could have told Dad that I was sorry for what I had done, but when I was in trouble with Dad or at school as a boy I seemed able to offer only excuses or to stay stubbornly silent.

I went upstairs to change my clothes as instructed. Undressing, I had great difficulty in undoing the very wet knots in my bootlaces, because my badly bitten very short fingernails were inadequate for the task. It took minutes of precious time. Then, when I had removed my knickers, I had a job to unfasten the stiff leather tabs of the braces to transfer them to my school corduroys.

I had just sat down on the bed to get my breath back before starting to tackle the braces, when Dad looked in the door. He must have misjudged the situation seeing me sitting in my bare legs, doing nothing. He probably thought I was either defying him or sulking. He went away but soon came back with his leather strap. It was then he saw the mess I had made of my knickerbockers lying on the bed. Seizing me, he got me face-downwards on to the bed, and, moving my shirt tail out of the way to expose my bare bottom, he applied the strap to it. When satisfied, he picked up my wet clothes and left me, asking "Aren't you ever bloody well going to do what you are told?".

When I had finally dressed myself, I crept down the stairs to the front room, where, placing two cushions on the sofa, I sat and sulked. Of course, Dad and Mum knew what I would be doing, and they let me be. The sun came out, and I became absolutely frustrated.

Later on, I heard Dad call out "Come on, Jack, dinner's ready". I knew from the tone of his voice that I had been forgiven, and the incident closed. So I went into the hot steamy kitchen to take my place at the table, sitting down gingerly on the hard chair. I was in a lot of discomfort, but I kept quiet, anxious for the incident to remain closed.

No reference was made to me during dinner or thereafter, for Dad, though violently bad tempered at times, bore no malice. Mum would have said nothing, being distressed at the trouble I had caused. Older sisters Jess and Kit were now young ladies, and the antics of a troublesome boy would have been ignored. Fred would have been quietly pleased it wasn't him. Ivy and Winnie were too young.

In the afternoon I went into the front room, out of the way, and to be able to arrange soft cushions to sit on. Being bored, I first looked through Dad's copy of the Popular Educator, but I was in no mood to be educated. I then tried the tatty copy of "David Copperfield", which I had found too difficult to read hitherto. But when I came across David's account of his schooldays at Salem House under Mr Creakle I was interested and it made me think less badly of my time at school. When I went back into the kitchen for tea, the sight of my best clothes on the metal guard, drying in front of the fire, was a reminder that I had been in disgrace again, this time on a Sunday.

Carts and waggons abandoned and rotting in the Nursery after they had finally been replaced by lorries. This photograph was taken in 1959. Fred and I as boys had many rides in the horse-drawn vehicles.

Peace Day, July 19th 1919. Two childrens' parties, the one immediately above, in Alberta Road, B.H.P.; and the top one in Sixth Avenue, roads where my mates lived, were typical of the many thousands of street parties given to children by parents and residents.
In the photo of Sixth Avenue is a tree. This had to be removed later because boys kept starting fires in a hole in its trunk, causing alarm to the residents, and calls to the Fire Brigade.

CHAPTER 15

Apart from the troubles I got myself into, I was living a very ordinary uneventful life as I approached the age of eleven. My total personal possessions consisted of my school and Sunday sets of clothes; an iron hoop and skimmer, a whipping top and some string, some marbles and five stones, some rather dog-eared cigarette cards, a stub of pencil usually very badly sharpened and an exercise book. I never seemed to have had any toys of consequence. I never had a scooter, roller skates, nor, of course, a bike. I had never any money of my own in my pocket, except perhaps a penny, which stayed there only the length of time required to get to the sweetshop. With the exception of my weekly Comic, and Dad's few uninteresting books, I had had no access to pleasurable reading matter until I started to obtain boys' papers and Comics without paying for them. I don't know if any of my mates were any better off but I knew that there were boys who must have been, judging by the Gamage's advertisements I saw in Dad's newspapers. I don't know if I thought it fair that I did not have at least a little of what some other boys must have had, but I do know that I thought it fair to help myself to small things if the risk was not too great.

Only once had I been to a public entertainment of any kind. The only music I had heard was sisters Jessie's and Kit's tinkling on the piano; the Church hymns, and the bands in the Town Park, Salvation Army and the Boys' Brigade. I had never been on a school outing, or on a Sunday School treat. I had never been inside another boy's house, except that of a relative, nor had any boy come in to mine. We did not celebrate birthdays, nor give birthday presents. I had never slept in any other bed than my own, for I had not at any time been away one night. The maximum distance I had been from my house was a few miles, except when I was able to scrounge a ride alongside the driver of a Nursery cart or waggon. Otherwise I walked everywhere, only getting as far as I could walk. I had never met any strange or eccentric grown-ups. All of them I met were boring and dull, except for my Uncle Charlie, my Mum and Dad.

Yet I am sure we Robinson children enjoyed ourselves once we escaped school in the afternoons. We were free to do as we wished, anywhere, as long as we kept out of trouble. We had no responsibilities, except to be back punctually indoors for dinner, tea or bed.

Perhaps it is because my life as a boy was so very ordinary in other respects that I can recall so much of those times when I was in difficulties. Or perhaps it is a guilty conscience. But I am still surprised how vague I am about the few events which should have been pleasurable and memorable. One such was Peace Day in July 1919. I had been promoted to the Seniors earlier than I had expected, and, as such, had became eligible to take part in the Procession. We all paraded in the school playground on the Saturday morning, in our Sunday best suits and boots, where we were given each a small flag to carry on a stick. We marched smartly off, for we were all patriotic. Each school in Enfield represented a different country of the Empire. I was disappointed to find that we were to carry Scottish flags, for I would have loved to carry the English one — my Dad had told me we came from pure English stock and that I was English.

We were joined by hundreds of other boys as we marched along Southbury Road, some from the George Spicer School. In the Town Park there was a Brass Band playing; and we gave three cheers several times during the morning. I regret I can recall nothing more of it. But in the afternoon I was free to wander the roads of Bush Hill Park and stare at the Peace Day parties given to the children by the parents and neighbours. Tables and chairs had been brought out from the houses; and, I suppose, bread and margarine, with a drink of some kind was served to the children. There could not have been much in the way of delicacies offered, because wartime conditions still prevailed in some respects. We Robinson children did not participate in any street parties, because at that time we belonged to no proper road, and we had no neighbours except for the horses.

Playing with 'fag' cards.

Leap Frog, one game requiring no equipment but strong backs.

CHAPTER 16

From personal unpleasant experiences, and observation, I soon learned in the Senior Boys what was expected of us. We were required to be punctual, respectful, and well-behaved both in the classroom and playground. We should be as tidy and clean as conditions permitted. In this the teachers made allowances for our dirty, sometimes muddy, roads, our lack of proper cleaning materials and facilities in our homes. Talking in class or whilst forming into lines in the playground, fidgeting, inattention, laziness and carelessness would earn one or two strokes of the cane on the hands. These were known as "handers". Swearing, dishonesty, cheating, truanting, lying, fighting and bullying could earn four strokes.

Looking back, I think that the teachers, conscientious as they were, tried to be fair most of the time, encouraging the boys who showed ability, and punishing them when they were lazy or careless. Those boys who seemed dull were expected only to show willing, and to behave themselves.

I realised that I should not stretch my luck too far, because when the cane, usually referred to as the stick, was not in use in our class, it could be heard in use in any one of the seven other classrooms separated by glass partitions from one another. The ominous whistle made by it as it came swiftly down through the air on to a boy's hand was the background noise during our schooling.

The stick was the only punishment used in our school. All the teachers were skilled in the art of inflicting the maximal pain on a boy's hand consistent with causing the minimal permanent injury, and I had learned the hard way that the severity and after effects of a caning could vary enormously, depending on the mood, the intention and the accuracy of the teacher. If the fingers were struck by intent, or by miss-aim, or if I had moved my hand, it was very bad luck for me. One vicious stroke could be worse than three ritual ones.

As I grew older I became less apprehensive when required to put my hand out for a caning after having committed a relatively minor offence, because this could mean the usual ritual one or two strokes were given on the palm of the hand so that the cane bounced up immediately upon impact. These were known as "stingers". The pain was intense but bearable, and soon abated — that was if you were not unlucky.

A severe caning was a different matter. One such punishment was in the Juniors when two of us had truanted one afternoon, and had failed to produce the required "excuse notes" next morning. We were sent to the head teacher. My mate Bill was first to be dealt with, and, after the first stroke, he jumped back away from the head teacher, and yelled out in pain. When told to put out the other hand, he cried "No Miss, please". This cry he repeated after every stroke, and he finished up snivelling. My first stroke was so heavy that the intense pain shot up my arm, and seemed to make my feet leave the floor. I backed away, blowing and spitting into my throbbing hand, protesting. How many strokes we got I do not recall, but they were enough to have us returning tearfully to our desks with red weals and swellings like cushions on our hands. I was grateful that my humiliation had taken place in the corridor and not in front of the class. I have to admit that I was rarely ashamed of being punished: it was that I preferred to keep the knowledge of it to myself. Boys did not speak to me about their canings. In our school they were not considered a disgrace — in fact getting the stick was thought "Just 'ard luck".

In the Senior Boys, I learnt to relax my fingers and cup my hand slightly just before the cane came down, in the hope that the little cushions of flesh thus formed would help soften the blows. In addition, if circumstances permitted when a caning was imminent, I would squeeze and rub on to my fingers and palms, keeping my hands in my jacket pockets, the small scraps of soap purloined from the scullery sink draining board, and wax droppings prised from the candlesticks. I never knew how effective either of these two operations were, just as I was never sure if it was better afterwards to squeeze my hands in my armpits or to hold them gently against the cold ironwork of desk or bench.

ENFIELD EDUCATION COMMITTEE.

RECORD OF CORPORAL PUNISHMENT.

(Revised 19th November, 1912).

Photo-copies of entries in two such Records, one of our Council School, the other from a neighbouring Enfield Council School. These have been selected from many hundreds as representative samples, and have been mounted on the page haphazardly, intentionally.

	Name of Child	Amount of Punishment	Mode of Punishment	Reason
5	Holloway IVR	with the tawse on his buttocks		Truanting
5	Cowley	1 each	on hand	Constant fooling
	S. Robinson, Cousins	2 each	on hands	Continued idleness.
	Higgs	1	" "	Laziness
	Harvey	4.	" "	Writing filth on paper.
6	Trump	2		Marking on desk.
	Worth	3	"	[illegible] conduct
	Lewis	1	" "	Hindering another boy in his work
	Leslie	2	" "	Whistling in classroom
	Cozens, Wignall, Capens	1 ea	" "	Writing [illegible]
	Robinson (S) ~~Feltham~~ (123)	2 ea.	"	Playing in lines.
0	Ruff	1	"	Laziness
	Harvey, Edwards, Ricketts, Gillam ~~[illegible]~~	4 ea.	* on buttocks in H-M's room	* Wilful damage to School wall
	Smith	2	" "	Playing with & spilling ink
6	Cowley	2	on hand.	Continued playing after caution
	Stevens B.	2		making silly faces after reprimand
	Taylor VIR Lewis VI	2.	" "	Fighting in Playground
	Sutton VII	3	" "	Persistent Talking
9	Edwards	2	On hand.	Striking matches in class
	Cowley	2	" "	Misbehaviour in Class
	Harvey	2	" "	Talking in Line
	Taylor IVR	4.	" "	Truanting
	Parker Robinson Salmes	2	"	Rough Play in Playground
6.	Clarke	2	On hand	Throwing paper across room.
	Fowler VI	4	on buttocks	Truanting
18	Collins, Daniels, Robinson	1 ea.	" "	Untidy or smudged work

When we were sent off to fetch the stick, teacher would tell us to bring back "the book"; this being the Punishment Record. But most of the times we returned without it, because it had gone astray in its frequent short journeys during the day between the classrooms. Teachers never seemed to notice its absence. Once when handed the stick and the book in a classroom, I slyly let it fall on to the Head's desk as I passed by — he being absent. I reckoned that the teachers usually made an entry in the book when a boy had been very naughty, but only sometimes made other entries. I have seen the book collected from our classroom by a boy from another class without any entry having been made for the several canings given not long before by our teacher.

I got the idea that the school staff acted on the assumption that more credit would accrue to them if it was shown, by examination of the Record, that they were able to maintain discipline in their classes without the need for much corporal punishment. I have not had first hand sight of the Record covering the period I attended the Senior Boys but I have photocopies of some of the entries showing my name, and also some from the Junior Boys. However, I have had the chance to closely examine one Record of a nearby school. I was surprised to see how slapdash many of the entries were, some almost illegible, and without care in noting down the initials of the boys. Some entries appear to have been made by the boys themselves, because it is difficult to believe that the writing is that of a teacher. It would seem that the Record was considered a nuisance.

Some entries show that the punishment did not conform to the regulations laid down by the Enfield Education Committee, even though seen and approved by the visiting inspector. These regulations state that the cane should be used only when other methods had failed. It must have been well known that no other methods were used in our Council School. They also stipulate that only an approved cane, on the hands, should be used. The entries in this particular Record show that boys were beaten on the buttocks with the strap. In fact once when we had a temporary teacher for a few weeks he used a strap. Fortunately I only fell foul of him on one occasion. One entry in this Record obviously had been put in by a very daring boy — he had awarded himself 1,000 strokes. I would have have liked to have known him. He does not seem to have been punished for making the entry. Perhaps this shows how incomplete these so-called Punishment Records were!

Mr Oliver, the head master, I respected and feared. He did not take any classes, and was not seen often in the classrooms. We saw him standing on the steps leading up from the playground to the school building, when he blew the whistle and supervised, with the aid of his teachers, the orderly formation of the boys into their class lines, before we marched in strictly enforced silence into the school hall for morning assembly.

It was here that we saw him most frequently, when, after prayers, he would call on to the platform in turn boys who had been waiting at the foot of the wooden steps at the side. He would cane them. We knew nothing of their offences, nor did we care. Sometimes in the corridor I saw him seated at his table when I was allowed to leave the classroom to go across the playground to the W.C., or if I had been sent out of the classroom to stand in the corridor until I was dealt with by him.

I was reminded of Mr. Oliver a few years back when his death was announced at the age of 100. Letters from old pupils at the Council School appeared in the Gazette extolling his virtues and saying what a wonderful man he was. They praise the strict discipline, and recount the lickings and cuffs they got. Looking back I am sure that the school was a well-run place; certainly very severely governed. In his school most boys were well-behaved, though some were daring and mischievous. The school was attended by hundreds of boys from working class families, many of whom were under-nourished if not actually hungry. Extreme wartime conditions still prevailed, we lived in cold houses, and sat in cold classrooms.

People who did not live in those times should not be hasty in forming judgements on how we were treated. Attitudes were so different then, and we were the product of our times. Boys left school knowing how to write, read and do arithmetic; a sufficiently sound basis to go to free night school

Wanderings down memory lane

Gazette 16.12.72

Sir,—I was pleased to note by their letters to the "Gazette" that at least three "Old Boys" of Bush Hill Park School have wandered down memory lane.

In addition to the masters they mention (Messrs. Beech, Searle, Leach and Allamandy), other notable "Sirs" were Messrs. Clapp, Jones, Dabbs, Marsh, Threadgold, Morrow and Tranter.

When I was transferred in 1923 from George Spicer School to Bush Hill Park School, Mr. Holding was headmaster but shortly after he retired and his place taken by Mr. Leach, Mr. Oliver being placed as headmaster at George Spicer which was converted to the "Central School."

I will agree that it was hard schooling in those days and I certainly collected my quota of cuffs and lickings!

There are many more memories which no doubt I could put into words but printing space being at a premium, I will content myself with the hope that the memories of other Old Boys, through these letters, may be jogged into the past for a brief spell.

I should also like to thank Mr. J. S. Stokes and Mr. J. Wilmot for their appreciation of my few lines of verse and, rather apologetically for my remissness, to "B.D." of Orchardleigh Avenue (Letters, February 6, 1970).—Yours faithfully,

H. J. Matthews.

27 Bridge Close,
Carterhatch Lane, Enfield.

Mr. J. Oliver, Headmaster of the Seventh Avenue, Bush Hill Park, Boys' School

Mr. Oliver, Head Teacher Bush Hill Park Boys' School.

Enfield Gazette
Nov 16 1972

'A wonderful man'

Sir,—It was with much regret that I read in the November 10 issue of the "Gazette" of the death of my old schoolmaster, Mr. J. W. (Jack) Oliver, who was one month short of his 101st birthday.

He came to Seventh Avenue School, Bush Hill Park, at the latter part of the time I was there and what a wonderful man he was, as were also the teachers, three of whom I remember, Mr. Searle, Mr. Leach and Mr. Allamandy. Any one of these was worth a hundred teachers of today and one thing is sure: there never will be another Mr. Oliver.

He hated slovenly behaviour or speech, and I have often thought of him when I have watched TV reporters interviewing teenagers.

He believed strongly in discipline and rightly so, but of course this must be started by the parents before their children are of school age.

When Mr. Oliver was my headmaster that was how it was: we went to school prepared to accept discipline.

So a class of 50 boys was no problem to our teachers; we paid attention and we learned quickly. We knew what was meant by honour, principle, integrity and to respect other people.

Herbert J. Matthews, in his poem in last week's "Gazette," feels as I do about "The Old School" and has found the right words to express his feelings, and mine, and I am sure, many others.—Yours faithfully,

John S. Stokes

11 Fillebrook Aven.,
Enfield.

I will agree that it was hard schooling in those days and I certainly collected my quota of cuffs and lickings!

Letters from old pupils

if they wished. They were able to enjoy themselves with simple pleasures without the aid of wireless (radio), tape recorders, television, the telephone or the motor car. They did not break up other peoples' property nor sniff glue to escape from the boredom of the affluent permissive society.

All my direct contacts with Mr. Oliver were disagreeable ones. There may have been boys who had agreeable ones — but I did not know any. I can vividly recall some of mine. I had been sent out of the classroom to stand in the corridor for some offence or other. He came along and asked what I had been doing. I answered "Nothing, Sir". He replied "I have some sharp medicine for boys who do nothing in my school", and he promptly gave me a dose of it in the form of two "handers" with his cane; one for being sent out into the corridor, and the other for not telling the truth.

Another time, just after the close of afternoon school, I stood watching two classmates George and Ernie messing about with the school gate padlock. I was a nosey parker, and offered some unwanted advice. Milsom, the caretaker saw us, and the next morning he waited alongside Oliver as we filed into the Hall. Oliver told us to go stand at the foot of the small steps leading up on to the platform, where we joined two other boys. After prayers, we were beckoned one by one on to the platform. The first two boys got a "hander" each. Then me. I protested vociferously, and offered my explanations, but got two "handers". George and Ernie followed me and got four apiece.

At playtime I kept out of the way of both boys for I was feeling guilty about what I had said to Oliver. Just before the whistle blew, I rushed off to the W.C., as was my habit. Whilst standing undoing my fly buttons I was seized from the rear. George pushed me into the corner aided by Ernie, saying "You're a rotten sod for telling Oliver you were only watching us — you're a bloody sneak — what shall we do with him? I know — let's pull the bugger's knickers down — then he'll be late and get another walloping!" At that moment the first whistle blew. I panicked, because if they did undo the stiff leather braces tabs, the strong elastic to which they were attached would make them spring up under my waistcoat out of reach, and I would have to undress to fasten them back on to my breeches — a time consuming task at the best of times.

I struggled, kicked and squirmed, pleading with them not to do it, but they were determined, and strong; one unfastening the front whilst the other did the back. The second whistle blew just as they dragged my breeches down, and left my long stockings draped over my knees. They rushed out, for they had no intention of getting into any more trouble that morning. Ernie shouted back at me "You're a shit — and don't you dare tell on us".

Desperately frustrated, I had to put my waistcoat and jacket down on to the damp W.C. floor before I could re-adjust my stockings and breeches — then re-fasten on my braces — a lengthy task with my left hand still painful from the earlier caning. At last I was able to hurry out of the W.C., but had to return to pee, before rushing across the deserted playground, up the stone stairs into the empty corridor. Oliver must have heard the clatter of my boots, for he emerged from my classroom and had propelled me back into it before I could gather my wits. I could only blurt out "Sir, please Sir", my usual introduction to a feeble excuse, before he had caned me again, though not severely. He then quietly told me to go back to my desk and stop being a silly boy.

When seated at my desk, I observed boys whispering to each other and casting sly glances at me when teacher's back was turned — obviously I was of interest to those who normally were indifferent to the goings-on of others. I had always tried to keep my troubles as private as possible, but this time I had failed miserably by getting caned in front of the school and then again for causing a stir by being absent after playtime. I had expected to be ribbed by the boys when out of the classroom, but I was wrong. It was then I decided no longer to worry if boys knew about me, as long as I managed to put on a brave face, and keep my troubles from Dad. Mr. Oliver did not know that he had done me a good turn by not allowing me to offer explanations, because I would not have trusted myself. As it was, George bore me no grudge, greeting me cheerily when I ran into him in the evening in the street, teasing me by asking "Did the old bugger 'urt yer?'.

One day three of us were to be caned for careless untidy work, so I was sent off for the stick —

Volunteer Force

To

Y.82620 L/Cpl. Sydney John Robinson

I am commanded by The King to express to you His Majesty's thanks for the services which you have rendered to the Nation during the great War as an enrolled Volunteer in the

1st V. Bn Midd'x Regt (1st Bn Midd'x V. Regt)

Winston S. Churchill

Secretary of State for War.

Certificate of Service

Enrolled 30 . 11 . 16. Discharged 28 - 6 - 18

Entered into an Agreement under the Volunteer Act, 1916, on 14 - 2 - 17 to continue serving in the Force for the duration of the War, and to perform the prescribed programme of training.

Entered into an Agreement under the Volunteer Act, 1916, on —— to perform temporary Service.

Served as a full-time soldier with a Volunteer Special Service Company from —— 1918, to —— 1918.

why always me I do not know. When I found it in a classroom the teacher told me that it was split and to take it to Mr. Oliver, which I did. He told me to wait whilst he got another. He went to his room and returned with a brand new yellow cane, but instead of giving it me at once, he took out a small spirit lamp, lit it and charred the end of the cane in the flame. I found out later that this was to try to prevent it from splitting. I hated new canes — they hurt more than the old bent ones.

The other time I can recall was, when standing outside in the corridor one afternoon, expecting Oliver to come along at any moment, I heard a commotion, and saw a big boy I knew hurrying up the corridor with Oliver behind him. Oliver was striking at him with the stick. He cornered the boy just across the corridor from me, and began belabouring him as the victim cowered. Oliver was shouting "Tell me where you have put it?". Oliver saw me; turned round, straightened the stick, gave me a "hander", and dismissed me back to my classroom. Sitting at my desk, as soon as the initial pain in my hand had become bearable, I whispered to the boy sitting next to me that I reckoned it was Daniels who had stolen the school football, and that Oliver was giving him "what for" to find out where he had hidden it. The news was quickly whispered around the class. My ability to impart this important information was some small recompense for getting a "hander".

Any boy who spent as much time in the streets as we did after school in the afternoon, and on Saturday mornings, was at risk of getting hit by an ill-tempered adult if thè boy annoyed in any way. A stinging clout round the head, a whack with a walking stick or a nasty poke on the back of the leg with the sharp end of an irritable woman's umbrella could be our lot. I can recall clearly two such times when I was on the receiving end.

Opposite our Cottage was an orchard, which extended down the lane to Porter's Cottage and beyond, to the railway bridge. The orchard was fenced off by chestnut palings joined together by wire, and was partly hidden from the road by a scraggy hawthorn hedge on an earthen bank. In the Autumn I had my eyes on the lovely apples on the cordon trees only just out of reach; and, having no money to buy such luxuries, wondered how I could get some. On one or two afternoons at the end of school I would wait until the boys who lived in Ponders End, and attended our school, had wended their way home past our Cottage. They were unlikely to return that day as they played in their own area; and were very rarely sent to Bush Hill Park for shopping as they had plenty of shops nearby. The people in the factories and nurseries would still be at work so it was the best time to study the fence, with the minimum of fear of being observed.

It was too wobbly to be climbed over, so I decided to try to untwist a joint in the wire between two palings near ground level, and push them apart just wide enough to enable me to crawl through. I was excited and nervous when one afternoon I sat on the bank, choosing a spot with a clear view down the lane, up Main Avenue and round the bend of Lincoln Road. I kept one hand in my jacket pocket, clutching tightly Dad's pliers borrowed unbeknown to him, fearful of losing them. They were essential for untwisting the wire joint in the fence. All I needed was enough courage to start the enterprise.

A man on a bike approached where I was sitting, and, as he passed me slowly, he cleared his throat and spat. Perhaps aided by the strong breeze in my direction, his spittle hit me smack on the face. I shouted at him "You dirty bugger". He stopped a few yards from me, dismounted, letting his bike fall against the bank, and came towards me. I knew from experience that I was going to be hit, so I tried to duck; but he did not miss. With the force of the blow, and probably because I had one hand in my pocket, I lost my balance, and toppled over down the bank. I was hurt, and furious. As I picked myself up, he re-mounted his bike. I shouted at him "You sod — I'll tell on you to my Dad!", and then scampered across the road to the safety of my garden.

Later that evening I had the opportunity to tell Dad, but I did not take it, for I had learned not to attract attention to myself if it could be avoided. Unfortunately Mum asked me why I had blood on my Eton collar, and on my ear. I didn't know I had, though my ear lobe was very painful. The man must have had a ring on one of his fingers. Mum took me unawares, so I had to reply with the first

Part of the class in the Senior Boys. Fourth left, third row is Ken Stevens, who became a life long friend, brother-in-law, and was an outstanding photographer. Second from left, second row is Charlie Hill, who became a Baptist Minister. First right, bottom row is Walter Sheen, who became a Wing-Commander R.A.F.

thing I could think of — "I've been in a fight". Dad heard me, and said, very tetchily, "Oh, so you're up to that lark now — are you? You had better watch it".

By next afternoon I was fed up for three reasons. One was that I had told Dad I had been fighting. I knew what he meant when he said "Watch it" — he was not worried that I should get a black eye, a bloody nose, or some kicks and bruises — he might even be pleased. What he was concerned about was any resultant damage to my school clothes. Another reason for being fed up was that after choosing carefully a spot where I could break through the fence into the orchard I had made an enemy of a spiteful man who could pass by the place at any time. The third was that I had to go to school in an Eton collar with prominent stains on it from Mum's amateurish efforts to remove the blood.

Not much after this, I got hit by another adult. We were messing about outside a shop when we were sworn at by a bad-tempered man delivering boxes to it. Suddenly my mates ran off, and I felt a sharp clip round the ear, at the same time told to clear off. It was a policeman, known by us as a copper, who had appeared from nowhere. I cleared off smartly, being scared of him.

◁ *This photograph was taken by me before Fourth, Fifth, Sixth and Seventh Avenues and part of Lincoln Road were demolished. It was the view seen from the corner of Main Avenue with Seventh Avenue, and shows Bush Hill Park Council School and the row of terraced houses in Seventh Avenue, one of which was our home until 1917. At the end of the terrace nearest the school lived the Toops, and they had a yard in which they kept their large horse-drawn Removals pantechnicons. There was no fire escape on the school building as now shown. And certainly there was no metal barrier alongside the kerb to prevent the children from running into the road and getting knocked over. In our day it would have been most unlikely for a child to collide with an occasional cyclist or a slow moving horse and cart. Opposite the school in Seventh Avenue were some shops, which when I was an Infant were: Sanders, the watch repairer; Bunn, the sweetshop; Harrisons, fried fish; Read, the butcher; Rumke, the barber; Bird, the baker; Barge, the boot maker, and Daniels the greengrocer. Rumke was German, and cleared out after his shop window had been smashed in the riots when the Lusitiania was sunk. The school playground was very large. It was bordered on the Main Avenue side by the Deaf Boys annexe; the outside W.C.s open to the weather; the caretaker's house, the shelter or sheds, and the Manual Room annexe. The playground surface was smooth, and in icy weather was a lovely skating rink. The slides we boys made in such weather extended from the railings in Seventh Avenue to the railings separating us from the Senior Girls. The teachers were not spoil-sports, and left the slides to us until they thawed.*

Some of the thousands of hot house plants being grown in the glasshouses at Low's Nursery. It was through these glasshouses that I would run as a boy without a second's glance at my surroundings, except if I saw a frog, a newt or a butterfly. I got to know only some of the names of the plants - though I did know those I helped Dad and Mr. Phillips to re-pot when I earned a few pence in an evening. In the picture are Gerbera plants, native to South Africa.

On the left is a view from our backyard. The low building with the chimney is one of the stokeholds with coal burning boilers needed to provide the hot water through large iron pipes running just off the ground through all the glasshouses. Dad spent many an hour, sometimes anxiously, discussing with Mr. Phillips the Nursery Foreman, whether or not frost threatened, and to fetch the stoker to fire the boilers. There was no reliable weather forecast in those days, and a wrong decision could cause considerable loss to the Company. At the Nursery Dad started work at 6.30 AM six days a week in summer and at 7.00 AM in winter, and sometimes overtime. The alleys between the greenhouses, one seen in the photo, would have growing weeds higher than I was, in summer, fertilised by the chemicals used in the greenhouses.

One view of part of our garden and backyard bordered on two sides by glasshouses, one of which protruded almost to our backdoor. This particular glasshouse was extensively used by Mr.Cook and his son for plant research. Both were important relatives of Mr. Stuart Low, and were fussy men. Fred and I often finished up with very sore backsides after Mr. Cook had complained to Dad about us throwing balls or other missiles at the glass panes, sometimes breaking them; also using bad language in which Fred, Ivy and I were very fluent.

CHAPTER 17

For a time we had a nice teacher who spoke encouraging words to me about my ability, but it was not long before I managed to upset her. One afternoon she took the class on the one and only outing I ever made from the Council School, to Epping Forest. During our play there, we used the one ball any of us had, but it got lost, and the teacher promised to replace it next day. As we started to walk back, the teacher stayed at a bus stop, to ride home. The boy whose ball had been lost nudged me, saying "I hope she doesn't forget my ball". I shouted across the road to the teacher "Don't forget old Smithy's ball, Miss". Next morning, the teacher called me out to the front, telling the class I had spoiled for her a pleasant afternoon, by my rudeness. I was sent to fetch the cane. I think this was the one time when I was ashamed of being punished.

I was now out of favour with my first Senior Boys' teacher, after having been thus in the Junior Boys with Miss Swaby, Miss Matthews, Miss Worfolk, and, of course, the Head Teacher, Miss Wye.

In spite of setbacks, I feel that the period between Dad's discharge from the Army, and the start of the Autumn School Term was my most carefree: although I disliked school, I had become used to it.

We lived amongst a large complex of greenhouses containing thousands of potted plants, some of them tropical, used for decorating rich peoples' homes, banqueting halls, expensive restaurants and conservatories. Lows had an extensive overseas business. Many of these plants were sent daily to Covent Garden Market, after being loaded into carts, and we could hear the horses being got ready in the stables as we lay in bed. One of our greatest pleasures was to climb up beside the carter, snugly dressed in our thick clothes, and have rides sometimes. I was not very interested in these plants or in the activities of Dad in the Nursery, but I did like the large water tanks set into the ground in each greenhouse in which Dad dipped his large can to water the potted plants. This was a tiring job. I can recall as a very small boy, when helping Dad to pull off his knee-high leather boots, smelling the wet corduroy of his breeches. These tanks attracted me because in them or around them were frogs, tadpoles, newts, toads and other small strange creatures.

If the men were working overtime in the Packing Shed I would visit them by going from our back-yard into the Acacia House to the Nursery. I would watch them preparing potted plants for despatch by van to the Railway Station. Around the plant they would build a large cage of thin green bamboos, and strong string, and then protect the delicate parts with Japanese moss; the whole cage wrapped in strong brown paper.

I liked also the alleyways between the greenhouses in which grew in the warm weather flowering weeds taller than I was, through which I would push to hunt the many species of butterflies. I was sometimes brought to a halt when I touched the stinging nettles or enormous thistles, and was glad of the protection of my thick corduroys and worsted stockings. The plentiful dandelions I would gather to take Mr. Tim Phillip's house in Main Avenue corner of Fourth Avenue where one of his hobbies was wine-making. I would use any excuse to visit him, hoping that he would allow me to stay in his garden and see his various types of chickens — he had hundreds of hens.

I regret now that we Robinson children did not value the surroundings in which we lived. We had a house which had a large garden all round it; it had a large shed in which we could play, oak trees to climb, bushes to hide in, and a Nursery in which to sneak. But even for the other working class families Bush Hill Park was an ideal area in which to let children grow up. In between it and Greater London were nurseries, orchards, green fields, and abandoned brickfields overgrown with grass on which we romped. We had a recreation ground, and were within easy walking distance of Enfield Town Park and the New River. There was the River Lea, and the marshes. But best of all was the Royal Naval aerodrome at the bottom of South Street where we could peer through the wire fence at the planes and the uniformed men. We were very disappointed when it finally closed

A common sight during and after the War were the ex-soldiers, sometimes disabled, reduced to playing a gramophone in the streets to get a few coppers from kindly-disposed passers-by. This soldier is in his uniform except for his cap.

Enfield boys playing five stones. Dad said that he called the game 'Buck and Gobs'

Girls played with the same set of four square stones and a marble, but in a different kind of pavement game.

down.

Bush Hill Park was divided into two by the Great Eastern Railway track on which there was a regular service to Liverpool Street. This track separated two classes of citizens. One class we called "Over the Line", where the better-off families lived in large houses in tree-lined roads. Some of our teachers, but not all, lived over there. Some lived in our working class district, which mainly comprised neat rows of small terraced houses, cheaply rented. The mothers and their children could shop within a minute or two's walk from their houses, either at the corner or in the several rows of shops. Most things to fill the mothers' daily needs were available. I was sent daily to Shelley's, the bakers, and to Atkinson's, later Mrs. Sharp's, on the corner of Poynter Road, to buy a pennyworth of firewood which was stacked high on the right hand side in front of the counter. I can remember that on the left hand side easily available there was a quantity of punishment canes stuck into a glazed earthenware length of drain pipe, priced at one penny. There must have been quite a turnover in these because the quantity varied from day to day.

With few exceptions, all the children attended the large Council School in Seventh Avenue, positioned no more than three or four minutes scamper from any of the childrens' homes. Almost all of us were Home Counties English children of identical accent, culture and class. If a boy, say, who had been brought up in Scotland came into our class he would have felt a foreigner. As for foreigners I only knew two; one was the German barber who disappeared after his windows were smashed; the other was a tall, thin boy, a Belgian refugee, I think, who was newly in our class. He looked different because with his knickerbockers he wore mens' ankle length socks, exposing the calves of his legs — a part of the body not seen on boys in our time. One day I got mixed up with this boy and another in the playground, and the Belgian complained to the teacher about something we had done. I had not considered it very important but we both got caned. I kept clear of him after that.

Grown-ups didn't move about those days, staying put for many years, so there was a continuity of neighbours and friends. Teachers also stayed at the same school, so they had in their classes from one year to another members of the same families, some large. Sisters Jess, Kit, Ivy and Winnie had the same teachers. Fred had the same ones as I had.

Until I developed a passion for reading, in the oak trees, I liked the streets best of all. After a chunk of bread, and a cup of hot drink when I got home from school, I would be made to see that my bootlaces were properly done up, before Mum let me go off, with my cap on my head. I would walk miles in the streets, which were the children's playground. The mothers were quite confident that the kids would be safe; well rid of them out of the way of their fathers when they came home to tea. In the afternoons the children had the roads almost to themselves, except to the odd bicycle or two. The coalman and the milkman had put away their horses and carts. At the front doors pieces of string would hang through the letter boxes, at the other end of which inside the houses would hang the front door keys. Thus the children could go in and out of their homes without annoying their parents.

In my expeditions I would have to dodge the children engaged in their various activities depending on the seasons. I might need to step off the pavements to avoid turning skipping ropes, possibly fastened to lampposts at one end; avoid children hopping about over chalk marks on the pavements; avoid the spinning tops being lashed at by boys with their whips; sidestep games of marbles or cigarette cards. The hoops, metal for the boys, wooden for the girls, could be real hazards. I would stand and stare at the wounded soldiers in their blue and white uniforms sitting outside St. Mark's Institute. I would stop and listen to the wheezy old gramophone on a pram played by a disabled soldier, with his cap on the pavement in the hope a kind passer-by might drop him a penny or two.

At that time I had to keep a wary eye open for two boys who thought they owed me a grudge. One boy would shove me violently off the pavement if he saw me before I saw him. He disliked me because I had told the teacher he had tripped me up as we were getting into lines in the playground.

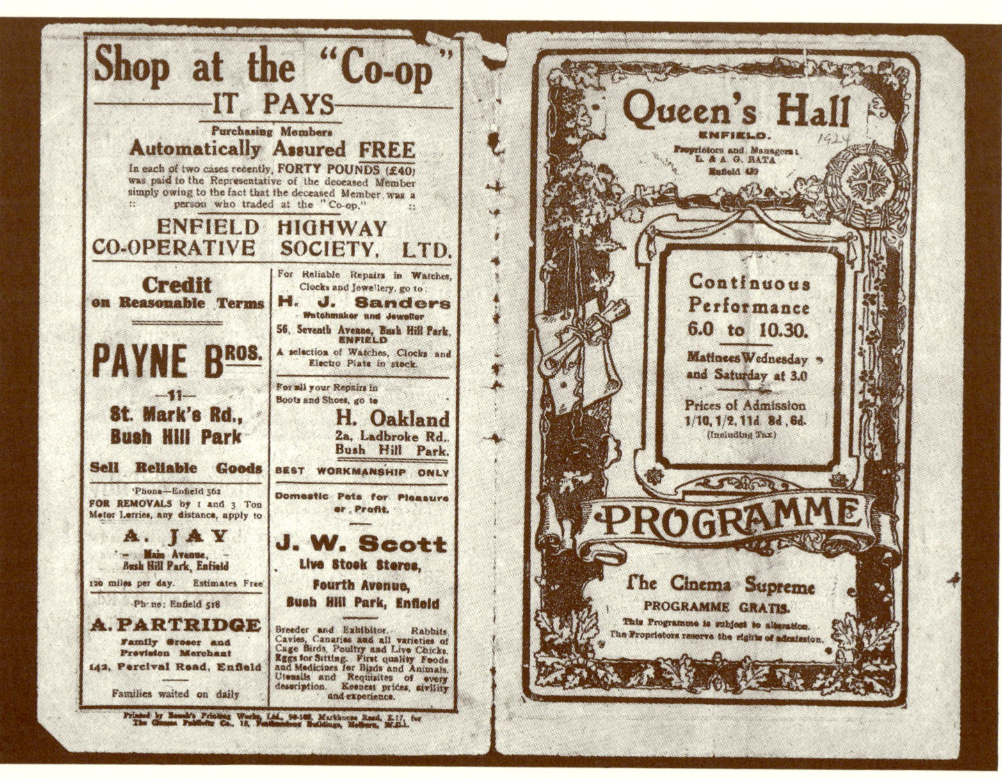

Shop at the "Co-op"

IT PAYS

Purchasing Members
Automatically Assured FREE

In each of two cases recently, FORTY POUNDS (£40) was paid to the Representative of the deceased Member simply owing to the fact that the deceased Member was a person who traded at the "Co-op."

ENFIELD HIGHWAY
CO-OPERATIVE SOCIETY, LTD.

Credit
on Reasonable Terms

PAYNE Bros.
—11—
St. Mark's Rd.,
Bush Hill Park
Sell Reliable Goods

'Phone—Enfield 562
FOR REMOVALS by 1 and 3 Ton Motor Lorries, any distance, apply to
A. JAY
— Main Avenue, —
Bush Hill Park, Enfield
120 miles per day. Estimates Free

Phone: Enfield 518
A. PARTRIDGE
Family Grocer and Provision Merchant
142, Percival Road, Enfield
Families waited on daily

For Reliable Repairs in Watches, Clocks and Jewellery, go to:
H. J. Sanders
Watchmaker and Jeweller
56, Seventh Avenue, Bush Hill Park, ENFIELD
A selection of Watches, Clocks and Electro Plate in stock.

For all your Repairs in Boots and Shoes, go to
H. Oakland
2a, Ladbroke Rd.,
Bush Hill Park.
BEST WORKMANSHIP ONLY

Domestic Pets for Pleasure or Profit.
J. W. Scott
Live Stock Stores,
Fourth Avenue,
Bush Hill Park, Enfield

Breeder and Exhibitor. Rabbits, Cavies, Canaries and all varieties of Cage Birds, Poultry and Live Chicks. Eggs for Sitting. First quality Foods and Medicines for Birds and Animals. Utensils and Requisites of every description. Keenest prices, civility and experience.

Queen's Hall
ENFIELD.
1924
Proprietors and Managers:
L. & A. G. RATA
Enfield 439

Continuous Performance
6.0 to 10.30.
Matinees Wednesday and Saturday at 3.0
Prices of Admission
1/10, 1/2, 11d. 8d., 6d.
(Including Tax)

PROGRAMME

The Cinema Supreme
PROGRAMME GRATIS.
This Programme is subject to alteration.
The Proprietors reserve the rights of admission.

I was not going to be the only one to get the stick when it was his fault. The other boy was one I had to be particularly wary of for a time. To avoid him I needed eyes at the back of my head, for he would creep up behind me, and shove me so violently and unexpectedly in the back that I have fallen flat on my face. He did this to me because one day, as a horse and cart passed me in Seventh Avenue, I saw a boy hanging on to its tailboard, cadging a free ride unbeknown to the driver. We all loved to do this. I shouted out, as was our practice, "Whip behind, Guvner". There was a sharp crack as the driver's long whip curled round to the back of the cart and slashed the boy's legs. It must have hurt. The boy dropped off the tailboard and turned towards me — I was off up the road like a shot — I sensed trouble. But he knew me, and he took a long time to forgive me, getting his own back by attacking me from the rear whenever the opportunity presented itself.

In my expedition I might sit for a while and talk with an old lady who could be found either sitting opposite our cottage on the earthen bank, or on the pavement outside the railings of the Council School. She made boot polish of soot and something else, which she put into old polish tins and offered for one penny each. In the summer I would wander up Lincoln Road, over the level crossing, to see if there was any cricket at Wellington Road. Then, if not, on to the Queen's Hall Picture Palace, where I would stand and stare at the coloured, exciting posters, and sniff the lovely perfume that wafted out through the entrance at which stood a smartly uniformed commissionaire. I would long to have a threepence to enable me to join the other people going in.

I can recall my first visit clearly. Somehow I managed to get hold of threepence halfpenny, honestly, possibly, because my mind was at ease when I spent a halfpenny of it on broken toffee from Vidal's before I hurried through the alley from the level crossing to the Pictures. I joined the queue, mostly of children, which stretched down to Adelaide Cottages where my Uncle Charlie had lived. I hoped the queue would not end like the Maypole queue did sometimes, when I got turned away. Reaching the steps of the entrance, I was helped up them by a shove in the back by some bigger boys who seemed in a hurry. I plonked down my threepence and went to the opening, but was called back because I had not taken up my ticket. As this caused a minor delay I was called a "silly sod" by the bigger boys behind me. Inside I sat down at the first empty seat, but was pushed off it by another boy who told me to "buzz off". I buzzed off and went down to the front row, which was empty. I wondered why, but it soon filled up. I was to learn that in that row I had to risk getting a ricked neck to look up at the pictures. There was a lot of confusion in the place and a hullabaloo until suddenly there was clapping. A stout lady came through a small door behind a curtain on a brass rail, and disappeared from view just to the left of the big rectangular coloured picture of a lovely mansion and garden on the wall in front of where we all sat. It must have been she who started to play the piano. The coloured picture rolled up and the lights went out. Sitting there, clutching my newspaper cone of broken toffee so carefully wrapped by old Mr. Vidal, I was as near to heaven as I ever have been since, watching my first Moving Pictures. I wanted them to go on for ever. I was really upset when one Picture ended when we were all shouting with excitement. I turned to the boy next to me and asked why it had ended like that. He replied "It's to make you come back next week, you silly bugger".

When I got back home, brimming over with enthusiasm, I had difficulty to persuade anybody to listen to me, and was rebutted firmly in my attempts to get any more money to go again the next week. My eldest sister Jessie, when she became a real "film fan" in later years told that she was very sorry for me at the time because I wanted to know what had happened to the woman who had been tied up on the railway line when a train was coming. She remarked that she did not know how I managed to get the money to go to the pictures, because I had been given only a penny during a whole week as pocket money. She added that I had been ten years old then, and that I was the first member of the Robinson family ever to have visited a Picture Palace.

From my very early days I had become familiar with flies that tickled my nose and tried to share my food. I would watch them struggling to free themselves from the sticky flypaper hanging low in our kitchen. But it was not until I was appointed chief shopper after sister Kit had started work that

A view of Main Avenue taken in the early thirties. On the left foreground are the railings of the St. Mark's Road C. of E. Church playground. On the right were: Harry Smith's Outfitters where Dad could buy a cheap work shirt, worsted stockings or a celluloid collar for me. Then there was Chaney's, the newsagent, who published postcards of Bush Hill Park; then the Dairy, followed by Mrs. Orland's Pork Butchers, and Rudlands where I was sent to buy paraffin for our oil lamps.

On both sides of Village Road from its junction with Park Avenue at St.Stephen's Church there were green fields towards Winchmore Hill. In the summer these fields were ablaze with colour of buttercups and marguerites. In one field near the road stood this unusual tree.

I realised how many there were.

My shopping errands took place either after I had my midday lunch, home from morning school, or in the late afternoon, mostly at a time when everybody else did. I therefore had to take my turn in the shops. In the grocers and bakers the assistants fought a continual war with the flies whilst measuring and weighing the cheese, the sugar, the loose jam, the bacon and other delicacies now available. Flypapers hung close to the assistants and sometimes to the customers. One afternoon, somehow having a halfpenny to spare of my own, I decided to enter a little baker's shop and examine more closely some jam tarts in the window. Once inside, I bent over to do so, and then saw some doughnuts which could be a better buy, so I moved along still bent over. When I straightened myself up my cap got entangled with a flypaper. The cap parted company from my head and stuck fast to the sticky strip; both then swinging to and fro like a pendulum. To separate them was a tricky and messy job, and my antics were strongly disapproved of by other customers, one of whom remarked loudly "What a stupid boy"; another threatened to clout me when I started to flick off the dead flies from my cap with my finger and thumb. Every time from then onwards that I put on or took off my cap I got a sticky finger, because it was impossible to remove the gooey dirty patch from it.

The flies which invaded our kitchen and the shops were probably the same ones which had previously feasted on the little heaps of horse-droppings in the roads. If we had given thought to that, I doubt if it would have caused us any concern. We knew nothing of germs.

When I became the family's regular shopping boy, the Co-op had started to emerge as the working class supplier of every kind of goods, and Dad joined as a member because he thus earned a small dividend on his purchases.

I didn't mind taking a pillow case to its shop at the end of Seventh Avenue to get our supply of bread, but I did not like going to the C.W.S. grocers in St. Mark's Road every Friday evening, because everybody went then — the men got their week's wages that afternoon. As soon as I arrived home from school Mum would write out her requirements in the Order Book. I would then wait until Dad came in with his wages, when the estimated money would be stuffed right down into one of my pockets together with the Order Book. Brother Fred refused to go shopping, so it was often Ivy who was given a ride in the box on old pram wheels to St. Mark's Road. As I neared the shop I would look to see how many similar conveyances, prams, and pushchairs there might be parked on the pavement outside the shop. I hated waiting, and was always glad to get myself inside on to the sawdust-covered floorboards. Being attended to was a slow job, for there were almost no pre-packaged foods, items needing to be weighed out and wrapped up or put into paper bags. The cost of each item was then calculated with the aid of a pencil and paper, and entered in the customer's order book. Any amounts of ounces could be ordered, and in the warmer weather, because refrigerators had not been invented, it was best to buy only small amounts of things we had just started to afford, such as butter, cheese,margarine, dripping and cheap cold meats like brawn and breakfast sausage. When home, these were put into what we knew as the 'safe', a small wooden cupboard fitted with a fine wire mesh door, intended to keep out the flies and wasps, and to provide ventilation for the delicacies stored therein.

When the order had been attended to in the shop, the items were totalled in the book, and a small slip of paper given to the customer with the total value of the purchases thereon. This was the Co-op 'check'. At the end of each quarter it was my job to add up all the checks; then Dad would see that I had reached the correct total before putting them in a special envelope to be returned to the Co-op.

Dad was still having to be careful with his money, but we certainly were now better-off than we had been during the first year Dad came out of the Army. We were having Argentine roast beef every Sunday for dinner, and often for Sunday tea a tin of salmon, followed by a tin of pineapple chunks, shared between the eight of us. The roast beef was supplying us with dripping to spread on our bread for breakfast. I loved it — especially the brown pieces in it.

This is a Library similar to ours except that we had no access to any books unless we followed the procedure outlined below.

Enfield Public Libraries.

Lending Departments.

The Lending Departments are open on weekdays from 10 a.m. to 8 p.m (except Wednesdays, 10 a.m. to 1 p.m only) but will be closed on Christmas Day, Good Friday, Public Holidays, and such other days as the Committee may determine.

The time allowed for reading this book is **14 days** from the date of issue. A fine of One penny will be charged for the first week, or portion of a week for which it is detained beyond the time allowed ; and Twopence for each subsequent week or portion of a week, until the book is returned. A book may be renewed provided it is not required by another borrower. Books cannot be exchanged on the day of issue.

Borrowers are required to keep this book clean, and to provide adequate protection in wet weather. They must not turn down the leaves, mark, stain, deface or otherwise injure the book. Damages will be charged for any injury done while the book is in the possession of the borrower. Readers must take the earliest opportunity of reporting any damage previously done, otherwise they will be held accountable for the injury. If lost the book must be replaced, or paid for, by the borrower or his Guarantor.

No person may use the Libraries while there is a case of infectious disease in the house, and must report to the Librarian any case occuring there, while books from the Library are in their possession.

Borrowers are asked to return or exchange this book personally. When this cannot conveniently be done, they are requested to send a responsible messenger, competent to deliver their messages and to take due care of the books. The Staff have instructions to refuse books to messengers whom they consider not qualified to take proper care of them.

H. HAMILTON CONNOR,
Librarian.

The Enfield Public Library in Cecil Road as it was when I joined it in 1919. There was no public access to the books themselves. On the right hand side in the photograph, the length of the building were glass cases in which were displayed in numerical order the catalogue numbers of the books - in blue for "IN", and in red for "OUT". The large catalogues, required to be consulted, are out of sight on the left hand side. There was no Juvenile Section in my day. If a borrowed book was kept beyond fourteen days, fines were rigidly imposed, irrespective of one's ability to pay.

CHAPTER 18

At the start of the Autumn Term I found myself with Miss Deane, a noted very strict disciplinarian. I came to learn that from this class boys were selected to sit for the entrance examination for free places at the Enfield Grammar School the following year. I had no such aspirations, so it came as a great surprise when I slowly learned that I was one of them. I quickly sensed that Miss Deane was going to have no nonsense from boys like me, and that I had better watch my step. Shortly, we began to get homework, unusual for Council School boys.

I did not greet this with any enthusiasm, because I did not want to compete in any way, especially with boys who seemed to like school, and who seemed able to keep out of trouble. At that time I could read and write quickly, and do sums, but had no ambition to study. I wanted to leave school and rear chickens, as my mate's older brother did.

As luck would have it, just at the time I started to get homework I reached the age when I could join the Public Library. I had looked forward to it and had had the Application Form to fill up as soon as I was eleven years of age. It needed a signature from a Ratepayer who was able to certify that I was a fit person, but I knew no ratepayers, because all we working class folk paid rents and weren't considered qualified. I persuaded Dad to ask Mr. Low, so I was able at last to hurry off after school to the Library with the Form and the penny for my ticket. I returned home dejectedly without either, because I had to wait a week for my ticket to be ready. A week later as I wended my way I couldn't believe that the Authorities, always, in my opinion, suspicious of boys, were going to let me loose amongst a lot of books so as to choose one — and I was right — they weren't going to let me.

I stood in the long entrance corridor of the Library not knowing what to do after I had received my ticket. I could see no books except those through the gap in the tall glass-fronted cases that ran the length of one side. I looked around for a friendly-looking adult, who told me that I must consult one of the catalogues on small tables on the other side of the corridor. I had to look up the title and author of the book I wanted to borrow, write its number down on a slip of paper provided and take it to the Issue Counter. I went home, very dejected, because I didn't know any authors or titles of books. When Dad came in for his tea I told him, and to my surprise (Dad was always surprising me) advised me to go back and look up books by Rider Haggard, Conan Doyle or W.H. Ainsworth. Back I hurried.

Consulting the catalogue I thought "King Solomon's Mines" sounded exciting so I wrote the number on a slip of paper, with a stub of pencil tied to the table with a piece of string, and placed it down with my ticket on the Issue Counter. A lady attendant went away, and I saw her climb up a ladder in front of tall bookshelves. She came back without the book, plonked down my ticket on the counter and said tetchily; "Don't you know the difference between red and blue? This book is out". Thus I learned that I had to consult the thousands of numbers in the glass cases to determine if the number of the book I wanted was coloured red or blue. Red was "Out" — Blue was "In". I had to have several goes in order to find a book whose number was in the desired blue colour.

I still recall the feeling of excitement I had as I looked through my first library book in its thick plain cloth cover and heavy leather gilt-titled spine. By the time I had reached the level-crossing on my way home I was well into the first chapter of "The Hound of the Baskervilles" by Conan Doyle. I was thrilled to find how easily I could read an adult book, understand and enjoy it. I had fallen in love with fiction!

The temptation to read these books made my homework a nuisance, but because Dad knew that I was a scholarship candidate I had to apply myself to it. He started to show interest in me when one evening to my surprise he was able to help me with my Algebra. He kept his eye on me from then onwards, often saying that I could do well if I was not "so bloody lazy and careless".

In class I seemed to be giving satisfaction, although I was getting more of the cane than most of

BUSH HILL PARK SCHOOL
SENIOR BOYS' DEPT.

SCHOOLS TO DROP LONG DIVISION

Only "very basic" calculations should be done on paper. Long divisions, which "many pupils find difficult and few really understand, should no longer be generally taught."

The inspectors fear that too many children leave school with little idea about measurement and estimation.

From the Daily Telegraph in the 1980's

Mr. Allemandy, on left, with his top class of Senior Boys, in the hall at Bush Hill Park Council School.

Miss A. Deane

the others, but very good scholars were not exempt from such punishment. The boy Sheen, a brilliant scholar, being coached by Miss Deane for the Enfield Technical School, got it sometimes. I kept hoping that my previous, severe Junior Boys teacher had not been in touch with Miss Deane and had not related how she had got me to work.

When Miss Deane sent a boy to bring back the stick, she kept it as long as she could; walking up and down the aisles with it in her hand. There was no chance for malingerers in her class. One bright day, when the sun was shining through the classroom window, I can recall seeing the dust rise from my mate Charlie's jacket as the cane fell across his shoulders whilst he sat hunched up over his desk writing in his exercise book, with the tears running down his grubby cheeks. It was unusual to see a scholarship aspirant being punished for carelessness during class time. We were usually kept back to be dealt with after school.

Months later, doing my homework, I carelessly made several errors in a long division sum and in trying to erase them a hole was made in the cheap wartime paper of the exercise book. Impetuously, I tore the sheet out, and re-did the sum on a fresh page. It was only then that I realised the enormity of my offence, so I carefully examined the book, finding that there remained small pieces of paper along the inside edge. After trying to remove these with my bitten short finger nails, it was only Dad's tweezers, borrowed in his absence, that facilitated the removal of the evidence of my crime.

Next morning it was raining so I stuffed the book up inside my waistcoat, tightening my jacket belt to hold the book firmly in place. Sitting at my desk I lugged it out ready for the arithmetic lesson. As the teacher collected them later in the day from us scholarship boys, and then the rest of the boys, for marking, I thought I noticed something queer with mine.

At the end of afternoon classes, as we were leaving, Miss Deane told Hill and me to stay behind. This did not alarm me more than usual, because at worst it could mean a couple of ritual strokes of the stick on the hands, or at best, to be asked to carry exercise books to teacher's home in Village Road where sometimes she would mark them in the evening. Hill was dealt with first, being severely reprimanded for careless work, and warned. Then, dismissed, he hurried off. I was then shown my exercise book lying open on her table, from which she lifted a loose blank sheet, and demanded an explantion. My face flushed up, and I blustered, realising I was trapped. I had not known that if a leaf was torn from such a book the anchorage of another leaf could be weakened and could fall out.

Teacher became angry at my failure to admit the truth at once, and she said she would report me to Mr. Oliver. I panicked, because this would mean being punished on the platform in the morning in front of the school — and of course Oliver could not allow me to continue as a scholarship aspirant. This must bring disgrace for me at school, and at home, for Dad would have to know. I pleaded with the teacher, saying that I would be thrashed, and that my Dad would never forgive me. She said I should have thought of that before. I continued to plead. Quite unexpectedly, she told me to go and bring back the stick, and "be quick about it".

As fate would have it, I had to search for it in what I thought would be empty classrooms, but when I opened the door of the big boys' room, I quickly shut it on seeing three or four boys lined up; one being whacked by Mr. Allemandy with what appeared to be a walking stick. I shuddered at the prospect of landing myself eventually in that class with him as teacher, as could be my fate if I failed the scholarship. For the first time in my school life I was desperate to find the stick and take it back to the teacher, in case, whilst waiting, she had second thoughts. It was only when I was coming back along the corridor, having failed to find it, did I spot it on Oliver's desk. I hadn't looked properly.

That evening I sat up in the oak tree fretting about my stupidity. The more I fretted the more I realised that my safety rested in Miss Deane's hands. Her goodwill was essential, something she had already shown me by waiting until all the rest of the class had left before telling me that she knew what I had done. She had punished me severely for my outrageous behavious, and so was she

BUSH HILL PARK BOYS' SCHOOL.

TERM REPORT.

Name. S Robinson Class.

Position in Class 6 No on Roll. 43

SUBJECT	Marks Poss	Obtained	REMARKS.
Writing	10	9	Improved lately
Reading	10	10	Very Good.
Spelling	20	20	Very Good.
Composition	20	19	Very Good
Arithmetic	10	10	Very Good
Recitation	10	7	F. Good
History	20	14	F. Good.
Geography	20	15	F. Good
Drawing	10	8	F. Good.
Totals	130	112	
Times late	0		Times absent 0

Remarks Generally does very good work, but is sometimes lazy, and troublesome.

A. Beane Class Master.

Parents Signature. S. J. Robinson

giving me another chance? It slowly sunk into my thick head that Miss Deane really wanted me to win the scholarship, and that she was being frustrated because I seemed unable to behave myself. She had made me learn thoroughly, and understand, vulgar fractions, long division, decimals, square roots and the rudiments of Algebra; but in much of my work I started off quickly and accurately and then trailed off carelessly. I was neat and tidy in my writing to start with but at the end I was scribbling.

If I failed her I could find myself in her class for another year — no pleasant prospect — then end up in Mr. Allemandy's class, with a bad reputation, and his walking stick. I had no choice but to try hard.

In class next day I sat uneasily, trying to look as bright and attentive as possible, and whatever happened, not to ask permission to go to the W.C. — not easy when I was so apprehensive. It was not until the next day that my mind became more settled, when teacher reprimanded me for making careless spelling mistakes, remarking that I would not pass any examination that way. From then on whilst working for the scholarship I was required to pay each time for the smallest failure to meet her expectations.

One Term Report has survived for that period. I was sixth in class of forty three boys in the end-of-term tests. The comments read "Generally does good work, but is sometimes lazy and troublesome".

In the Spring of the next year we sat the examinations at separate desks in the hall of the George Spicer School. Shortly afterwards, in my weekend suit and very shiny boots, I appeared for an interview in front of an examining board at the Grammar School.

Much to my surprise, later, Dad received a letter saying that I had been awarded a place at the Grammar School, commencing in September. I found it difficult to believe; my emotions were mixed. I was pleased to have done something right for a change, but did not want to go to the new school. If only I could stay at the Council School, having had the distinction of winning a scholarship!

My best mate had failed, and I was sorry, but within a day or two whilst we were doing drill in the playground, I saw his Mum striding towards the Senior Boys' Entrance in a determined fashion. I was to learn quite soon that she had obtained an interview with both Mr. Oliver and Miss Deane, and had asked why her boy had not been successful when I had. She claimed that her boy was as bright as I was, and better behaved. She was told that her boy had just failed by a narrow margin. Nobody knew that I had been driven on to do my utmost for fear of the consequences of failure. My mate did not have that fear, otherwise he may well have done even better than I had.

Ivy 1920

Senior Boys' School, Seventh Avenue, Bush Hill Park

'backed away instinctively fearful of getting some more'

My mate, Arthur, whose Mum marched into the school to complain when she learned that I had passed for the scholarship when her boy had not.

CHAPTER 19

For the remainder of the school year I was to find myself with a male teacher for the first time, and I was surprised to find him less severe than the women teachers I had before. It was unfortunate however I had the knack of upsetting all my teachers early on in our association, and this time was no exception. One afternoon we were clattering down the stone staircase of the main building to go across the playground to the Manual Room when I had to retrace my steps by pushing my way up through the descending boys to get my cap which had been forgotten on my desk As I reached the bottom of the stairs again most of the boys were disappearing into the playground, but two of the boys remaining in the lobby were peering closely through the glass of the door into the hall. One of them who knew me said "Come and see old Deanie". I joined them, peering through the glass. I saw a group of girls making gymnastic movements in rhythm with a piano, led in front by a female figure dressed in the briefest of gym slips showing stout legs and thighs encased in black stockings or tights — or something like them — I wouldn't have known.

This could not be our austere, upright, tightly corsetted teacher, who was only known to us to wear a skirt down to her ankles. I had never seen a lady's legs before — even young Ivy showed only a short length of leg between the top of her laced-up boots and the bottom of her dress. I immediately said in my cocky voice "That ain't ole Deanie". But it was — I was wrong — and I could not take my eyes off her, prancing thus a few yards away. And what was she doing with girls — she was the boys' teacher?

Our entertainment came abruptly to an end. A loud male voice came down the stairs asking what we boys were doing and for us to come straight back up to him. Alarmed, we did so, following our teacher, Mr. Tranter, into the corridor and to the Head's desk, from which he picked up a cane. Following my usual practice to try to escape retribution, I blurted out something like "Please Sir, I was only passing Sir — I had just been back to get my cap Sir". Ignored temporarily, he gave my two companions a "hander' each, and dismissed them, both hurrying off. Momentarily, I thought how smart I had been — my ploy had worked. But I had misjudged easy-going Mr. Tranter, for as I involuntarily made a movement as if to follow the other two boys, he stopped me. He said that they had made no excuse for their obvious misbehaviour, but that I had, and ought to be ashamed of myself. I misjudged Mr. Tranter for the second time. He was a skilful caner, giving me such a whack on one of my hands that I instinctively backed away from him, with the hand squeezed tightly into my armpit, fearful of getting some more. That fear was justified, for I suffered two more strokes. He then told me that I had better get across to the Manual Room otherwise I would be in further trouble, this time with Mr. Beech.

I took heed and chased off, praying that I would be able to sneak in and get to my bench before being noticed. I was lucky, but I badly wanted to press my throbbing sore hands into my armpits in an attempt to alleviate and spread the pain in them but could not bring myself to do so, because the other two boys would have noticed I had got the stick in spite of my excuses, and more than they had. I was glad nobody had witnessed my humiliation.

The Manual Room was not my favourite place to spend an afternoon. Mr. Beech, the Woodworking Teacher, discovered that I was no good at carpentry, and moreover accused me of not trying. But even if I had tried I could not have sawn a piece of wood straight, nor have made a plane do its job. All the tools seemed blunt to me. Perhaps I was not instructed properly, for I can recall receiving no personal attention. though I doubt if it was that. I could not sharpen a pencil properly until I was older. My manual ability was limited to writing well and quickly, and to drawing. Young brother Fred had all the manual aptitude — I had the mental aptitude not properly used.

This lack of manual dexterity manifested itself every morning when I was dressing, for I had difficulty in handling the wide, curling Eton collar around my neck so as to position it correctly enough to be able to push the small slot at the back over the stud in my shirt neckband. This was

A Piggyback Fight

Fred and Ivy
1920

'that lousy jersey'

made more frustrating because I could not see what I was doing.

One morning having arrived tardily for school to the playground I told my mates Eric and Stan of this, saying that some boys were lucky — they had to wear stiff collars only at weekends. Eric said he didn't mind because it saved him having to wash his neck. Stan said he liked to look smart, which I agree he always did. He also told me I was half-baked — why did I not do what he did — which was to leave the back of his collar studded to his shirt when he took it off at night to put on his nightshirt. I romanced, replying that my Mum made me keep my shirt on under my nightshirt because our bedroom was damp and cold. I was not going to tell anybody that Fred and I slept in our flannelette vests and shirts because we had no nightwear.

What prompted me to start talking with Eric and Stan about collars was because I had been reprimanded in class for fidgeting with mine, for I was wearing a secondhand starched linen collar from Sid Phillips, which was so worn out that it had developed an edge like a saw, and it was cutting into my neck. Both Mum and Dad knew that it was very uncomfortable but were making me wait for a new one, Dad telling me that it would teach me a lesson to try to look after my clothes — he wasn't made of money.

In fact, Dad was losing his patience with me. He had only recently bought me a new collar, but the second day I wore it for school it was ruined in a piggy-back fight. The boy who was riding me was about to be pushed off my back, and in an effort to save himself, he grabbed my new collar. The celluloid split at the front stud slot.

After many complaints to Mum about more sore neck, she persuaded Dad to relent, and he gave me the money to go to Harry Smith's little outfitters, in Main Avenue, and buy the cheapest one he had. Only a few days later, one morning, I couldn't find my back stud, which must have come adrift in bed. I was notorious for losing things and not finding them, as was sister Ivy. I asked Mum if she had a stud. She hadn't, so I went off to school with no anchorage of this stiff, deep collar at its back. I managed bearably in class, but at drill the collar got jammed between the top of my jacket and my ears. During the midday dinner time Mum asked Dad to lend me his spare back stud, which he did, but accompanied by mutterings about my stupidity. I moved away from him smartly into the scullery to put my collar on securely, but all my efforts failed, because, however much I forced it, the borrowed stud would not go into the collar slot. Examination showed that the brass stud knob was too big for the new collar; so I decided to make the hole larger, searching for a suitable tool for the purpose. I dared not disturb Dad again.

Under the stairs I found a screwdriver, a very unsuitable tool for the job even if in the hands of an expert; but it had to do. I placed the collar on to the wooden draining board, and tried to keep uncurled the three inch wide strip of celluloid, to enable me to see the hole which I wanted to make bigger. I nearly wet myself with anxiety and frustration, but eventually found myself able to make a stab at the hole. There was a sharp cracking sound — and instead of a slightly larger hole there was a large split. Celluloid wouldn't take such treatment.

In utter despair I put on the collar, and went back to school with it precariously held by the front stud. In the evening I kept clear of Dad hoping that Mum may be able and willing to find a way out of the mess I was in. But when bending down to undo my very tightly laced boots before going to bed, the collar shot up to my ears. Dad saw it. There was brief questioning and bad language; my reply being evasive. I was told to get upstairs and into bed. I did not have long to wait before Dad came up. He then vented his feelings by walloping me on my bare backside with his strap. I must say this for Dad — he was predictable. He could easily have stopped my pocket money when I misbehaved — but he never did — he was not that kind of a Dad.

For some days I was made to attend school in my tatty jersey, until Dad relented again and bought me another collar. When he saw the class photograph taken by bad luck during those few days he said I looked like a "bloody tramp", and he refused to let me go up the road with him anymore on his occasional trips to see Mr. Phillips until I had taken off "that lousy jersey" and put on my collar and jacket.

Collars

Above; Some of the boys in our class who were sent to school in jackets requiring Eton collars and which perhaps had not been returned from the laundry. It was more likely that money was too scarce to buy them.

My mates, including Stan and Eric.

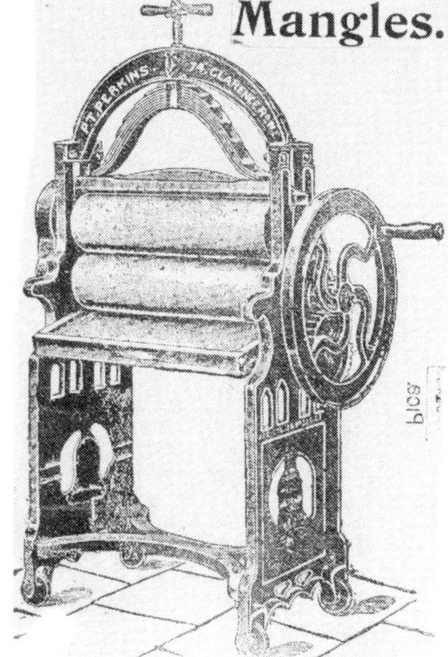

These collars needed only the occasional wipe over with a moist cloth, or so it was claimed, to keep them clean. They seemed to satisfy Mum whose aim was to keep the amount of clothing needing washing to the very minimum. She made this clear many times, and to me twice, I recall. Once was when I asked her on a hot day, although I anticipate here, if she would get me a soft collar like the one my scholarship mate Ted had now been given she replied "I can't wash things like that — I'll never get them clean". On another day, again ahead of my story here, I asked Mum if I could have some underpants. She replied quite tetchily "I have enough washing to do without these — at any rate you don't need underpants with breeches". After that I gave up asking, because without Mum's support Dad would certainly not have granted any such requests.

It is only as I write this account of my boyhood do I realise what a dreadfully exhausting, uncomfortable and frustrating task Mum must have had doing the family wash for eight of us. The washing in those days was done without the aid of any labour-saving devices. In most working class homes like ours there was a copper, a permanent fixture in the scullery, in which clothes could be boiled after it had been filled by pots and pans from the cold mains tap, and a fire lighted underneath it. After boiling, the clothes would be transferred to the sink for soap to be rubbed on to them, then put back into the copper. If there was any warm water available from kettles and pans on the kitchen range the clothes would be rinsed off properly in the sink — otherwise in cold water, which would be squeezed out from the wet clothes by means of the mangle. This was an essential piece of apparatus for the housewife, and it occupied a prominent place in the scullery. It consisted of a heavy large framework with two big rollers, usually of smooth wood which were made to revolve by turning a large iron wheel fitted with a handle. The wet clothes were fed and guided through the rollers with one hand whilst the wheel was turned by the other hand. Afterwards the clothes would be pegged out on the clothes line, hopefully to dry.

Mum had a mangle in Seventh Avenue, but not when we moved to the Cottage. Our removal from one home to the other took place on a very miserable foggy Saturday afternoon, and was carried out by Dad and a workmate with the help of a horse and small cart loaned by Dad's employer. Both men were tired after having laboured seven hours in the Nursery before starting loading our belongings, and it was late evening before the last trip was made. The mangle, a clumsy, heavy iron thing, could not be got on to the cart, so it was left behind, in the expectation that Dad would be able to borrow the cart on another day. But Dad was called up in the Army.

So Mum had to do without, and to make things more difficult for her, there was no spare fuel, due to war-time shortages, to light the copper. Therefore she had to carry down the passage water in kettles and pans heated on the top of the kitchen range, and do the best she could in the sink with a piece of household soap, rinsing the clothes in cold water. Then she wrung them with her hands, before pegging them out. I can recall seeing the clothes line sagging with the weight of the dripping garments. In inclement weather they dried out not at all. and we seemed to have so many foggy days in Bush Hill Park during those years. During the awful winter of 1917 the clothes hung frozen as stiff as boards on the line for days, until in desperation Mum brought them in a few at a time for them to be propped up to thaw out before draping them precariously over our brass fireguard where they would steam from the heat of the fire. Whatever official records show, I feel sure that we had much more harsh weather in my days than we do now.

When the clothes were finally dry, Mum would make room on the cluttered kitchen table for her old piece of blanket on which she would press them with the flat-irons heated on top of the kitchen range.

As during the whole of my schooldays my shirt, vest and long stockings were washed once every fortnight, I expect they must have been fairly grubby and perhaps a bit smelly by then because I had worn them night and day for the two weeks. But perhaps the dirt didn't show much because my jacket or waistcoat buttoned right up to the neck so that only little of the shirt showed. Mostly my stockings were black.

The Manual Room, across the playground from the main school building at Seventh Avenue, Bush Hill Park Council School. In the rear are standing Mr. Beech, the Woodworking Teacher and Mr. Oliver, the headmaster. This room was the scene of a near disaster for me, and caused many anxious moments for about two months.

*Mr. Beech,
Woodworking
Teacher
Bush Hill Park
Boys' School*

CHAPTER 20

After the collars incident with Dad, and near the Summer holidays, the Manual Room was the site of some really serious trouble for me.

It was towards the end of afternoon classes, when the teacher, Mr. Beech, was coming round to inspect our work. I found I could not make my plane do its job to finish the task set us, so I did something stupid, breaking the strict rules that boys should not interfere with the tools. I hit the blade with the mallet. To my horror, when I tried the plane on my wood, it made horrible jags, because I had forced the blade out too far. I panicked, and, seeing a plane lying idle on the other side of the bench, I exchanged it for mine. But I could not smooth out the damage done to my work. Within a minute or two the teacher examined my work, and looked puzzled. He peered closely at the plane I had picked up from the other side of the bench, and asked me to explain how I had so damaged my wood. I was stumped for an answer, having had insufficient time for even my fertile mind to think up an acceptable explanation. I blustered and lied. As fate would have it, the plane I had abandoned was picked up by the boy across the bench — he had been absent for only a minute or two — I thought he had gone off for some reason or other. He probably became suspicious on overhearing the interrogation I was having, and he tried the plane to finish off his work. He complained, and my fate was sealed. The teacher knew what I had done but I would not own up, so I was sent off to bring back the cane.

I went off as told, but unhurriedly in the hope the bell would ring and my classmates dismissed before I got back with the stick. The clatter my metal-shod boots made on the hard surface echoed loudly across the playground, disturbing the absolute quiet in Bush Hill Park at that time in the afternoon. It made me anxious the noise would arouse the curiosity of Oliver who was usually in his room above the corridor just before the close of classes. As I went up the stone stairs to the corridor I hoped he would not be there to ask what I had been up to. He was not, so I did what I usually did, which was to listen for the swish of the cane coming through the partitions. I could not hear it, so I peered through the classroom doors until I saw one in use. I had to wait for it to become free, and then very slowly wended my way back across the playground, but without the punishment book which, as usual, had gone astray in its travels during the day.

As I went back to the Manual Room I was hoping that the school bell would go for the end of afternoon classes; but it did not do so until I had handed the stick to the teacher. On hearing the bell the boys grabbed their caps and headed for the door to escape from school, but the teacher shouted at them to come back, and to gather round him in the centre of the room. He announced that I had been very disobedient and had lied. He would see that I knew that such behaviour did not pay because he especially disliked liars. He appeared not to be so very angry as he said this; in fact he seemed pleased that he had at last caught me in a punishable offence. I knew he did not like me because he thought I was too lazy and careless, but he was easy going. I do not remember him caning any other boy in my class.

The actual punishment I cannot recall. Perhaps my mind went blank, as it did sometimes when events seem to overwhelm me and retribution was imminent. When the teacher had finished with me I stood hurt and sullen whilst the boys, without permission, clattered off noisily from the room, no doubt irritated by being kept in just to see me caned. The teacher, not unkindly, told me to return the stick to Mr. Oliver.

As I went into the main building I realised that all the boys had gone, so I had to creep up the stairs as quietly as I could, hardly daring to hope that I would meet nobody. My luck held, and I was able to put the stick alongside another on the desk, and scuttle off as quickly and quietly as my studded boots would allow. I did not know what I would have said if I had met Oliver — I believe I would have lied again.

As I wended my solitary way homewards with my mind in a bit of a turmoil, it came to me that I

Mum and Dad in the backyard at Low's Cottage. I suspect Dad must have found that hat - he would never have bought it!

One of my mates, Charlie, who told his scallywag of a brother that I had been walloped by Mr. Beech. This was to cause me considerable embarrassment.

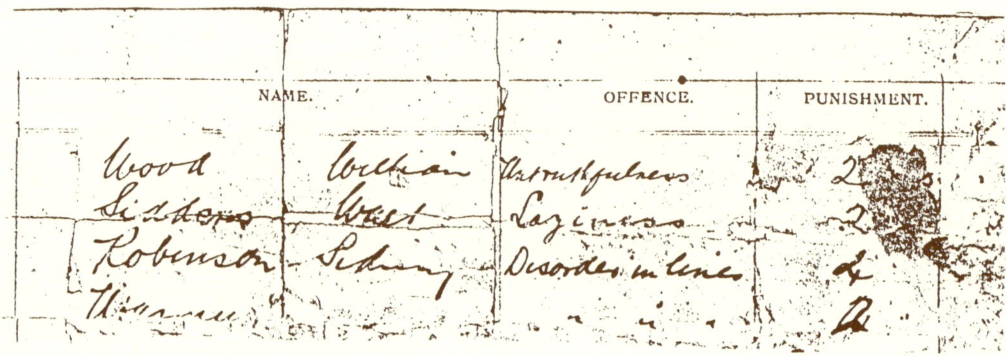

NAME.		OFFENCE.	PUNISHMENT.
Wood	William	Untruthfulness	2
Sidders	West	Laziness	2
Robinson	Sidney	Disorder in lines	4
[illegible]		[illegible]	2

did not seem to be able to keep out of trouble, with either my Dad or school, for very long at a time. But until recently I had been able to keep the knowledge of most of my troubles reasonably private, more by luck than anything else, although I was artful. I had always done my best to give the impression of being a good boy, using any excuse to avoid punishment. How was it then that I had lied so barefacedly this afternoon when it was obvious what I had done? Why had I not tried to excuse myself instead of refusing to own up? How had it happened that I had behaved so outrageously that it made a normally good natured teacher cane me severely in front of forty or so other boys who had been kept back after school hours because of me? Why was I not ashamed, but only anxious about further consequences? As I thought of all this, I experienced an inexplicable feeling of excitement, short lived as it was to be. It scared me a bit.

At home, I sat up in my oak tree with a crust of bread and margarine, thinking about the incident, and nursing the red and purple weals on my hands. Suddenly I came over all hot, and I could feel my face flush. I had a dreadful thought that I could be in peril. What would happen when Oliver learned of my behaviour? Was it possible that he would not know? Surely the teacher would be pleased to make the entry in the punishment book, even if he had to put himself out to do it? Oliver would then see it. The teacher might tell Miss Deane! I could not see how it was possible for the scholarship place not to be taken away from me and awarded to another more deserving boy. What about my mate and his mother? I understood that she had told Oliver and Miss Deane that her boy was better behaved than I was — now she could return to them and prove that she was right. I could not recall if my mate had been in the Manual Class that afternoon to witness my disgrace, but Charlie, another mutual friend had, and he might pass the information on.

During that evening my thoughts ran riot. At one time I thought of brazening it out by telling Dad that I had been fighting, got into trouble, and had decided I didn't want to stay at school any longer than I could — that I wanted to start work.

I had a restless night trying to think up an acceptable excuse if Dad received official notification that I had misbehaved and that the place at the new school had been given instead to the runner-up. As I tossed and turned I thought I might anticipate the trouble by plucking up enough courage to tell Dad a story based on an event that had happened the year before when I had annoyed a boy as we were forming into lines after the whistle had blown in the playground, and he had knocked off my cap in retaliation. Impetuously I had then knocked off his; my action being seen by the duty teacher who whacked me when we got into the school building. If I could get going on this story to Dad I could get carried away with the romancing and become quite convincing, having had a lot of practice. I would add that the scholarship boys should not fight, and because of what I had done my place at the new school might be given to the runner-up. Perhaps I dare add that I didn't want to stay at school until I was sixteen? Dad never need find out the truth because he was not the type of man to ask questions of the school.

But when morning came I became scared again. At school I could not concentrate, and I panicked every time I saw Oliver. I waited anxiously at postal delivery times, fearing a letter may come.

The school holidays started without any developments, and in consequence I felt a little safer, but I was still worried. To add to my misery, Charlie told his scallywag of a brother. Every time he saw me in the street he shouted after me "Wotto Grammerite — did ole Beechy wallop yer?" He was so fleet of foot that I could not catch him if I had so wanted. Perhaps it was for the best because probably he would have punched my nose, for he was bigger than I was and he might have called after me all the more. I was very embarrassed when he shouted at me when I was with the family, but I just had to put up with it.

VILLAGE ROAD, BUSH HILL PARK

One of the trams which provided a regular service from Enfield Town to London, passing through the wealthier part of Bush Hill Park. It was a real treat for me to ride on the top deck of one of these trams.

PHOTOGRAPH OF BEARER.

SIGNATURE OF BEARER.

Dad's Passport photograph taken for his trip to Belgium in 1920 when he was thirty nine years of age, and in his prime.

CHAPTER 21

The Summer slowly passed, uneasily for me, but as each day went I felt a little less anxious. One morning, when Dad came into breakfast a letter came for him. I nearly wet myself to see that it looked like an official letter. Dad read it carefully, turned to me and said "Jack, I want you to go to London for me and collect my passport. I am going to Belgium with Mr. Phillips, the foreman of the Nursery. Here's the money for your tram fare, and a shilling for yourself. Get the tram at St. Stephen's Church and ask the way when you get off in Tottenham Court Road".

I was absolutely thrilled. Fancy going to London by myself on the top of a tram, and having a whole shilling to spend! I never had such an amount of my own in my whole life. I went straight upstairs to put on my Sunday suit, then asked Mum if I could wear the wide, starched linen Eton collar which had belonged to Sid Phillips — though it was a bit sharp-edged it looked smart. I polished my boots with real pleasure for once. The August weather was miserable, so I asked Dad if I could wear his new leather gloves, and he agreed that I could do so on condition that I tried not to be my usual careless self, and lose them. I promised.

It was suprisingly cold on the top of the open deck tram but I felt beautifully warm and secure in my jacket and waistcoat buttoned up to my neck under my collar; my strong webbing braces holding up securely my thick tweed close-fitting knickers fastened firmly below my knees over my extra long woollen stockings; my recently acquired Bolsom Brothers boots with their metal studs carefully hammered in by Dad, and Dad's lovely leather gloves. My happiness would have been absolutely complete if I had been still an ordinary Council School boy, and had not been frightened into working hard for the scholarship that still threatened my safety.

I collected the passport without difficulty, and on the way back to the tram stop I passed a Lockhart Restaurant from which emanated a tempting smell of dinner. I went in to sit at a marble-topped table at which I was served a plateful of steak pudding and "two veg". — receiving a bill for sixpence from a waitress who called me "Duckey". From another waitress I accepted apple-pie and custard, priced on the list at threepence.

When I finished I picked up the bill and my cap from the seat beside me, then went to the Pay Desk. As I presented the bill I realised that it had not included the price of the apple-pie. I succumbed to temptation and paid only the sixpence. I looked around, saw nobody interested in me, and left the restaurant. I walked very slowly along the pavement, so guiltily that I turned my head away from a policeman who was passing by.

I could not resist glancing back. Somebody stood outside the restaurant waving something, in my direction. Ignoring it, I hurried on; only feeling safe when I was seated on the top deck of the tram on the way home.

Sitting there I felt very contented, with my belly full of the finest food I had every tasted, and threepence extra which would enable me to go to the Pictures. The wind seemed colder than ever on the top of the tram, so I felt in my jacket pockets for Dad's lovely gloves. I panicked. Where were they? I could not think properly. Then I knew. The person waving at me with something in the hand was not calling me back because I had failed to pay fully for my meal, but because I had left Dad's gloves in the restaurant. I deserved everything I had coming to me. I had so looked forward to giving Dad his passport — being told that I had done things right for a change — of telling the family of my first solo trip to London — of my meal in a London restaurant. Everything had gone wrong. I thought of the family knowing how stupid I had been; of the chagrin to be felt when young Fred and Ivy got to know of it.

At home, when Dad came in I gave him the passport, and he was genuinely pleased with me. I did not dare tell him about the gloves, and he did not mention them. All the rest of the day, and whole of the next I could not settle to anything, and was so nervous that I could not bring myself to steal my usual weekly "Magnet" laying so temptingly on the newsagent's counter. I kept thinking of my

Photograph of Southbury Road looking towards Enfield Town, taken from about where the A10 now crosses it. On the right is a lone building never occupied in my boyhood, believed orginally to have been intended for a pub, but the license was not granted. On the left side of the road orchards and nurseries extended to Bury Street - on the right disused brickfields and open country.

Photograph taken at the terminus of the Metropolitan Electric tram line which ran between the High Road, Ponders End and Enfield Town. The fare was one penny. The Great Eastern Railways Goods Yard hides Enfield Town Station and Ebenezer Gibbons' shop.

Clarence Road, Ponders End where my best mate lived. These photographs will give some idea of the peace and quiet of our roads before the motor car pushed everything else off the roads and off the pavements sometimes. These photographs were taken in 1925.

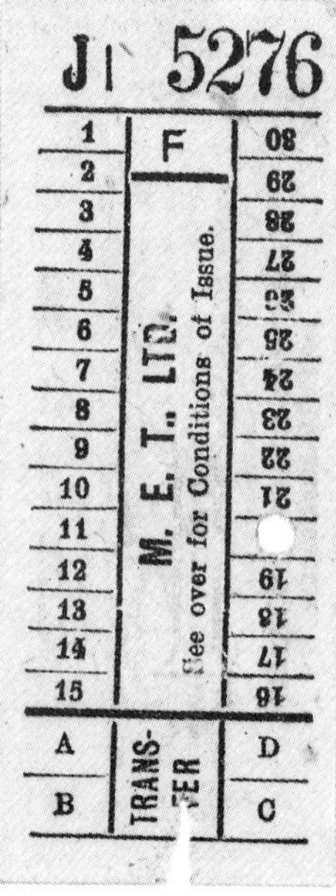

The Metropolitan Electric Tramways ticket costing 1d. (one old penny).

deceit, Dad's disappointment in me again, his quick temper, and my disgrace.

On the third day I could stand the anxiety no longer, so I told Mum at breakfast time what had happened; and would she tell Dad when he came in for his "Oxo" drink mid-morning? She said she would see, but I must stop being such a troublesome boy, and stop annoying my father who had enough problems. I was still being artful in spite of my anxiety. It was Thursday, and Dad was leaving for Belgium very early on Saturday morning, so he would be very busy getting ready in addition to all the work he had to do in the Nursery. I thought that if I went into the kitchen as soon as Dad knew, he might be wild enough to thrash me there and then when Ivy and Fred would be out to play and Kit and Jess would be at work. Thus my disgrace would be secret.

When I went into the kitchen Dad glared at me, saying I was a lying, careless little bugger, and he would deal with me later. But I used every subterfuge to keep out of his way; going to bed early that evening saying I wasn't well; keeping right out of his way on Friday. I think he was so taken up with his trip to Belgium that he forgot about me once his temper had subsided.

To my surprise I received a postcard from him in Belgium saying that he had a present for me. I looked forward to it very much, but was disappointed when he came home, for it turned out to be a little wooden model of a Brazilian native river craft, of no interest to me because it couldn't be played with. It stayed on the front room mantelpiece for nearly forty years, gathering dust. Dad had been with Uncle George and Aunty Lizzie in Belgium during the time they were preparing to depart for Brazil, where Uncle had inherited from his step-father an Orchid Nursery. I learned later that they had asked Dad if he would allow them to adopt me. Looking back, I think it must have been that they had not been blessed with a son after more than ten years of marriage, and they thought that Dad had so many children to have one to spare. They probably chose me because of Aunty's and my strong family resemblance. Dad and Mum would not agree to part with me. At that age I doubt if I would have agreed had I known, because I would not have left Mum — and I would have reckoned that I belonged to my Dad in spite of everything.

Cousins Edith and Doris Firman, daughters of Dad's sister Jessie, who married our Uncle Arthur not long before the outbreak of the War. Uncle was prisoner-of-war in Germany for four years, whilst his first little daughter was an infant.

On hot summer days a Council Water Cart, drawn by horses, like the one above, would come along our roads to lay the dust; much to our enjoyment.

View of Main Avenue seen from the Lincoln Road junction in 1934, showing the surface of the road now made up. In the left top foreground can be seen the very tip of one of the oak trees in our garden and the stable next door alongside the entrance to the Nursery. Beyond there are Council Houses built on land that was allotments in my boyhood. My sisters could not have lived nearer to their school - their playground was almost opposite the Nursery entrance.

CHAPTER 22

During the summer holiday of seven weeks, a period which I should have thoroughly enjoyed as the longest time I had been away from school since starting in the Infants, but which was spoilt for me by the scholarship menace, I had my first trip ever in a motor car, though it was very short. One Sunday afternoon, Dad shouted at me from the front door "Come here, Jack". I went with some trepidation, wondering what I had been up to, which was about to be found out. To my surprise I found Dad with a smartly dressed man in a dark green livery, peaked cap and shiny leggings. Dad said "Show this chap the way to the Hawthorns". I went back to get my cap, and hurried out to the front gate.

To my astonishment and joy he was standing by a magnificent limousine, with gleaming brass head lamps and radiator. He shoved me up into the front seat, and mounted the other side of me. The engine was purring, and within a minute or two we were in the entrance to Stuart Low's house, the driver helping me down on to the gravel path. He said "Ta — lad", and went to open the door for the occupants in the rear of the automobile.

Before they dismounted I saw them seated. One was a lady in a large pink flowered hat with a matching veil, alongside a gentleman in a very light grey suit, not of the type I had ever seen worn in Enfield, and he had a flower in his button hole. Opposite him were two smart boys in Norfolk suits with red school caps. The perfume emanating from the car was heavenly. It was the briefest glimpse of another world.

As I walked past I could not take my eyes off them. They took no notice of me, thinking probably that I looked exactly like their gardener's boy dressed in his best clothes for obligatory attendance at Sunday School. They were nearly right, except that I went voluntarily. I had been reading in my Comic about such a boy who had to go to Church twice on his only day off from working in the greenhouses of the Manor.

Nobody had a motor car in Bush Hill Park. Everybody walked or biked; the teachers, the doctor, and Mr. Stuart Low who had plenty of money. For longer journeys there were good services of transport, trams, buses and trains, if one could afford them.

At that time our roads were not properly made up, being very dusty in summer, and muddy in winter. Our joy as kids was the visit of the Council water carts to lay the dust. There were plenty of drenched boots, stockings, trousers and dresses then. Small heaps of horse manure could provide a hazard for the unwary, though most of them in our area were quickly shovelled up by the children for use on their Dad's garden or allotment. Our Dad said that manure was just the job for rhubarb.

One idle early evening I found another use, if that is the right word, for some manure. I came across my mate Bill outside Vidal's sweet shop blowing into a paper bag. He intended to wait until there was a passing adult unlikely to be aggressive; then burst the bag to make a minor explosion, in the hope that the unwary person would jump out of his skin. I proposed that we try another stunt I had heard about; that was to put some dried-up horse manure in a bag, seal it up, and lay it on the pavement. Then to wait. He agreed, and I soon found nice manure. Unluckily I filled the bag up too much, so when I began to close it by taking hold of the two sides, and twirling the bag over several times like the greengrocer did, the bag burst open, shooting the manure all over the place in the forecourt of the little shop. Bill had another bag, and this time he did it properly, putting carefully into the centre of the bag embedded in the manure some small stones from his front garden, to give it some weight. We gently laid the bag in the middle of the pavement across the road, and moved away, trying not to give the impression we knew anything about it.

It was not long before a woman pushing a pram came along. She avoided the bag. Then along came a gent in a bowler hat. He stopped; poked it with his umbrella; didn't like the look of it, and went on. Then came running along diagonally across the road a boy carrying a folded newspaper he obviously had been sent by his Dad to buy from Hoopers. He ran past the bag, observed it out of the

46 *Advertisements.*

Great Eastern Railway

2/6 Day Excursion 2/6

Excursion Tickets are issued daily during the Summer Months from London (Liverpool Street and Fenchurch Street), Bishopsgate, Bethnal Green, Coborn Road, Stratford, Forest Gate, and from the Stations on Enfield, Walthamstow, Loughton, Tottenham and Hampstead, North London and Woolwich Lines to

SOUTHEND-ON-SEA

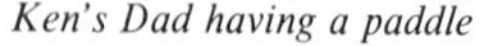

Ken's Dad having a paddle

Fred	*Ivy*	*Mum*	*Dad*	*Win*	*Sid*
10	*8*	*41*	*39*	*4*	*12*

We Britishers may have been an island race, but for some like us the sea may as well have been thousands of miles away, because though train fares were relatively cheap, they were mostly beyond the reach of working class folk like us. I saw the sea for the first time when I was twelve - I doubt if Dad and Mum had ever seen it before.

corner of his eye, stopped and went back. He did not at first pick it up, but moved it along gently with his boot. Then, his interest awakened, he looked up and down the road before picking it up and placing it carefully within the folds of his newspaper. He ran off homewards, turning into Lincoln Road, where he lived.

Bill was disgusted, saying that it was a waste of a bloody good bag. We were bitterly disappointed that no adult had opened the bag whilst we were watching because we wanted to see the look of utter disgust when it was done. I did wonder what had happened when the boy got home. If he were like me he would have sneaked upstairs to his bedroom and slipped the packet under the blanket until a convenient moment presented itself to open the treasure trove.

Whilst recording these recollections of some seventy years ago, I have come to realise that my memory can play me false about dates. I have always been quite sure until now that Mr. Cook, Dad's employer, gave him a complimentary ticket on two occasions for afternoon performances of some sort of entertainment, and that I used both of them. One I felt sure was for a rehearsal of Sanger's Circus in Churchbury Lane, and I had played truant from school to go to it, expecting that Mum could be persuaded to give me a note of excuse next morning. I thought this had happened during the uneasy summer, but on checking my dates it could not have been the Circus I went to, because I was not able to get Mum that morning to write out a note before Dad came in for his breakfast. I got a walloping at school for truancy. The Circus, I find, took place in late August when I was still on school holiday, so the walloping must been on another occaison somewhat similar.

The weather that summer had been generally very poor, in keeping with my depressed mood; and August started cool and cloudy, so we were surprised when Dad announced on Saturday lunch time that we were going to Southend for the day on Sunday.

Next morning, after Dad had done his watering in the Nursery, had inspected our boots to see if they shone, and if our stockings were free from wrinkles, we walked the short distance to Bush Hill Park station, where we got seats in the steam train. The excursion fare, return, was 2/6d (twelve new pence). I know that Ivy and I enjoyed the train journey, Ivy being constantly reprimanded for putting her head out of the window.

I do not think I was very impressed by my first sight of the sea. It seemed a long way out. I had read about the sea, and had drawn maps showing it at school, but had never seen it. I am not sure if Dad and Mum had ever done so before. We went on a short motor boat trip; but I enjoyed best of all the "sausage and mash" lunch we all had on the sea front.

It had turned out a really lovely warm day, but in spite of the blessed sunshine, there were very few people in the sea, though there were a few children with their stockings and boots off paddling about in the muddy puddles left where the tide had gone out. There was a man or two doing likewise with their boots hanging around their necks by the laces.

I don't think it would have occurred to me to ask Dad if he would allow me to do the same. The act of putting on my stockings and boots and the removal of them were done only as an essential but disagreeable part of life. I wasn't fond of water anyway, nor was Ivy — she fell into a Nursery tank once and was rescued by Fred — I think that put her off water.

By the sea I can recall feeling no discomfort sitting in the hot sunshine in my tweed suit, and I doubt if Ivy was any more ill at ease in her several layers of clothes and her high boots. This was in an age when all garments were made of wool, or of cotton mixed with wool, and they were thick and heavy, for there were no man-made fibres.

Working class men and boys did not remove their jackets in public, for there were no self-supporting trousers in those days, and to appear in a waistcoat, or with the essential but rather ugly braces and prominent braces buttons showing would be undignified.

As for sunbathing — we had never heard of it — the exposure of any part of the adult human body for the purpose of acquiring a suntan would have been considered eccentric, and possibly offensive.

We boys wore the same clothes on the hottest as on the coldest day of the year — there being no

REPO[illegible]

[illegible] Girls' School
Bush Hill Park

Name I. Robinson.
Class 3 Date 15.12.21.

V.G. = Very Good; G. = Good; F. = Fair
W = Weak

Subject	Max	M.G.
Arithmetic	10	5
Reading	10	8
Writing	10	7
Spelling	12	11
Composition	10	7
Recitation	10	8
Geography	20	13
History	20	13
Drawing		G.
Needlework		F.
Handwork		F.

Attendance V.G.

Punctuality V.G.

General Conduct F.

Ivy must to ~~become~~ a more steady girl.

Remarks Ivy works well, but lacks steadiness.

E. M. Hake.
Class Teacher

[illegible] Turner.
Head Mistress

Ivy was nine years seven months old. She did not like this teacher, who so aptly described her pupil. It is interesting for me to observe that with Test Results equivalent to 72% Ivy was considered a good worker. My Test Results, at the same age, of 82% earned me the classification of 'very lazy'.

concessions to the seasons although we did have overcoats for the winter.

It was about this time that Dad acquired a small plot of ground at the far end of the Nursery for growing vegetables, and Fred and I were co-opted to help clear the numerous weeds. During the operation Fred accidently drove a tine of a garden fork through my boot into my foot. This occasioned me to limp badly for a couple of weeks, and I thought it was a pity it had not happened whilst still at the Council School, because I would have liked to have told the teacher in the hope that I would have got some sympathy for once. The damage left a permanently distorted big toe.

On the Nursery site and in the orchards work had now started to divide both of them by the construction of the section between Bury Street and Southbury Road of the new Cambridge Arterial Road as it was to be called, later to become the A10. The activities were of great interest to us, and the site provided a splendid playground when the watchman was out of sight after work had finished for the day. One day Dad told us that in the morning when he had been about to ring the bell for work to start in the Nursery at 6.30 a.m. he encountered a stranger, who said "I'm looking for me bleedin' steam-roller. Some bugger's pinched it". Dad told the man, who turned out to be the road night-watchman, that it wasn't likely to be in the Nursery. Later Dad informed us that the steam-roller had been moved very quietly, in the night to the Southbury Road site, where it was then to be needed, and the night-watchman, who had been over-imbibing at the "Salisbury" Public House, had not been in a fit state to observe anything upon his return to his hut.

Our cottage home seen in 1925, when the end of Main Avenue had been developed, and the Cambridge Arterial Road (now the A10) had cut the Nurseries in two. Our postal address was then to become 195, Lincoln Road, Bush Hill Park, but the Enfield Council workman fixed the road nameplate 'Main Avenue' in such a position on our cottage front fence that we were 195, Main Avenue. It stayed that way until the cottage and nurseries were demolished in 1959.

CHAPTER 23

Young Ivy and Fred were due back at the Council School shortly, at the end of their summer holidays. The thought that the teachers and Headmaster may be getting together to talk before the Council School re-opened, caused me further anxiety. I could imagine Miss Deane talking of the success she had in getting six of her boys places in the Grammar School of the twenty available, and my name being mentioned in the hearing of Mr. Beech who apparently had not entered my offence or punishment in the book. I felt that my award could still be withdrawn.

I could not forget that my best mate had only just failed. He should not have done when I had passed. Neither could I forget what his Mum had told him after she had complained to Oliver and Miss Deane; this was that I had only just passed by the narrowest of margins. This questionable achievement had come about because I had made every effort for all those months, for fear of the consequences if I had failed. This seemed the best I could do even after being driven on by frequent canings, to which my mate had not been subjected. I recalled that Miss Deane had said she was going to be hard on me, after I had behaved so badly; so she was. I remember how, as afternoon class came to an end each day, I would look to see if the cane was still on Miss Deane's desk, for this would mean that one or more of us less satisfactory scholarship hopefuls was going to get it after the rest of the class had been dismissed. Sometimes I knew quite early in the day that I was likely to be one of them as soon as I looked inside my exercise books handed back to me that morning after Miss Deane had marked them at home the previous evening.

My two other mates were delighted they had passed, but I could not share their enthusiasm. Their success seemed to have encouraged them to be very studious during the holiday. They discussed the contents of the Childrens' Newspaper, which I thought was dreadfully boring. Sometimes I would make up for my ignorance by use of my vivid imagination, agile mind and ready tongue, but rarely with any success. I envied their ability to keep mostly out of trouble at school — but not otherwise. I think they missed a lot of fun by not reading all the boys' weeklies I managed to scrounge; the books I borrowed from the Public Library which I had joined as soon as I could when I was eleven, and the lovely Pictures I saw at the Queen's Hall. My head was full of school, detective, adventure and historical tales and characters. The only drawback was that they kept coming to the fore when I was supposed to be paying attention to less interesting subjects in class: I would daydream.

When I thought of all this I started to worry about landing myself at the new school in a class of very bright boys, who found it easy to learn without the strict supervision and individual attention I needed and was accustomed to. I would soon get stumped, stop trying, and revert to my old natural indolent ways. How nice it would be if, having got the honour of winning a scholarship, I had an excuse not to go to the new school, and stay at the Council School? Perhaps I could get Dad to tell Oliver that he could not afford to equip me and keep me at school until I was sixteen? After all, he had started work at thirteen and he was good at his lessons. Sisters Jess and Kit had left school at fourteen, after getting very good Reports. Why should I be any different? If he did that, perhaps the teachers would be sorry and be more kind to me.

I waited an opportunity when I thought Dad might be in a good mood. Nervously I told him that I could not go to the new school in my corduroys but that I would need a new suit, a school cap, a satchel and plimsolls; perhaps some other things. More nervously I said that if he thought he could not afford them nor keep me at school until I was sixteen he could write to tell Mr. Oliver. I did not have to go — and I did not really mind. Dad said that he would see.

I was not being honest with Dad. I was using him to try to stay at the Council School in what I thought favourable conditions, and to remove any chance of exposure of my very bad behaviour which still might threaten the scholarship award, and my safety. Offering to stay at a school where I would start work at fourteen should tempt Dad to write the letter. To me at the age of twelve, fourteen was an eternity away. I did not know I was to learn of moves which may have changed my ideas.

My mind was in a turmoil that night and the next day. I was uncertain what I wanted to do, as I disliked school anyway. I could not tell Dad emphatically that I did not want to go to the Grammar School, because whilst studying for it I had not said I was not keen. I had to use subterfuge somehow. What did Dad mean when he replied that he "would have to see"?

That evening however my fate seemed to be sealed. When Dad came in from the Nursery after his usual exhausting long day on his feet, he curtly told me to go up the road to Mr. Phillip's house at about 6.30 p.m. and bring back a parcel, which was for me. I could hardly wait. On the way back from the errand I passed young Ivy playing on the corner of Seventh Avenue, and Fred playing fag cards in Lincoln Road, so they were out of the way. Dad told me to go upstairs and put on what was in the parcel. To my delight it was a Rugby suit, and an Eton collar. It was smashing. As I went down to Dad I thought I must not let my liking for the suit settle the matter — that it was to be the new school for me. I can recall what I said to him; "Oh, it's all right, but I wish it didn't blinking well stink of moth balls!" (Its smell didn't bother me in the least but I wasn't going to say so).

Unexpectedly Dad became furious, probably because of the way I answered him, and my apparent ingratitude. He got up to get his strap, shouting "There's no bloody grammar school for you, mate. Get into that front room — I'll tan the bleeding hide off you". I went to prepare myself for the belting, thinking what a daft bugger I was. As I waited with the jacket and waistcoat off I hoped that Dad meant it when he said I was not going to the new school. I was going to hang on to the suit anyway, even if it did stink.

As I waited I heard Mum and Dad talking. To my surprise, Mum not Dad came in to me. She picked up the jacket and waistcoat, and, before going out again, she told me something she had so many times told me since Dad came out of the Army, which was that I should stop being troublesome to my father to make him lose his temper — all the family suffered as a result.

There was more talking and then I heard Dad shout "Come back in here, you". I re-adjusted my breeches and went back into the kitchen, where Dad bad-temperedly said that the suit did smell, and that Mum would air it in the garden whenever possible. I could wear my Sunday suit for the new school until the smell had gone.

I was disappointed. There was no escape from the new school. My dream of staying at the Council School, honoured with having won the scholarship but being too hard-up to take advantage of my success, had vanished. I would have put up with a hiding and no new school if I could have hung on to Sid Phillip's suit, smell or no smell. Mum was to have little success in getting rid of the moth ball stink, but that did not worry me. Nobody seemed to be annoyed by it at Sunday School, which I was about to give up anyway. I suspect that Dad did not forget my attitude to the Phillip's suit. From then onwards I was aware that he searched around and bought for me clothes at bargain prices regardless of my wishes or of fashion. I must have looked odd at times amongst well-dressed fee-paying boys. Not that anybody cared. I didn't. There was no uniformity of dress at schools in Enfield.

I had not seen my best mate for some time, as I had been going around with the others who had passed the scholarship. So I called on him, and he divulged to me that he was not staying at the Council School, but going to a newly formed Central School at George Spicers in Southbury Road, together with my cousin Harry Anthony, and all the other boys who had sat but failed the examinations. I was shattered, for that was where I wanted to go, and there would have been no need to worry about a new suit. I could have gone in my corduroys, and possibly leave school at fourteen or at the very latest fifteen. What a mess I had made! I got on fine with both him and Harry — they were on my level. I could now never pluck up enough courage to raise the matter with Dad.

I suppose it served me right that I was not allowed to forget my outrageous behaviour in the Manual Room for months. My mate's brother continued to taunt me every time he saw me in the street with his shout "Wotto grammerite — did ole Beechey wallop yer?" Unfortunately he spent

THE GREAT BUNTER MYSTERY!

SEARCHING FOR THE MISSING CHANGE!

(A Very Amusing Scene in the Magnificent Long, Complete School Tale of the Chums of Greyfriars.) 26-7-19 all of his time when out of school playing in the very streets I had to traverse, and he was always artful enough only to shout at me when he was at a safe distance. I am sure my new school cap was an affront to him. but he eventually got bored with it, and gave up, much to my relief.

Dad seemed to be getting a bit better off, sending me more frequently to the newsagents, thus giving me increased opportunities to acquire illicitly boys' weeklies, for I could not satisfy my appetite for boys' school stories, the money for which was lacking. I hated school yet loved to read about it. Then one day, the only weekly I could easily pick up was a copy of the "Union Jack". From then on I had a new obsession, that for Sexton Blake, Detective. I must have known the risks I was running, because a boy I went to school with had been charged at the Juvenile Magistrates Court with petty stealing, and he had been taken down to the basement, where he had been given four strokes of the birch on his bottom. He said that he had been scared not knowing what the four policemen were going to do to him.

When I had a newly acquired copy of a boys' weekly paper and had been reading it in bed, I would put it under my pillow before extinguishing the candle. Sometimes, when half-awake, I could hear it gently rustle as I moved my head, and I would go hot all over with visions of being escorted home from the newsagents by a policeman, who would tell Dad that I was to be charged with stealing. I could envisage being at a boys' reformatory school, feeling very sorry for myself. I would resolve not to be tempted again, but unfortunately my good resolutions came to naught when I saw the weeklies in neat little piles on the newsagents' counters.

When carrying my valued boys' weekly papers, which I wished to keep very much to myself, I would stuff them inside the top of my breeches and under the bottom of my waistcoat. This would give me an unjustified appearance of stoutness.

BUSH HILL PARK SCHOOL,

SENIOR GIRLS' DEPARTMENT.

REPORT. [illegible]

Name I. Robinson Class I

Subject.	Marks. Maximum	Obtained.	
Arithmetic	10 / 10	4 / 6	**ATTENDANCE.**
Reading	10	10	Regularity. [illegible]
Composition	20	[illegible]	Punctuality. [illegible]
Writing	10	6	
Spelling	10	10	**GENERAL CONDUCT.**
Recitation	10	4	
History	20	17	
Geography	20	[illegible]	REMARKS.
Drawing	10 / 10	[illegible]	a steady, persevering [illegible]
Needlework	10	7	
TOTAL	150	102	

No. of girls in class. 34

Position in class. 11

Class Teacher A. H. Gooch.

Head Teacher E. J. Groome.

Ivy at eleven no longer lacked steadiness, and her conduct was considered excellent. Her surviving school reports from this time onwards show that she was a very satisfactory pupil in the senior girls school.
1920 photograph - Ivy is 4th right, 3rd row.

CHAPTER 24

The Grammar School re-opened three weeks later than the Council School, so whilst young Fred and Ivy were back at school I was able to pass my time looking after the chickens, pigeons, reading fiction and working on Dad's allotment.

Eventually the morning came when I joined my two scholarship mates at the top of my road to walk the mile or so to the new school. All three of us were equipped with our new school caps, and cheap canvas satchels. We were an assorted group, but probably a representative sample of boys of our age in those days. Stan wore short knickers with long stockings over his knees, Ted wore short knickers and bare knees, and I had my knees covered with long stockings and breeches. We all three wore footwear of the kind boys had worn for twenty years — ankle length laced-up black boots, highly polished. Mine had metal heel plates and studded soles.

Our satchels were empty that morning, possibly so for the only time for the following three months. Recalling how untidy I was, it could be that my satchel was not empty for the next fifty eight years, because when it surfaced after the death of my eldest sister it had in it some exercise books, my last Term Report from the School, and a copy of "The Magnet" boys' weekly published in 1919.

On arrival at the school we joined hundreds of other boys in the playground, waiting for the bell to ring. After morning prayers in the Hall we somehow found out what Form we were in. I think that was our introduction to our new school life. I was surprised and somewhat disturbed to find myself in Form 2a with my two scholarship mates who were very good scholars: I had hoped I would be put into a lower Form with the less keen boys.

The system was very different from that of the Council School. The Class or Standard as I had known it was here called a Form. We sat at individual desks instead of shared desks, and the blackboard was fastened on to the wall, not placed on an easel. We did not have one teacher, here called master or mistress, for the whole year teaching us all subjects, but different ones for each subject, and the lessons were of forty five minutes length, when our instructors changed. Mrs. Richman, our Form Mistress, took us for History and English and I think she tried her best. Miss Atkins took us for Nature Study. As for the masters — they rambled on at the blackboard for forty minutes — then set the homework. But I found that it was all so boring.

There was no individual attention, so only the keen boys were going to learn much. It was then I realised what a splendid teacher Miss Deane had been, for even if she did walk about the classroom with a cane in her hand, she did sit down at our desks and show us our mistakes. I soon knew that I was not in the right environment. Lord Jenkins of Putney, who was at the school at the same time, and was my age, remarks in his autobiography that the teaching was appalling. Since reading that, I have become easier in my mind.

Whilst sitting in the Form Room my thoughts would wander to the brown-capped boys at the new Central School, with whom I would have been at ease. But one morning on the way to school one of my scholarship mates told me that Oliver was now Headmaster at the new Central School, having been transferred from our old School. So I stopped that particular line of wishful thinking and started to wish once again that I had persuaded Dad to say that I could not accept the scholarship because he was too hard-up. This wishful thinking was strongly reinforced when I heard that Miss Deane had been moved to the Girls' School because she had been considered too severe with us boys. But when I remembered seeing Mr. Allemandy hitting boys in his top class with a walking stick, I gave up, and resigned myself to being a Grammar School boy.

Lord Jenkins, in his same book remarks that although he passed the examination, his father wanted his son to get the same treatment as the sons of gentlemen, so he paid for him. My experience was that although the teaching was poor, there was no difference between the treatment of fee-paying boys, and boys like me obviously working class and hard-up.

The Enfield Market Place, and part of the Town, as I saw it four times a day there and back from school. Any Grammar School boy seen riding a bike in the Market Place was caned by the Headmaster. This was one of the offences I could not commit as I couldn't ride a bike. There were no motor cars needing parking places, so the Church Commissioners got no revenue from this source. In the left of the photo can just be seen the railing of the Gents' Public Convenience. This Convenience was closed on the Sabbath, much to the inconvenience of boys like me, whose bladders could not tell what day it was.

Mum in the backyard. In the background are the Nursery stables.

In the Form Room sitting just across the aisle but slightly in front of me, so that he was always in full view whenever I looked up from my desk, was a boy exactly as I would have wanted to be. I could hardly take my eyes off him. He was fresh, clean complexioned, and good looking, with fair hair neatly brushed back. I could smell his expensive hair oil from where I sat. He had a brown, fine quality tweed sports jacket with leather buttons, his breeches of matching material so perfectly fitting at and below his knees that they must have been made for him. He had on a brilliantly white starched linen Eton collar. His fine woollen stockings were turned over at their fancy tops, neatly, just below the knees. On his feet were not boots but brown brogue shoes.

He was exactly like the boys pictured in my boys' weeklies. When I sat looking at him, sometimes I could visualise him boarding a train in a first class carriage with his parents on their way to stay at a seaside resort in a good hotel for a month's summer holiday; or being bought the magic lantern advertised by Gamages, as a Christmas present. Or being taken to the Pantomime in the West End. I admired him, but sometimes my envy hurt me inside.

We never spoke to each other and I sometimes wondered what he thought of my short cropped hair and fringe, my celluloid collar, my rough suit, long black worsted stockings and boots. He at times took out with a flourish from his breast pocket a handkerchief and blew very loudly into it, causing the master to rebuke him. One master would call out "Stop trumpeting, boy", and he would reply in his cultured voice, quite cheekily, "Sir, Oh sorry Sir, I can't help it, Sir". I did not know names of boys in my Form except some of the scholarship lads, but I knew his, and it was exactly what I had expected it to be. I was constantly reminded of it by seeing the initials on the corner of his handkerchief. I will not divulge it because some time later he was called to the Headmaster's study, and when he returned he was tearful and flushed. Not long after that he disappeared, and did not return. Months later I heard he had been involved in some missing money, and his father had removed him from the school. My illusions were not shattered but it made me feel good that such a boy with no obvious need should succumb to temptation, when I so frequently succumbed, but with need, in my opinion.

E. M. Eagles
The Headmaster
(Beak)

G. Livermore
(Maths 4b)

J. Arthur
(German)

Next Term begins Tuesday, 4th May.

ENFIELD GRAMMAR SCHOOL.

Founded 1557.

THE Grammar School possesses the advantages of being a very old Foundation and also of being thoroughly up-to-date. It endeavours to cultivate in its Pupils a high standard of efficiency—moral, mental and physical.

STAFF.—Edwin M. Eagles, M.A. (Head Master), S J. Coysh, B.A., B.Sc., S. Smith, M.A., L.-es-L., A. L. Watson, B.A., J.P., A. M. Godsell, B.A., T. Lakeman, B.Sc., C. W. Livermore, B.A., E. Perfect, J. M. Arthur, B.A., D. W. Rosling, B.Sc., C. H. Dearing, H. Partridge, D. S. Hemmings, B.A., E. L. Mellersh, M.A., F.R.G.S. D. C. Ellis, M.A., R. C. O. Leonard, B.A., Miss M. J. Swift, L.L.A., Miss M. Hocking, B.A., Miss J. Atkinson, B.A., and Visiting Masters.

Fees, etc.—The inclusive Fee is £4 4s. per term; there is an Entrance Fee of 7/6. The Head Master will be pleased to supply further information on application.

In order to derive the fullest benefit from the School Course, boys should enter when they are between 11 and 12 years of age. The School Year begins in September, and boys cannot be admitted at any other time unless under very exceptional circumstances.

Miss Mare
(Music)

E. Mellersh
(Maths 3b)
known as 'Bubbles'

S. Smith
known as
'Cheesy'
(French)

Miss Swift
(Maths 2a)

Miss Atkins
(Nature Study)

D. Rosling
(Science)

H. Partridge
(Woodwork)

A. Watson
known as
'Old Watty'
(History)

C. Dearing
(Gym)

CHAPTER 25

There was no school uniform, boys wearing a variety of outfits, though a school cap was obligatory. Very few boys wore the school tie — I never had one. I learned that there were a number of offences for which punishment was certain. One was riding a bicycle in the Market Square — the other was talking to the County School girls, whose school was just at the back of ours. These were two offences I could not commit, because I couldn't ride a bike, and I did not know any girls — certainly not County School ones. Arthur Ellis told me years later that he got caned for both offences.

Little by little I learned the ropes, without directly being informed. Discipline was obviously more relaxed here, but there was a procedure which caused me anxiety, and this was the Weekly Record, I thought unfair. On Monday morning of each week we were given a printed form on which we were required to enter our name, Form, and the date. We were required to enter on it anything unsatisfactory in our work or in our conduct during the week, this being initialled by the Master. On Friday evening this Record was to be taken home, and brought back on Monday duly signed by a parent.

I learned that impositions and detentions were awarded freely. Three detentions in one week brought the Lab. Boy to the Form, with the Headmaster's request for the boy to report to his Study, if he could be "spared". A caning usually resulted, duly entered on the Record.

I found that we had "Break" and not playtime. We had a "Quad" and not a playground, the surface of which was unsuitable for me to slide on with my iron-shod boots, but excellent for us to raise as much dust as we could; done to annoy those in charge, especially when rehearsing for the Empire Day March Past. I was good at this.

Along the length of the school building at the rear was a terrace bordered by a sloping grass bank, along which two masters in gowns and mortar boards would stroll during "Break". Woe-betide any boy who trespassed thereon, something we could do quite impetuously chasing after a ball in play. The Quad was bordered on two sides by neighbours' gardens, one in Uvedale House being the cause of boys getting caned. I was eventually to be one of them — for the temptation of ripe walnuts hanging ready on the tree — requiring only a quick throw upwards of a loaded satchel, was too great for me.

As the fee-paying boys had been in the school a whole year before I arrived, they were familiar with the masters' little habits, but I had had no warning, putting me at a disadvantage. I tried not to look too embarrassed when called out to the front of the Form for some misdemeanour, and to receive the ritual face-slapping on each cheek. This was known as getting "ginger", the name given to it by the administrator Mr. Smith, the French Master. I hated being treated as a small boy.

This same Master, daily, would summon a boy out to the front of the Form, remove from his purse with a flourish a penny coin, and, with a theatrical movement, say to the boy "Go at once to the sweetshop in the Market Place. Give the lady my compliments, and obtain for me one pennyworth of acidulated tablets, the square ones, and do not eat any of them, because I shall know".

The Science Master, Mr. Rosling, came to the school on a new bicycle. He was a tall, handsome man, who wore knee breeches, smart turn-over socks and very expensive looking boots. He objected to the noise, some of it deliberate, made by boys when walking up and down on the floor of the laboratory, and he hated the noise of squeaking leather boots. In spite of the fact that I made as little noise as possible with my metal studded boots, he always called out to me "For goodness sake, Robinson, get your father to pay for those boots". There was a saying that squeaking ones had not been paid for.

Mr. Watson, our elderly History Master, was an expert at lobbing the hard-backed blackboard duster at any boy who had dropped off to sleep from sheer boredom. Some of the fee-paying older boys would lob it back to old Watty, but I dared not trust myself — I was not accurate enough.

Before the year 1920 it would have been unusual to see a school girl with hair other than in a way nature intended, long and uncut.

Suddenly in the very early nineteen twenties fashion changed, and within quite a short period most girls had had their hair shorn to the level of their ears, in a style known as the "bob". However, our Dad took the same unfavourable view of short hair for girls as he had done of bare knees for boys; so as a result Ivy and Winnie stayed in long hair just as I had stayed in knickerbockers or breeches.

It can be observed from the photograph of Winnie's class at the Council School in 1924 that she is very much in the minority with her long hair amongst the girls with the new style. Both Win and Ivy wore long hair for years after fashion had changed. Win had her tresses brushed down over her shoulders; Ivy with her light brown hair reaching down to her waist plaited into "pigtails" tied at their ends with brightly coloured ribbons. These pigtails would bounce up and down as she ran or played.

Winnie, first from right, top row.

Ivy and Winnie
1927

Winnie
1929

Winnie
1928

1931
Win Unshorn — Ivy Bobbed

Mr. Dearing took us for "Gym" in the Hall. For this, all we did was to remove our boots, placing them out of the way against the wall; then don plimsolls. I soon got accustomed, together with seven or eight boys, to remain upright when the rest of the Form performed "knees bend" exercises, because of the tight knickerbockers or breeches we wore. Fashions were changing quickly, most boys being in short knickers and bare knees within a year or so — but I remained one of a decreasing number in the minority. Dad was required to spend another two shillings and sixpence on a pair of wooden Indian clubs, which I made feeble efforts to swing. I did not do very well with them, nor did most of the others. Some boys managed to vault over the horse but many of us just scrambled over it. Nobody told us how to use the wooden spring-board for the purpose.

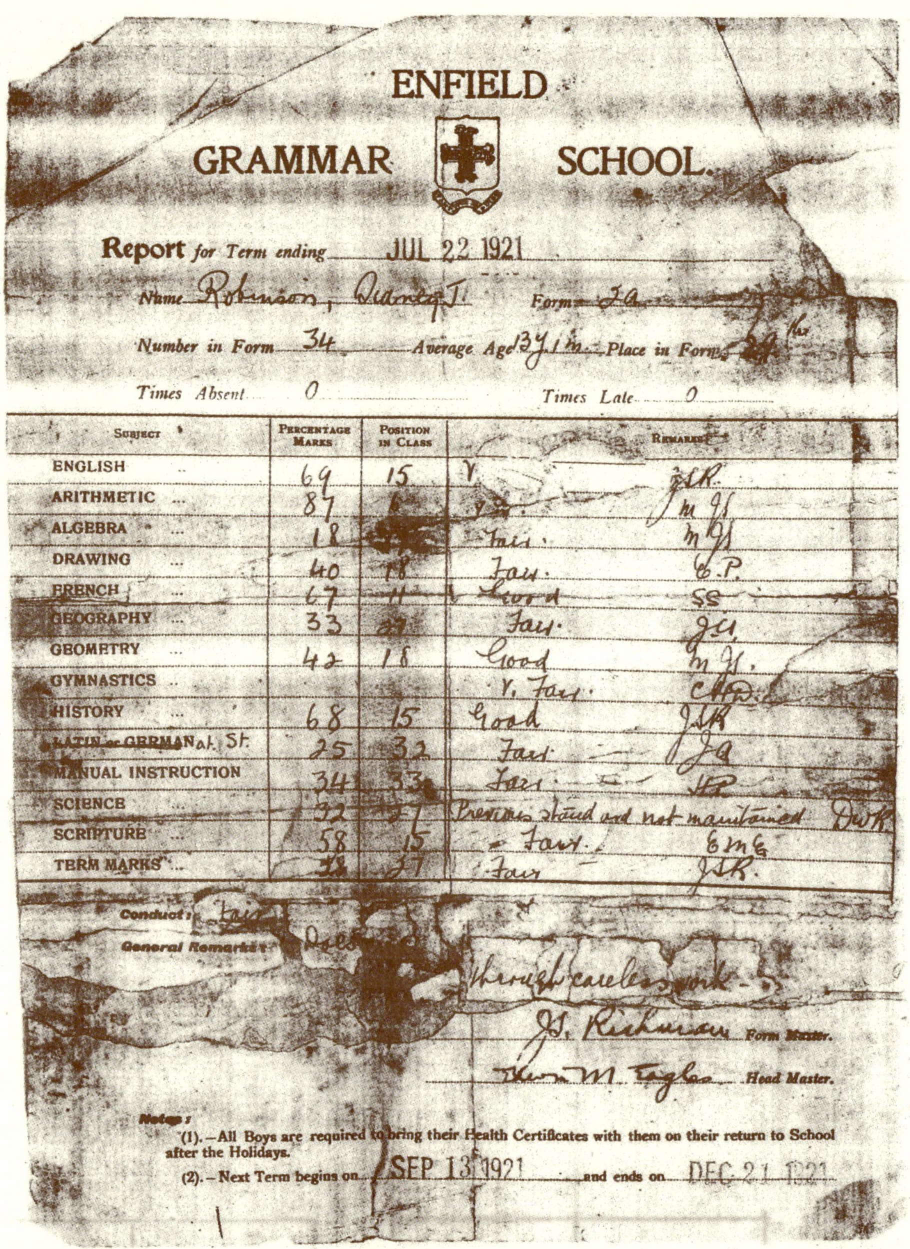

ENFIELD GRAMMAR SCHOOL.

Report *for Term ending* JUL 22 1921

Name Robinson, Stanley J. *Form* 3a

Number in Form 34 *Average Age* 13y. 1m. *Place in Form* 29th

Times Absent 0 *Times Late* 0

Subject	Percentage Marks	Position in Class	Remarks	
English	69	15	V. [illegible]	JSR.
Arithmetic	87	6	V.G.	MJJ
Algebra	18	[illegible]	Fair.	MJJ
Drawing	40	18	Fair.	E.P.
French	67	11	Good	SS
Geography	33	29	Fair.	JG.
Geometry	42	18	Good	MJJ.
Gymnastics			V. Fair.	[illegible]
History	68	15	Good	JSR
~~Latin or German~~ Art St.	25	32	Fair	JG
Manual Instruction	34	33	Fair	HP
Science	32	27	Previous stand not maintained	DWK
Scripture	58	15	Fair.	EMG
Term Marks	33	27	Fair	JSR.

Conduct: Fair

General Remarks: Does [illegible] through careless work.

J.S. Richman **Form Master.**

[illegible] M. Eagles **Head Master.**

Notes:

(1).—All Boys are required to bring their Health Certificates with them on their return to School after the Holidays.

(2).—Next Term begins on SEP 13 1921 and ends on DEC 21 1921

This Term Report, after surviving by accident, and in bad storage, for more than sixty years, was nearly destroyed by carelessness, and had to be repaired after some of the pieces could not be found in the dustbin. It had already shown some signs of being boyishly tampered with in an attempt to disguise or improve the Remarks. I can recall it reading. "Does not try hard enough nor concentrate properly, and loses marks through careless work".

CHAPTER 26

By the end of the first term I had begun to be more at ease. I had managed to give some sort of satisfaction, in spite of Mrs. Richman's remarks on the Term Report that I "had lost marks through careless work". I am sorry that this Report has not survived, because, if I recall correctly, it was the only one I ever had which gave me "Good" for conduct; this in spite of the fact that I had just started to get into mischief, but not seriously enough yet.

I think it was during the November of that Term that there was a very short cold spell in an otherwise mild month. It happened the day the school central heating system briefly broke down. I was so warmly dressed that I had not noticed its failure during the morning but some boys did, and apparently so did the staff. After dinner time we were all marshalled in the Market Place. Led by Mr. Edwin M. Eagles, the Headmaster, we meandered, scuffled and shuffled our way through Church Street, up Windmill Hill, part of the Ridgeway, then back to the School, where we were dismissed earlier than usual, greatly to my joy.

At home for the holidays, on the Sunday morning near Christmas, I sat in the kitchen, coming to the end of my library book. To my dismay I realised that I would have nothing else to read the rest of the Sunday. A little later in the morning Dad threw across to me a couple of coins and told me to go up to the newsagent and get him a newspaper. I asked him if I could have tuppence for a boys' weekly, because I had nothing to read. I caught him on the wrong foot. He refused. On reaching the shop I had one of my uncontrollable impulses. I took the newspaper and moved it along the counter with my right hand, whilst I fished about in my breeches pocket with my left for the coins. With my right hand I picked up the paper and whatever I had managed to take hold of underneath it. I passed the money to the shopkeeper as I did so. This time it was especially risky, as what I had purloined was something bulky.

As I left the shop I felt a thrill of excitement, but a reaction set in as I approached home. I looked back, nervously, my knees quivering slightly with the thought of the danger I was so often running. When I reached my backyard I took the Strand Magazine, for that was what it was, from the newspaper, and stuffed it up into my jacket. I gave Dad his newspaper when I got into the kitchen, then quietly went upstairs, putting the magazine under my pillow.

I fretted in the afternoon knowing that there was something interesting to read but could not do it because there was nowhere else but the warm, lighted kitchen to be in on that winter's day. In the evening my frustration turned to anxiety when Mum unintentionally moved Fred's School Report to a more prominent place on the mantelshelf. I knew that Dad had not seen it but I had no thought for Fred's well-being at that moment; it was that it might remind Dad that he had not seen mine.

As luck would have it, Dad rose to light one of his rare cigarettes, took the Report and read it. He turned to Fred, and said grumpily that he knew Fred was a lazy little bugger, and now the teacher knew — he had better watch out. Dad sat down, and I sighed with relief, short-lived because he turned to me saying something to the effect that mine would be better — where was it? Reluctantly I fetched it and gingerly passed it to him. He exploded, and said angrily that we were a couple of bright buggers. He added that if I continued to lose marks at school he would have to give me some on my backside.

Mum became irritated that we had made Dad angry, so she told us to clear off to bed. Undoing our boots and leaving them by the kitchen fire we went off with alacrity — I for one glad to escape the tense atmosphere.

Within a minute or two Fred had thrown off his jacket, waistcoat, collar and breeches and was under the blankets, whilst I fumbled about under my bedstead for the little tin lid, and my stump of candle. This I lit carefully from the small flame of the oil-filled night light, and fixed the stump on to the lid with candle wax, placing them both on the seat of the chair beside my bed. When I had removed my jacket, waistcoat, collar and breeches I draped them over the back of the chair with

8 April 1983

The British Journal of Photography,

Acknowledgements

The detailed examination of the Cottingley Affair contained in this ten-part series, a length necessary to extract a solution, has only been possible through the co-operation the writer has had from various quarters. Primarily he is indebted to Mr Sydney J. Robinson who placed at the *Journal's* disposal not only the cameras and other source material purchased at Sotheby's in 1972 but also his complete dossier on the subject comprising material from 1920 to the present day, and without which it would have been quite impossible to assemble the article. Mr Robinson tells how as a knickerbockered schoolboy of 12 in 1920 he read the *Strand* article by flickering candelight in his draughty cottage bedroom, while owls hooted in the oak tree a few yards from his window, and how he felt let down by the facts emerging from the article that his favourite boyhood hero, the author of Sherlock Holmes, had come to believe in fairies and gnomes. For some 50 years he travelled extensively around the world in his work. He began collecting books when he retired and spotted Doyle's *The Coming of the Fairies* listed in a Sotheby's sales catalogue in 1972. On making a few enquiries he was astonished to discover that the Cottingley mystery was still 'unsolved' after some 50 years and he considered it a little bit of a challenge. He was responsible for pursuing the matter with Brian Coe, whose conclusions given in correspondence with Robinson, have been quoted in the course of this article. It was Coe who recommended to him the present writer should be be approached to see if the *Journal* could conduct a full investigation. After visiting Mr Robinson and seeing the evidence, which led to the realisation that although the photographic world was content to dismiss the pictures, the affair looked like continuing indefinitely in the national media, the writer decided to see what could be done to bring about a solution to this prime photographic 'mystery'. Mr Robinson co-operated extensively throughout the article, commenting meticulously on each section before publication. He has been such a good devil's advocate, that the writer at times wondered on which side he stood. The successful conclusion is therefore very largely due to S. J. Robinson's assistance and encouragement.

the idea of throwing a shadow over the door hoping to stop Dad seeing the candle-light as he passed our room on the way to bed. On starting to settle in bed to open the magazine I heard Mum come upstairs to answer a call from young Ivy, and had to wait. Finally I opened the purloined item, very nervously, thinking of the mood in which we had left Dad, and the fear that he might discover me with a strictly prohibited lighted candle. It was asking for another sore backside.

To my utter dismay The Strand Magazine did not contain another Sherlock Holmes story, but an article, soppy I thought, in which Conan Doyle explained his belief in fairies. I was disgusted — what boy would want to read about such things? Unfortunately however, I had nothing else so I flicked over the pages to see if I could find any mention of Sherlock Holmes. Instead I learned that Doyle based his beliefs on some photographs two children claimed they had taken of fairies. I thought Doyle must be bonkers — fancy believing what children had said! One of the girls was my age, and if she were anything like me, she would have been able to romance easier than to tell the truth. I felt sure that it wouldn't be long before Sherlock Holmes took out his magnifying glass and had explained to Dr. Watson how the photographs had been produced.

I feel I must digress for a moment from the story of my boyhood to relate the extraordinary sequel to the events of that day. Many, many years later when elderly and retired after long periods overseas, I began to collect books. I came across in an old bookshop a copy of The Strand Magazine containing the Doyle Fairies article, and my memories came flooding back. My curiosity was aroused sufficiently for me to make a few enquiries, mainly to confirm that the children had been found not to be telling the truth.

To my astonishment I learned this was not so — in fact Doyle had written a full length book on the fairies, and had remained convinced of the genuineness of the fairy photographs until his death. The girls, now elderly as I was, had stuck to their story that they had seen, played and photographed real fairies.

This was too much for me, so I began to research the strange affair. I was able to acquire two of the primitive cameras the girls used, made experimental photographs, and consulted experts from time to time over a period of six years. I was still unable to prove the photographs fakes, though from the evidence I had gathered I was convinced that the last three of the five photographs had been taken with the intention of deceiving Doyle and his collaborators. I began to fear that the ladies or I would die before the truth could be established, so I appealed to Geoffrey Crawley, the Editor of the British Journal of Photography, for help. He wanted a lot of persuading, but after three years he set to work as an investigating sleuth. So successful was he that after two years the ladies finally admitted that they had faked the pictures which they had taken sixty two years before.

The ladies have now passed away. I am left with nothing but admiration for them. When they had been young unsophisticated girls they quite unexpectedly found themselves involved with an educated, experienced gentleman from London, a collaborator of Sir Arthur Conan Doyle, the famous writer; both men being anxious to believe as genuine two photographs the girls had taken as a childish prank. The girls were persuaded to take some more photographs, with cameras and plates given to them. The youngsters, willing to please such famous people, enthusiastically produced brilliantly conceived fakes. Both men were surprisingly gullible, and chose to ignore what the older girl's father had said after efforts had been made to convince him that the photographs were genuine. He remarked "Those girls have been up to summat". He knew his daughter better than strangers — he had taught her all she knew about photography — and he had developed and printed all her work, but he loved his only child. If some people wanted to be deceived — so be it!

Lady Conan Doyle, after the death of Sir Arthur, claimed that he had been the real life Sherlock Holmes. If this had been so, the world famous detective had met his match with those mischievous cheerful youngsters.

The astonishing affair of the Cottingley Fairies, as it came to be known, was brought to a con-

ENFIELD

GRAMMAR SCHOOL.

Report *for Term ending* DEC 21 1921

Name Robinson, S.J. *Form* 3 b

Number in Form 28 *Average Age* 14·5 *Place in Form* 24th

Times Absent 0 *Times Late* 10

Subject	Percentage Marks	Position in Class	Remarks	
ENGLISH ..	67	19	Fairly good.	[illegible]
ARITHMETIC ...	38	25	Satisfactory progress.	[illegible]
ALGEBRA ...	46	25		
DRAWING ...	41	23	Fair	[illegible]
FRENCH ...	59	11	Good.	[illegible]
GEOGRAPHY ...	23	27	Poor	[illegible]
GEOMETRY ...	60	19	Quite satisfactory	[illegible]
GYMNASTICS ..			Good.	[illegible]
HISTORY ...	42	16	Good.	[illegible]
~~LATIN or~~ GERMAN	67	26	Fairly good.	[illegible]
MANUAL INSTRUCTION	49	16	Good.	[illegible]
SCIENCE ...	33	27	Fair	[illegible]
SCRIPTURE ...				
TERM MARKS ...	32	28	Poor	

Conduct: Fair [illegible]

General Remarks: [illegible]

[illegible] *Form Master.*

clusion only because I had been a naughty boy and, in attempting to steal a boys' weekly paper, had been obliged to make do with a Strand Magazine.

Now to return to my boyhood story. The remainder of the first school year passed without any memorable incident. It seemed that I had paid enough attention whilst the mistresses or masters rambled on at the blackboard to get by with my homework. In Mathematics I was holding my own, but with increasing difficulty, because I was not sure what I was doing. The Mathematics teacher, Miss Swift, had no particular talent for passing on her knowledge to boys like me.

The final Term Report for the year showed me "very good" in English, "good" in French and History, but for the overall results I finished 29th in a form of 34 boys, and 27th in Term Marks, getting only 28%. I ought to have been ashamed to have obtained only 25% for Nature Study and of being 32nd in the Form. I was growing up on a Nursery Garden, surrounded by plants.

Kind Form Mistress Mrs. Richman seemed unable to make any comments better than "Does not try hard enough nor concentrate properly, and loses marks through careless work". My conduct was classified as "fair", though I do not now recall why I merited this.

I had however managed to avoid getting three detentions in one week, which would have had me in Beak's, the Headmaster's study, for a caning. For other reasons I had been summoned there. One was for me to tell my parents that the Medical Inspection had revealed the need for my ears to be cleaned out. Amongst the others was to tell them that my teeth needed attention. Of course I did no such things, having no intention of allowing my Dad to probe angrily into my ears — nor of being sent to the dentist.

One of the photographs in the Strand Magazine which convinced Doyle fairies existed.

'the stern face and the shiny yellow cane on his desk'

Aged thirteen.

CHAPTER 27

At the start of the new school year I was not surprised to find myself in a lower Form than my scholarship contemporaries, and I started to drift away from my mates.Mrs. Richman had been replaced by Mr. Mellersh — known as Bubbles — who took us for Maths. Miss Atkins for Nature Study was replaced by Mr. Arthur — who took us for German.

It was an unfortunate incident which made me first fall foul of Beak. I was leaving the school grounds at the end of the afternoon school one day, just about to go through the small gate into Church Walk when I received a very painful knock on the back of my leg. Impetuously I shouted "You clumsy bugger", and a few more swear words, to a boy who was scooting his bike with one foot on a pedal, trying to squeeze past me through the narrow opening. By sheer bad luck two red-capped prefects were a yard or so away. They took our names and Form Numbers.

Next morning Powell, the Lab. Boy came into the Form Room and said to the master: "Sir, the headmaster sends his compliments and would you spare S. Robinson to report to his Study". I could be spared.

As I entered the Study I had only eyes for Beak's stern face and the shiny yellow cane on his desk. He told me that he had a report of unseemly behaviour on my part, for which I was about to be caned. I said that "It was not my fault — the boy should not have been riding his bike — and he hurt my leg". Beak replied that the other boy would be dealt with, but there was no excuse for me. However as it was my first offence I would be dealt with lightly.

Afterwards, sitting in my hard desk, feeling very uncomfortable, I did not think I had been dealt with lightly. The walloping I had received with the shiny yellow cane on the tightly stretched seat of my breeches had been very painful. Every movement I made at my desk seemed like another whack. Later, in the lobby, I saw the lady secretary take down from the Notice Board the small card on which were typewritten the names of the boys who had recently received corporal punishment, and saw her pin up a fresh one on which my name and that of others had been added. I was glad that no boy mentioned it to me — I was to learn that boys were not interested in others' misfortunes. The secretary Florrie Wallace knew me, because her father worked in the Nursery with my Dad, so I was always a little uneasy that she may mention my troubles at school to my father, because she was well aware of them.

The following weekend I kept my Weekly Record, on which was Beak's entry of my caning, in my satchel until the last moment on Monday morning when I got Mum to sign it, to my intense relief.

Doing my homework one evening whilst Dad was reading his "Daily Chronicle", he suddenly snorted and started to swear. He then told Mum that it looked as if Kate had said goodbye to her savings, because that bloody scoundrel Horatio Bottomley has been arrested. Being very inquisitive and easily distracted from my homework especially if Dad was swearing about somebody other than me, I asked him why. He explained that Aunt Kate, like thousands of other ordinary people during the War, had invested in Bottomley's Victory Bonds, and they had been swindled out of their money. I was sorry for Aunty Kate, because she was always very nice to me, in spite of behaving badly with her when I was smaller. She had then been going to Jarvisbrook at the invitation of Uncle George and Aunty Lizzie to spend her week's holiday with them at Low's Orchid Nursery, and they had particularly asked for "young Sid" to go along too. I had agreed, but at the last moment, my little bag packed, I had refused to go, much to Aunty Kate's disappointment. Aunty Kate had not married: the young man she was engaged to having died in tragic circumstances after being bitten by a poisonous snake when searching for rare orchids in China for Kew Gardens. Aunty would sometimes let me call on her at the lovely large house where she lived in Bagshot Road as housekeeper and companion to Madame Hovelt, the proprietor of the Enfield Purity Laundry.

The first Report of the second year showed me bottom of the Form for Term Marks. I was

BY KEN STEVENS
FOR SYD ROBINSON

The Wicked Headmaster
A fairy tale of Enfield Grammar School

Once upon a time [illegible] in Enfield Grammar School, a wicked, [illegible] man called Beak. He lived all alone in a study called 8, and had no companion except a big stick of which he was very fond, and every day at 4.15 a boy called Syd would knock at the door, and enter, and [illegible] him and say whack, whack, whack [illegible] little boy didn't like [illegible]

ENFIELD GRAMMAR SCHOOL

WEEKLY RECORD

Name S. Robinson Form III b [illegible]

	Monday.	Tuesday.	Wednesday.	Thursday.	Friday.
English					
Arithmetic					
Algebra					
Drawing					
French					
Geography					
Geometry					
History					
Latin (or German)					
Science					
Scripture					
Home Work					
Punctuality					
Conduct					
Detention	✓				

REMA[RKS]

caned for neglecting homework
E.M.E.

Wh[ere no remark] is made, Work an[d] Conduct are considered satisfactory.

Signed ... Robinson ...
Parent or Guardian.

In the remarks column of the original of the Weekly Record can be discerned, in faded red ink and through a heavy stain, the words 'caned for neglecting homework' and initialed E.M.E.

pleased to be considered "good" at gymnastics however. But I had started to find my homework a nuisance for I was borrowing exciting books by W.H. Ainsworth, which were also very lengthy, from the Library, and I begrudged the time I had to spend on soppy subjects like History and Geography.

My homework had already been the cause of me getting a number of detentions, and eventually I got into trouble over them. I recall Dad wanted me to help in the Nursery, carrying away and stacking plants as they were re-potted by Mr. Phillips and him. Dad often did this during the light evenings but he always asked me first if I had any homework to do because he knew I was very lazy. I would lie to him and say that I had not if I especially wanted some money, as I often did.

On the first occasion I worked two evenings, and went to the Pictures on the third, with a bag of toffee. As a result my homework was so badly done that I received three detentions, and these, together with one other for being late without proper excuse, made certain that I would be outside Beak's Study the next Monday at 10.45 a.m. or at 4.15 p.m.

Lord Jenkins refers in his autobiography to the Headmaster being a sadist with a collection of whips and canes lining his Study walls. I must admit that I did not see these, but when I was duly summoned there this time, I did see three assorted sizes of canes lying ready to hand on his desk. I did not observe which one he used on my seat, but I felt it was the stoutest! I wished more than ever that Dad would buy me some thick underpants or even thin ones!

This Weekly Record with "Caned for neglecting homework" written on it in red ink had to be kept from Dad at all costs. Neglecting my homework was bad enough, but to have been punished at school for it after I had told Dad clearly that I had none to do was really asking for trouble. I had lied to Dad two evenings running.

I was anxious at the weekend, and tried to behave well, making a special show of doing my homework in front of Dad. However, late Sunday afternoon he took his special marking pencil out of the cupboard, and angrily asked "Which of you two young buggers has been at this?", showing the badly scored wood and broken lead. As neither Fred nor I replied at once he said that he would clump the both of us. I backed away instinctively but young Fred stood his ground declaring that he had a sharp penknife and knew how to sharpen pencils. Dad knew this, and became furious because I did not own up. He pushed me into the front room, saying before he left, "And get your bloody trousers down quick". He was not long in coming back with his leather strap.

I spent an uneasy night worrying about the Weekly Report. It just had to be kept from Dad; absolutely vital for my well-being after my disgrace the previous evening. In the morning I found it less uncomfortable to stand to eat my crust of white loaf and drink my cocoa, before carrying out my plan. I watched Mum carefully, trying to choose the right moment in her harassed state as she tried to get four children off to school on time. I was so anxious that I got into a mess. Whilst moving around after Mum with the Record on the top of my satchel with the left hand, endeavouring to keep the offending remarks covered with blotting paper at the same time, I suddenly seized what I thought the right second to thrust the pen into her hand with my right. I had forgotten to dip it into the ink. This gave Mum time to say that I ought to get my father to sign it: "He'll be in to his breakfast in a minute". I panicked, pleading with her, complaining that I would be late for school. She relented, and signed it. Stuffing it into my satchel and grabbing my cap I was out of the house and running up the road within seconds.

That day I sat in the Form Room feeling frustrated. I kept asking myself how I could help Dad in the Nursery on those two evenings a week, earn the badly wanted shilling, and yet still get my homework done. That shilling was more important to me than anything else, never having had such a sum of money except on the day Dad sent me for his Passport. The few pence pocket money I received was hardly enough to buy sweets twice a week and buy a boys' weekly paper if I had not been able to purloin it, though I did occasionally manage to scrounge a few pence to obtain admission half-price at the Pictures.

I could not see a way to do my homework. I did not get home from school in the afternoons until

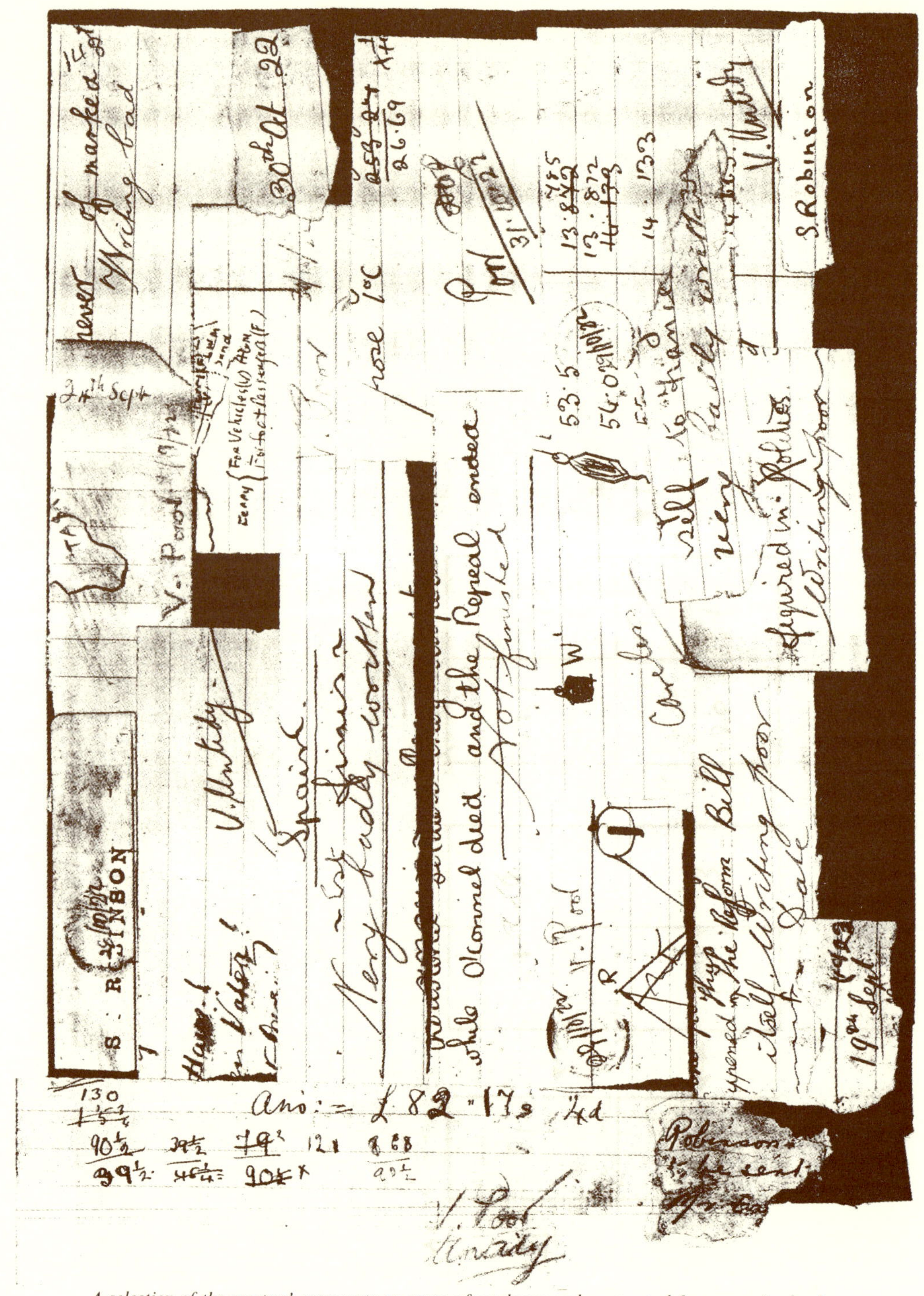

A selection of the masters' comments on some of my homework, extracted from exercise books.

4.45 p.m., but later still if I had a detention, not unusual. Dad came in to his tea at 5.30 p.m., and it was only then that I learned if he wanted me in the Nursery at 6.00 p.m. for roughly three hours. Dad insisted that we went to bed at 9.30 p.m. because we were so much trouble to get up in the mornings in time for school. Moreover, he and Mum needed a bit of peace and quiet before they themselves retired. Dad rose daily at 6.00 a.m. to rake out and rekindle the kitchen fire before going into the Nursery to ring the bell and to collect the employees' tickets as they came into work.

I suppose that other boys would have told their Dads the truth they they had homework to do, and that they would get it done by getting up early in the morning, but I was in no condition to do that, because when expected to be asleep in the late evening, I was sitting in bed reading by the light of an illicitly obtained stump of candle, exciting stories in books borrowed from the Public Library. Having no reliable watch or clock I did not know the time when I pinched out the flame of the candle and finally settled down to sleep.

I could find no solution to my problem; so it was not long before again standing outside Beak's Study at 4.15 p.m. on a Monday, waiting my turn to be called in. This time Beak asked me why I was not doing my homework some evenings. I told him that my father wanted me to help him. Beak replied that it was not an excuse — many boys helped their fathers — and they got up early to do their homework. He asked me what my father said about me being punished for neglecting it. I said he threatened to thrash me. Beak caned me, but to my surprise he did not seem angry.

Part of Church Street and the market place in Enfield as it was when I was a young schoolboy. The shop Pearsons Bros. was only a drapers cum haberdashery then. The International Tea Stores was rather an upper class grocers patronised by people who had a superior taste for various blends of tea. If I recall correctly, the market place was not crowded with stalls as it is today. The poorer people could choose to walk the two miles or more to the Edmonton market if they could not afford the tram or train fare. We walked down Lincoln Road to Ponders End, and then along the High Road to Edmonton.

Ken

A panoramic photograph was taken of the boys and staff at the Enfield Grammar School in October 1922. My copy of it, given to me by kindly M. Le Bas, our French Master at that time, is unfortunately in bad condition after being unrolled for the first time in about 60 years. I show here part of the photograph, the extreme right hand end. From it one can observe how few were the boys to wear the school tie, even on such an occasion. The tie is easily recognisable - it had broad lateral stripes (in red and white). It cost 2/6d. (12p). Surprisingly Ken Stevens, who was to become my best friend, always wore the tie though he hated the school. I cannot recall ever being aware of any of the school spirit which I read about in my boys' weeklies, but I do remember occasions when, after Monday morning Assemblies, Beak reproaching us for failing to give sufficient support to the school cricket or football match on the previous Saturday.

CHAPTER 28

I did not realise how poor my hurried homework must have seemed to the masters until one afternoon whilst walking home with two of my old scholarship mates I saw their exercise books about which they were arguing. I was astonished at the neat, almost copperplate writing exhibited therein, and if such excellence was expected, it was no wonder I was in trouble. But I couldn't be like them — they didn't read boys' weeklies, nor library books nor go to the Pictures. They didn't keep chickens nor have an allotment.

A little later, one of the boys, when we were talking outside his house, offered to show me his encyclopaedia. He knocked on his door, and to my surprise his mother asked me to go in with him. This was the first time I had been inside another boy's house, for normally, amongst working-class people, the friends of the children got no further inside than the front porch. The boy took me up to his bedroom, where, in addition to the very neat, clean bedroom furniture, there was a table covered by a fancy cloth and a chair. Over the table was a gas mantle and, to my astonishment, a fire alight in the grate. These were the conditions in which he did his homework — a little different from those in which I did mine.

My homework was done in the kitchen, the only room in our cottage with a table, chairs, heating and lighting. This kitchen was the centre of activity and leisure for our family of eight; three children younger than me. There was a coal-fired kitchen range alight summer and winter on which all the cooking was done and the water heated as well as the flatirons for the fortnightly wash. On the metal fireguard there was always washing airing or clothes drying. On one side of the range there was a food cupboard, but its contents were often to stand on the table because Dad could not control the ants which invaded it, getting into the sugar and into the condensed milk. On the other side of the range was a cupboard on which sometimes stood a wire netting apple box contraption in which I tried to rear day-old chicks, with the help of an oil-lamp. These chicks were bought from Curzons, up the road, for a penny each. The rest of the cupboard belonged to Dad. He kept his strap, easily available, in it. The table was near the wall alongside which ran an home-made wooden form used by the children when eating or playing. Dad and Mum had two wooden armchairs, and these with two ordinary kitchen chairs filled up any other space available.

In the warmer weather, moving about the room could be hazardous, because a flypaper hung quite low from the chain on the gas mantle light in the centre of the room. Captured flies, buzzing away, struggling to free themselves, could be within a few inches of somebody's head when seated.

In all but inclement weather we children could be playing outside, probably in the road early on; but later when time demanded that I got down to homework, there could be eight of us in the kitchen. By then Fred and Ivy would be getting tired, and probably quarrelling. To do my homework it was necessary for me to make room on the cluttered-up table for my pen, inkpot, blotting paper, pencil, ruler, rubber, exercise books, protractor and text books. My satchel went on to the floor, providing another hazard to the unwary. I can imagine with what enthusiasm I got down to drawing a map of the Provinces of India; or explaining the principles of the fulcrum, or of setting out in my best handwriting the causes of the Wars of the Roses.

Sometimes there would be a real diversion when Dad threw his boot at a mouse climbing up the curtain, or Ivy screamed because one was creeping along the picture rail. The mice were plentiful and friendly in the always warm, cosy kitchen of our cottage. Their forebears had established their secure home years before we moved in, and if they were at times unable to find suitable nourishment from the floor of our kitchen they only had to nip across the garden to the stables where there was always plenty. If we were quiet, one or two would appear from nowhere, and sit contentedly washing themselves until we banged the floor, or threw something at them. During the baby chick rearing period they were especially provided for by ideal food which the chicks carelessly scattered

ENFIELD

GRAMMAR SCHOOL.

Report *for Term ending* 12 APR 1922

Name Robinson, S.J. *Form* 3 b

Number in Form 28 *Average Age* 14 8 *Place in Form* 20

Times Absent 6 *Times Late* [illegible]

SUBJECT	PERCENTAGE MARKS	POSITION IN CLASS	REMARKS	
ENGLISH	55	13	F.G.	JMC.
ARITHMETIC	58	19	Untidy – can do well.	E.L.M.
ALGEBRA	34	25	Untidy & disappointing.	E.L.M.
DRAWING	60	12	Good.	[illegible]
FRENCH	41	[illegible]	Fair.	[illegible]
GEOGRAPHY	45	[illegible]	Fair	E.L.M.
GEOMETRY	54	14	Untidy. Some progress.	E.L.M.
GYMNASTICS			Fair	CHD.
HISTORY	30	[illegible]	Fair	ALW.
~~LATIN or~~ GERMAN ...	47	[illegible]	V. Fair	JMC.
MANUAL INSTRUCTION	42	17	Fair	HP
SCIENCE	27	25	Fair	DWR
SCRIPTURE				
TERM MARKS	51	21		

Conduct: Fair.

General Remarks: [illegible]

[illegible] *Form Master.*

[illegible] *Head Master.*

Notes:

on to our very worn linoleum.

Although I studied very thoroughly all the articles on chicken rearing in "The Smallholder" loaned to me by a mate's older brother, I was very ignorant of the correct rearing method, and many died. Then I acquired some secondhand chickens which I hoped would be able to supply us with eggs, but I found myself saddled with a mixture of tired hens and active cockerels, the latter fighting amongst themselves like billy-o. There were lots of rats around the Nursery and sometimes I found chickens disembowelled by them when I optimistically went to the large shed in the hope of collecting eggs. I read in "The Smallholder" that if a chicken got "crop-bound" it could be operated on, and the corn removed so I persuaded Dad to have a go, but the patient soon died. Fred and I kept pigeons, also acquired secondhand. We both got frequent hidings from Dad because we broke panes of glass in the greenhouses when throwing stones at the pigeons to try to make them fly off from the loft. We never gave up hoping that they would produce eggs and baby pigeons, but they never did. I was able to get hatched out some baby ducks by putting eggs under a broody hen. All these activities were far more interesting than homework, and these, with my obsession for reading fiction, made it a burden.

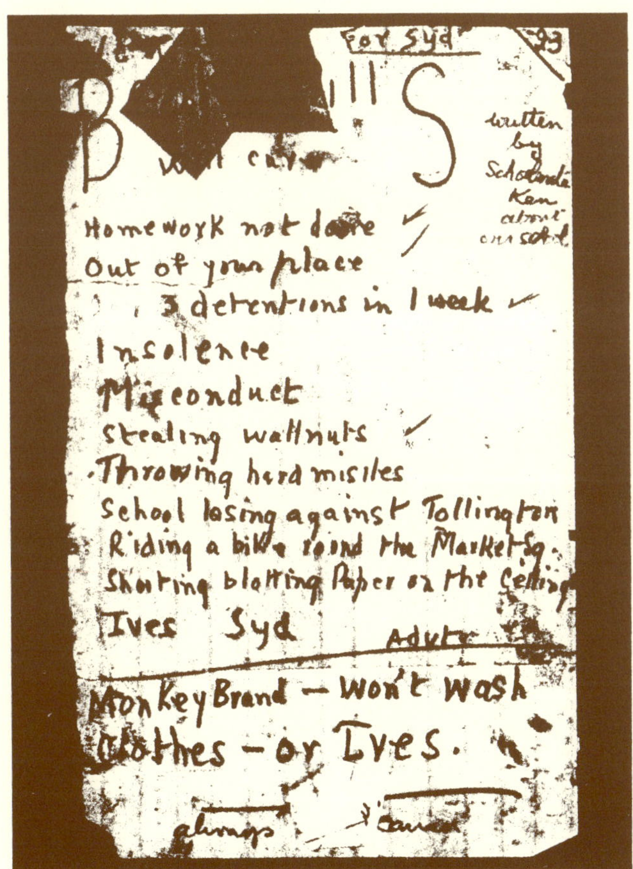

Ken Stevens, a boy of fifteen with a great sense of humour, wrote up this small advertisement in an attempt to extract a little fun from our troubles with Beak. The ailments from which we suffered, and for which we received pills in the form of whacks on our backsides, are ticked. Ives was another trouble-prone boy.

'No flick of an electric switch to flood the room with light'

'The Venetian blinds and the long, thick lace curtains made a room very gloomy on dull days.'

'To nervous children the flickering shadows cast by the candle could be very frightening'

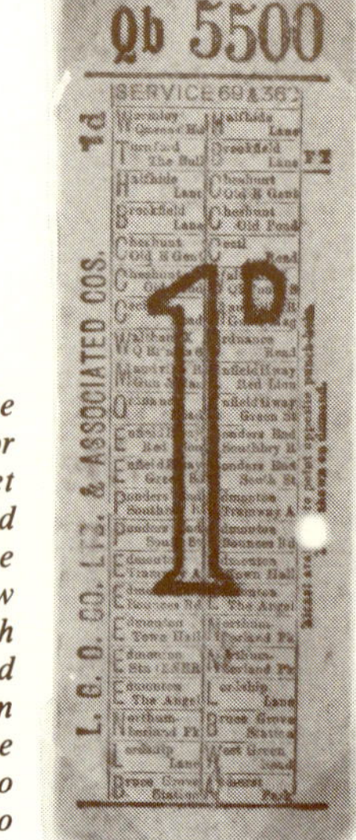

'A bus ticket issued by the London General Omnibus Co. for a journey from South Street Ponders End to Bounces Road Edmonton. The fare was one penny (less than one half new pence). Along this route, as with many others, the Co. suffered intensive competition from "pirate" buses which would race each other along the roads to reach the next bus stop first to pick up waiting passengers.'

CHAPTER 29

For any reader of these recollections unfamiliar with the times of which I relate, it would be difficult for him or her to imagine how different everything was then to what it is now. The facilities and comforts every child enjoys and takes for granted today were unknown to me, my brother and my sisters.

I knew there was such a thing as electricity, because the trams worked on it, but I had not seen it used elsewhere. Our roads, shops, trains and houses were lighted by gas. There were gas lamps in our classroom, but even on a dark, foggy afternoon they were only lit reluctantly. It was quite an experience to sit in a gas lit classroom. Our cottage had gas in the kitchen, and the rarely used cold parlour. The other rooms had no lighting, except a small oil lamp, or by candles when essential. Mostly, apart from the kitchen, our cottage after dusk was absolutely dark, except for a candle on a shelf in the scullery at the end of the passage. If anything had to be fetched, or searched for, the candle would have to be carried. To nervous children the flickering shadows cast by it could be very frightening. Nearly all the rooms were very gloomy except on sunny days, because visibility was reduced by the use of thick lace curtains, and by the Venetian blinds made of brown wooden slats, which after some wear became inefficient and refused to go fully up, leaving the windows partly obscured.

Ivy and I were always mislaying our things, I, especially at school times, but on gloomy days I often was not allowed to carry upstairs to the bedroom a lighted candle to search about for my Eton collar, a stud for it, my braces or my cap; sometimes on my hands and knees under the bed — and there was no flick of an electric switch to flood the room with bright light.

In the gloomy passage and up the stairs the wallpaper had peeled off the walls when we moved into the cottage, so Dad got our Uncle Charlie to gloss paint over them. After that they ran with water in all months except those of midsummer. I suppose the pointing of bricks was defective, but not rectified whilst Dad and Mum lived there.

The W.C. was in the backyard, ten yards from our scullery door. Its door had large gaps top and bottom, through which the wind would whistle, unimpeded across a vast expanse of greenhouses. It was an eerie place to visit at night, for owls would hoot in the oak trees, stray dogs be encountered which could easily enter our backyard from the Nursery or from the street. Any stray passer-by could wander in. Young Ivy refused to go to the W.C. in the dark, unless accompanied by another member of the family. In the W.C. we used newspaper — we did not know of the existence of toilet paper.

About a year after the end of the War Dad got a bit better off, so on rare occasions he could take Ivy, Fred and me to the Edmonton Empire, where we queued down the alleyway for the cheapest seats. As there were four of us, and the Circle above was supported by a lot of pillars where we sat, it was usual for one of us children to be seated behind one of these, risking a sprained neck and back to see anything on the stage. Young Ivy joined in all the comic songs. One comedian delighted Ivy by shouting to the audience; "Ow's yer muvver — and 'ow's yer Dad?" The audience, including young Ivy, would shout back "Orl rite thank yer". I loved the magicians.

To get to the Edmonton Empire we could go two ways — one by train from Bush Hill Park Station to Lower Edmonton — fare for us one penny. Or we could walk down the lane and get the bus, same fare. The public transport service was now excellent, designed and run for the maximum convenience of passengers, there being stops, both bus and tram, within easy walking distance of most homes and factories.

In an advertisement Dad saw boys' extra strong leather boots offered for sale at very low prices at Bolsom Brothers in Holborn. To get them Dad took Ivy, Fred and me on top of the open deck tram, an adventure we all thoroughly enjoyed.

MONEY!

W. P. HOBBS, Pawnbroker, Jeweller and Clothier :: ::

82 & 90, Lancaster Road, ENFIELD.

Money advanced on Diamonds, Jewellery, and all kinds of valuable property.

Large stock of Jewellery, Clothing, Boots, etc., at competitive prices.

TELEPHONE 384 ENFIELD.

PROGRAMME

For week commencing October 10th. 1921.

Monday, Tuesday and Wednesday—

The RETURN OF TARZAN

BY

EDGAR RICE BURROUGHS.

EPISODE IX. PATHE'S GREAT SERIAL

"THE PHANTOM FOE."

PATHÈ'S PICTORIAL.

Thursday, Friday and Saturday—

CHARLES CHAPLIN

IN

"A DOG'S LIFE."

GLADYS BROCKWELL

IN

"WHITE LIES."

EPISODE III.

"THE ROMANCE OF THE HOPE DIAMOND."

The Management Reserves the Right to Refuse Admission.

THORN'S

KNITTING WOOL, 3½d. per ounce.

Usual Price, 9½d.

20 LOVELY SHADES IN STOCK.

ENFIELD TOWN.

Telephone: ENFIELD 391.

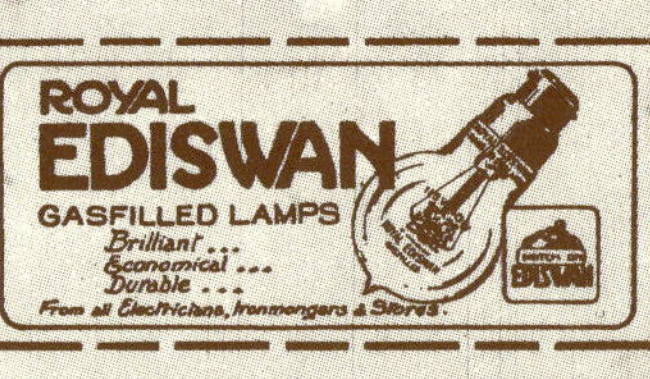

THE

RIALTO

PICTURE THEATRE.

MARKET PLACE AND

CHURCH STREET, BURLEIGH WAY.

ENFIELD TOWN.

THE HOME OF HIGH-CLASS PHOTO PLAYS

CONTINUOUS PERFORMANCE.

Monday, Wednesday, Thursday, Saturday, 3 to 10.30

Tuesday and Friday, 5.45 to 10.30

Entire Change of Programme every Monday and Thursday.

Full Orchestra. Grand Pipe Organ.

THE TEA ROOM & LOUNGE

Are open to all, whether visiting the Pictures or not, from 3 p.m. daily.

DAINTY TEAS AT POPULAR PRICES.

TELEPHONE: ENFIELD 711.

PRICES OF ADMISSION:

Balcony, Front	1/6	Entrance Church Street
" Back	1/10	
Fauteils	1/3	
Stalls	9d. & 1/-	Entrance Market Place

ALL PRICES INCLUDE ENTERTAINMENT TAX.

Children under 12 when unaccompanied by adults half price to Matinees only; when accompanied by adults half price any time, except Saturdays, when full price will be charged after 5 p.m.

No half price at Bank Holiday Performances.

PRINTING. Stanley Woodfield, Enfield. BOOKBINDING.

All enquiries and applications respecting ADVERTISEMENTS on this Programme must be addressed to STANLEY WOODFIELD, Printer and Advertisement Contractor, Windmill, Hill, Enfield. Telephone: Enfield 59.

Stanley Woodfield, T.U. Printer, Windmill Hill, Enfield.

The apparent small improvement in Dad's economic situation had not resulted in any increase in my weekly income, which was a pity because my need for funds had risen, for I could no longer worm my way into the Queen's Hall Picture Palace at half-price — it was now costing me sixpence and not threepence. Worse still was the new Picture Palace, the Rialto Cinema, which charged ninepence for the cheapest seat although it was a plush velvet one compared with one of wood at the Queens.

On a Wednesday there was an afternoon performance at the Rialto, and I envied the adults waiting at the entrance of the cinema as I wended my way reluctantly to school across the Market Place to sit in the Form Room whilst Beak rambled on about the Bible. He took us for Scripture. I couldn't imagine Mr. Oliver at the Council School doing that.

I wondered how Oliver would have dealt with two situations in which Beak found himself. One afternoon towards the end of school time as usual, the boys with watches pulled them from their waistcoat pockets to keep them in view. As soon as these boys started to get their satchels ready for departure we all did likewise. But this time the school bell did not ring. There was a chorus of "It's 4.15 Sir". Still no bell, but we heard a commotion in the corridor, and sensing that the other boys were on the move, we went out. There was a crowd of boys pushing and calling out "Come on — get a move on". I could just see Beak waving his arms at the front. Suddenly he seemed to disappear, and the boys flooded out through the exit into the Quad. As I passed I saw Beak standing out of the way, his face red and angry-looking. We heard next day that some mischievous boy had hidden the brass handbell which should have been rung as usual by Mr. Joe Lugg, the Caretaker. Beak had been trying to stop us leaving until the bell had been found — but he had been brushed aside by the boys in front who were propelled by those in the rear.

The other situation was about the bike shed. There was always plenty of shouting at the close of school each day as the boys retrieved their bikes, but one afternoon the din was so loud that it brought Beak to the scene. He couldn't get into the shed because there was a small heap of bicycles laying on their sides blocking the entrance, with boys trying to push their machines over the tangled mass. He shouted instructions but he was unheard because of the angry arguments, the clanking of metal and the ringing of bike bells within the shed. He withdrew from the scene, his gown billowing behind him, leaving two red-capped prefects to deal with the mess. But only the boys themselves, who knew all about bikes, were capable of getting out of the tangle — which I heard they did after much argument.

BOYS

KNICKER SUITS

In Rugby style, or Sports model with half-belt at back—fine appearance—hard-wearing quality. In splendidly serviceable Grey, Browns and Lovats. Lined throughout. Stout pockets. Ideal for school wear. For boys 7 to 13. Sold elsewhere, 35/- All Sizes. Post Free.

SPECIAL SALE PRICE **19/11**

Super Quality, 28/11 & 39/11

Post orders—state age, total height, shade of cloth, and if Rugby or Sports Shape required.

All Orders over £1 Post Free in U.K.

Horne BROTHERS

...E WEEKLY DISPATCH

JULY 16. 1922.

THE CAPTAIN.—Vol. XLVIII. March 1923

Youths. For Comfort, Wear a

GAMAGE SUIT

These suits are splendidly made from carefully selected tweeds in shades of medium and light Greys, Fawns, Browns, and Heathers. Skilfully cut and tailored for hard wear. Jackets cut sports shape as illustration. Knickers either the popular full shape with band at knee or breeches shape. To fit Youths from 12 to 16 years. A really splendid suit. Gamage Price... ... ... **29/6**

Patterns sent post free on request.

KNICKER HOSE

All-Wool Knicker Hose with turnover tops, in attractive Greys and Heathers, reinforced toes and heels—excellent for hard wear. Reduced from 2/6.

SALE PRICE ALL SIZES 1/9
3 pairs 5/-

Postage, 3d.; 3 pairs, 9d.
Post orders—state size of boot worn.

I was wrong about the suit, I found it comfortable. The knicker hose which came with it were of the type I wanted when older. They were knee length turn-over stockings, easier to wear than the long ones over the knees that Dad preferred.
Dad didn't like them because, he said, they were too short, exposing an inch or two of my bare legs. But their cheapness (they cost nine pence in today's money) outweighed his feeling of disapproval of my newly acquired look of partial nakedness.

In my fourteenth year I was no longer required to go out with Mum, Dad and the younger ones at weekends, except when clothing was to be bought for me. The photograph shows Mum, Dad, Fred, Ivy and Winnie on a trip to Southend on a charabanc in 1922.

CHAPTER 30

At the end of the Summer Term in which I had so much trouble with detentions, and the canings from Beak, my School Report was bad. Beak sent for me and told me he was very disappointed. For the last two terms, he said, my school work and behaviour had been unsatisfactory. He asked me why it was so. I replied "I don't know, Sir". He said I had plenty of brain, and if I did not show immediate improvement at the start of the new school year, he would know how to deal with me. When, some sixty five years later, I read in Lord Jenkins' autobiography that Beak was a sadist, I wondered if Beak liked to have, in the school, boys who merited punishment, and had parents who would not complain. Perhaps it had been unwise of me to tell Beak early in our association, in answer to a question from him, that my Father would be very angry if he knew I was caned for neglecting my homework or misbehaving, and that he could thrash me for it.

This Report showed that I was absent six times. As I was a wiry, very healthy boy all the time I was at Grammar School, I can only assume that these absences were when I feigned sore throats, stomach aches or headaches so that kind-hearted Mum let me escape school some mornings or afternoons. I cannot recall if and when I truanted — I certainly would have done if I thought I could have escaped retribution.

During those two years at the new school I can recall one Sports Day, held in the field which we shared with the Girls' County School. I remember seeing Mr. Edwin M. Eagles, performing expertly on the parallel bars, dressed in a white blouse, white satin knee breeches and white stockings. One Prize Giving was held at the Bycullah Athenaeum, when Colonel Bowles, Chairman of the School Board of Governors, presented the prizes. I didn't get one.

During the summer holiday I spoilt my school suit by badly tearing the jacket pocket and the knee of my knickers. I asked Mum if she would ask Dad to buy me another but she told me to ask him myself. When I plucked up enough courage I did so, and I got a reply to the effect that he was not going to spend a week's wages on a suit that I would ruin, and that he would look out for a cheap odd jacket and knickers. I saw myself in corduroy breeches again. It was a good job that he did not know that my clothes had been torn squeezing through the palings across the road, to scrump apples.

I told Dad that I knew he could get a suit for under one pound, 19/11d to be exact; and I ran off to find my hidden satchel. I fished out from it a piece of newspaper I had torn from the nail whilst seated in the W.C. one day, and had started to read it instead of putting it to the use for which it had been hygienically intended. I did not use it but kept it. Enthusiastically I showed the advertisement on it to Dad. (Both the advertisement and the satchel have survived). Dad said that it was weeks' old, and the suits advertised thereon were so cheap for my size, for a boy of thirteen, that they would have been sold out long ago.

Anyhow, he did send off for one, and for a pair of stockings, as thus the post was free. The parcel arrived, but with a note to the effect that those suits advertised, my size, were not available, but enclosed was one from a fresh batch, just as good, even more hard-wearing. To me it looked very juvenile, moreover the jacket really needed to be worn with an Eton collar, which I hoped I would not have to wear anymore. Dad was very satisfied, and I dared not protest. At that stage I was very anxious not to revive his interest in me, something which I had detected was waning. I wanted him to ask no awkward questions, sensing that he was getting weary of rearing children, for he had been at it for twenty years.

St. Matthew's Infants, Ponders End 1912

Ken - a wonderful friend.

Ken was christened Benjamin Kenneth Stevens. His mother died when he was very young and he was brought up by his aunt in his father's house at 45, Clarence Road, Ponders End. Ken as a child was very stubborn and self-willed, and refused to answer to the name Benjamin. He first attended the St. Matthew's C. of E. School and afterwards the Senior Boys' School in Bush Hill Park, where I first saw him across the other side of the corridor, waiting like me to be dealt with by the headteacher. I can recall how dejectedly he looked - no doubt I looked likewise. He was an unusual figure in his very expensive looking Norfolk suit, untidily worn, his collar several sizes too big for him, and his rather unfashionable long hair.

Although Ken was in a very low Form at the Grammar School, he was very intelligent, with a keen interest in photography - having his own darkroom at the age of twelve. He loved music and could play the piano and compose. He had a vivid imagination to write funny stories, and all his life he could joke about Edwin M.Eagles, alias Beak, and his cane. He hated school as I did. He was always a boy at heart. He shared a double-bed with his father until he married our youngest sister Winnie after courting her for many years. During the many, many years I was overseas we corresponded every week, and after his death I found he had kept all my letters to him. I was privileged to have him as a friend. He was shy, kind-hearted, generous and gifted.

CHAPTER 31

On the first day of school after the holidays, with my Term Report which Mum unwillingly had signed, I went back, wondering in what Form I would then be. If I had done only averagely well I should have been promoted to Form 4b. But it turned out to be Form 4c, which I knew as the laggards' class, where for the first week or two I was lonely. All the boys most probably were fee-paying, and had fallen by the wayside in their slow progression from the First Form. Perhaps this had an advantage as I found it easier to give some sort of satisfaction amongst boys not too bright and who were probably as lazy and careless as I could be. I did as well, or as badly, as most of the others. My problem was still my homework, and my unpredictable misbehaviour. Some of my old exercise books have survived, and I have extracted from a few of the pages the adverse comments on my homework by the masters.

In Form 4c I met Ken Stevens, who was eighteen months my senior, and by any standards should not have been in a low Form with me. I had come across Ken when he was in the Council School years before, in a situation in which we could not have failed to notice each other as we stood forlornly in the corridor waiting to be dealt with by the head teacher. We had not spoken and Ken disappeared from the school not long afterwards. He had been removed from there to the Grammar School because he complained that he got into so much trouble with the teachers. I learned this later. We met again when both of us waited outside Beak's Study for our turn to be called in to be punished for some misdemeanour or failing. This time we did speak, and at "Break" that morning we commiserated, for we both hated school. We walked home together that afternoon: and thus started a friendship which was to have an immeasurable influence on both our lives. It was strange that we took to each other immediately, because in many ways we were very different boys. Ken started to lend me boys' papers, making it no longer necessary for me to purloin them from unwary newsagents.

Most Saturday afternoons I was not required to go out any more on shopping trips with the family, so I would take the opportunity to do things that otherwise I would not dare do. One was to go through the greenhouses to the Nursery Office, where I would tip out the contents of the sacks containing the Company's waste office paper for the week. Low's had a very extensive and prosperous overseas business, and had lots of mail. I would tear off from the envelopes all the stamps to add to my collection. My behaviour as a boy very often surprised me because, for some inexplicable reason, I seemed to ask for trouble. If I had been caught in the Company Office Dad would have tanned the hide off me, and I am not exaggerating. He was very fussy about the behaviour of his children towards his employers.

Dad had to be strict, because the backyard, our playground, was part of the Nursery. One important glass-house was in our garden almost at our scullery door. Ivy, Fred and I were noisy, argumentative, prone to use bad language, and to throw mud and horse manure which often landed on the glass. Stones could be hurled; and it was in this regard that Fred, who recalled very little of his boyhood, told me in recent years that he did remember glass being broken, and although he did not know if he or I was guilty, it was he who got the thrashing. I also could have got it there and then if I had not sensed trouble when I saw Dad approaching. I shouted to Fred "Let's go — he's coming", and had run off into the street. Of course I eventually had had to return to the kitchen, but not until I reckoned that Dad would have had his tea and, hopefully, be in better temper. When I did however, I was greeted with "Right mate — it's your turn — now get up those stairs". I had only postponed the retribution. Fred had not known this or did not remember it.

I am unable to recall much of Fred. We were very different boys. He did not share my love of reading; my long walks about the streets, or my interest in clothes, chickens or the allotment. He hated being put into his best outfit to go on the Saturday afternoon shopping trips. He was restless, thus attired, being cooped up in the kitchen on Sundays. He never went to Church or Sunday

ENFIELD

GRAMMAR SCHOOL.

Report *for Term ending* 25 JUL 1924

Name Robinson S. L. *Form* 4b

Number in Form 21 *Average Age* 16 *Place in Form* 5

Times Absent *Times Late*

SUBJECT	PERCENTAGE MARKS	POSITION IN CLASS	REMARKS	
ENGLISH	61	6	Satisfactory work	DCE
ARITHMETIC	30	15	Weak	a
ALGEBRA	57	9	V. fair	a
DRAWING	62	9	Good	EP
FRENCH	63	2	Good	[illegible]
GEOGRAPHY	37	11	V. fair	ELm
GEOMETRY	57	6	F. Good	a
GYMNASTICS	63	10	V. fair	CHD
HISTORY	67	2	Good	afw
~~LATIN~~ or GERMAN ...	51	20	F. Good	Ima
MANUAL INSTRUCTION				
SCIENCE	40	9	F. Good	DWR
SCRIPTURE	54	7	V. fair	a
TERM MARKS	48	18	fair	a

Conduct : F. Good

General Remarks : His work & progress have been satisfactory. Chas. W. G. Livermore Form

Edwin M. Eagles. H

Notes :

(1).—All Boys are required to bring their Health Certificates with them on their return after the Holidays.

(2).—Next Term begins on 16 SEP 1924 and ends on 19 DEC 192

This Term Report for the final months at the Grammar School was the best I had had; but I was more than a year behind my scholarship contemporaries. However it seems that I was no worse than many of the fee-paying pupils, because the average age of the boys in the Form was sixteen, and I was not then sixteen.

School — he wanted to be amusing himself with Dad's tools — or in his old patched corduroys, out playing the street games at which he excelled.

As I write this I realise that I was never completely at ease with Fred being at the Council School when I was there, and very relieved he had not reached the Seniors during my first year there when I was in so much trouble, for he would have been in the hall to see me take my turn to be punished when called on to the platform after morning prayers. If my scholarship place had been taken away from me due to my misbehaviour, I would have been made to stay in the Seniors, a marked boy, and judging from my reports for the first two years at the Grammar School, I would have been in plenty of trouble, some of it for Fred to see or know about. He was so honest and ingenuous, but so quick-tempered, that I always had feared, when arguing with him at home, he would have blurted out in Dad's hearing what he knew of me. There was some small recompense in being a Grammar School boy, because Fred knew no boy in my Form — my scholarship mates having left me behind. Moreover Beak had stopped making public the names of boys who had been punished.

When some of our old school reports surfaced Fred did not want to be reminded that he also had had an uncomfortable time in the Juniors.

At school, after the previous bad year, I settled down better with Ken as a friend. He introduced me to Reg, who like himself, was eighteen months my senior, and also seemed to have lost his way up from the First Form as a fee-paying pupil. Both boys had a great sense of humour, and were mischievous. They infected me, as a result of which we got into scrapes together. These together with my inability to satisfy completely in regard to my homework, got me a number of detentions, but fortunately, seldom enough in any one week to oblige me to appear in front of Beak. During the school year, apart from a bad start, I had thought I had done reasonably well, but it seemed the masters did not think so, because at the beginning of the next and final year at the school, when I would have expected to have been moved up from Form 4c to Form 4a at the very least, it was to be Form 4b — a token move only. My earlier scholarship contemporaries had reached Form 5a.

During the final year Ken left school to start work, and Reg was taken away and sent to Clarke's Commercial College in Winchmore Hill, because his father considered he was in too much bother at the Grammar School. In the last Term I realised it was advisable to have a satisfactory Report to produce to prospective employers when I looked for a job in an office, the fate of most Secondary School boys. I therefore swotted up for the Term Examinations.

On the last afternoon of school, as I walked home with the Report, it pleased me to see that I was fifth in the Form Examinations. But by the time I got home I was depressed, for in Term Marks, which measured form-work and general behaviour, only three boys were as low or lower than me. I decided not to use the Report.

Thus ends the story of my eleven years of attendance at school. Whilst writing about them, I have come across some more of my old exercise books, and am pleasantly surprised how good my work could be when I was trying, or was interested in what I was doing.

Youngest sister Winnie (front row, first left), won a place at the Enfield County School in 1928. She was the only Robinson child to participate in school team sports. This photograph was taken on the field adjoining the County School, in the early 'Thirties.

A reduced size copy of a pencil sketch I made in 1926 of Mum and Dad sitting in the kitchen of our cottage on Low's Nursery, listening on their earphones with the aid of the crystal set to a programme broadcast on the wireless. Nothing could be heard from the B.B.C. in those days which could have caused the sightest offence to anyone!

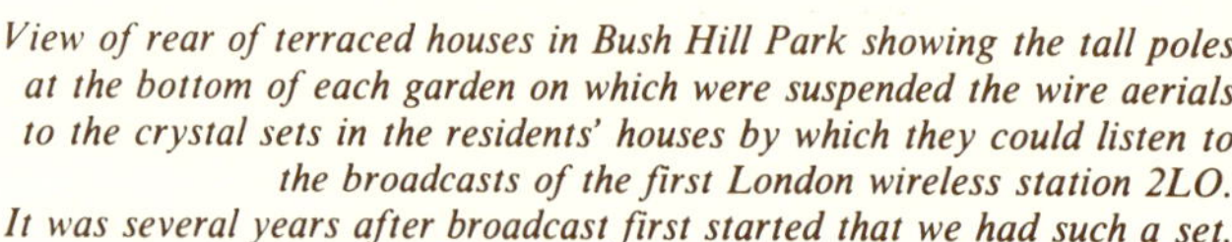

View of rear of terraced houses in Bush Hill Park showing the tall poles at the bottom of each garden on which were suspended the wire aerials to the crystal sets in the residents' houses by which they could listen to the broadcasts of the first London wireless station 2LO. It was several years after broadcast first started that we had such a set.

CHAPTER 32

As Ken had outside interests he soon got a job with a London firm taking photostats of documents, especially in the Public Record Office, and he was able to improve some faded poor prints I had of myself as a boy when I had been so keen to squeeze myself into any photograph. For me to find a job, I took my time, applying for office jobs in writing, but got no replies. Lord Jenkins says that he was in and out of work. Norman Lewis, also, who left school when I did, says in his autobiography that he had to turn his hand to anything. He bottled elixir for his faith-healing mother.

I found work as an odd job errand boy at a factory just starting to make wireless valves, at a rambling complex of smallish buildings on the banks of the River Lea in Ponders End, spending most of my time outdoors in all weathers doing errands between factories, sheds, warehouses, workshops and laboratories along the banks, often fog bound in that low-lying area with chimneys belching forth smoke. Because of the need to step over steam emitting from pipes at ground level, and trudging through mud, I spent part of my second week's wages to buy some secondhand Army Cadet breeches from a little old lady in a junk shop near Bush Hill Park Station, and these, with Dad's discarded leather leggings from under the stairs, were my protective clothing.

Brother Fred left school and started work at the same time, at the Nursery with Dad, and there was no jealousy between us, for we both had dirty outside jobs, and both were getting about the same wages, fourteen shillings (seventy new pence) per week. Nobody remarked that Fred, leaving the Council School at the age of fourteen, and I, leaving the Grammar School at the age of sixteen, were getting roughly the same wages, and in unskilled jobs. Both of us disliked stirring ourselves from our beds to brave the elements in bad weather, I on my secondhand bike, and Fred going into the cold, draughty Nursery.

We each gave Mum ten shillings a week (50 pence) out of our wages and with our first few shillings we bought two packets of cigarettes a week each at the cost of one shilling (5 pence). Almost all males smoked, many boys doing so as soon as they left school and went into long trousers. I started to smoke regularly from then onwards for thirty years, and thoroughly enjoyed doing it. So did my brother Fred. I spent 1/3d (6 new pence) for the entrance to the Pictures on Saturday evenings, and reluctantly put one shilling (5 new pence) away each week to buy clothes. I soon found a cheap supply to satisfy my needs; a pair of ex-army boots, a bargain price tweed sports jacket with leather buttons, and two pairs of army surplus long underpants, the type Dad always wore summer and winter. I got Fred two pairs too. These were the first underpants we had ever worn, and we needed them because we both had work outside. This collection cost about twenty shillings (£1), and together with my ex-army cadet breeches they kept me going until I could afford the blue serge double-breasted suit I had had my eyes on.

On Sunday mornings I would borrow Dad's walking stick, and go off hiking for as much as ten miles, before returning to our crowded, steamy kitchen where Dad had been cooking the Sunday joint in the kitchener oven.

I do not recall spending any money on food or drink, though I must sometimes have paid a penny for a mug of tea to have with hard-boiled egg sandwiches Mum made for my lunch. Food did not seem to have played a very important part of our lives — I certainly could go a long time each day without much to eat or drink. Sister Ivy seemed to have a good appetite though — she would eat anybody's left-overs. She was a strong, healthy girl, and when seeing her changing her stockings in front of the kitchen fire, I wished I had sturdy calves as she had — mine were a bit too slim. We were all very healthy in spite of our frugal diet and lack of variety. None of us had any imagination food-wise, and luxuries played no part in our lives. There were no potato crisps, roasted peanuts, ice-creams, cornflakes, baked beans or suchlike available to us — nor canned soft drinks.

My brother Fred stayed working at the Nursery for fourteen years, which was a pity, because he had talent. He had been lazy at school, though unlike me, he gave every satisfaction in his last year

NORTHAMPTON POLYTECHNIC INSTITUTE,
LONDON, E.C.1.

SESSIONAL COURSE CERTIFICATE

This is to certify that

Sydney John Robinson

attended an organised Evening Course of Study in

General Electrical Engineering (First Year)

during the Session 1925-6, satisfying the conditions as regards attendance and classwork and passing the sessional examination in each subject of the course as follows:

Magnetism and Electricity
Mathematics
Engineering Drawing

L. A. Sebastian Chairman of Governing Body.

Principal.

This certificate, one of three, survived only because it had been used as backing to a framed picture on the wall in our Cottage.

PERSONAL. 7th January, 1929.

Mr. S.J. Robinson,
Inspection Department,
New Southgate Mail.

I enclose herewith, steamer's ticket covering a second class passage in the s.s. "OROPESA", leaving Liverpool on January 17th.

Luggage labels are also enclosed in this connection.

The embarkation notice giving time of special train from Euston to Liverpool, will be forwarded later, as soon as information is received from the Shipping Line.

The amount of this passage namely £56. 0. 0. will be charged to your personal account, and you should voucher it in the regular way. You will have to purchase your own ticket at Euston for Liverpool, the cost of which should be included on your voucher.

R.A. MILES.

Actg. Head of Central Works.

Enclosures.

there. If, at the right time, he had responded as I had done to the severe discipline to which I had been subjected, he would have won a place at the Ponders End Technical Institute, and have become a brilliant engineer.

The five boys who had been at school with me at some time, and who lived close by, all got jobs without trouble, as they managed to get satisfactory reports from school. Two of them, with jobs in London offices became unemployed in the Great Depression. One then took up house decorating; another joined the Army as a private soldier.

As for me, after some time at the factory running errands, one day the foreman asked if it was so that I had been to the Grammar School. When told I had, he said I should not be wasting my time, especially as I was bright, but should take up an electrical engineering course, the coming thing. I took his advice, and enrolled at the Northampton Polytechnic Evening Classes, attending three evenings a week; and to my surprise I found that I had absorbed a lot of knowledge at school which I had been too idle to use, I managed to pass examinations.

By sheer chance one evening I did something I didn't usually do, that was to look at the Notice Board. On it was pinned a small card on which a Company invited applications from young technical students for training and work in a new technology. I applied, and got a job, which entailed a very long bike ride to and from work in all weathers. This was a hazardous journey on my very old machine, with an unreliable oil lamp.

I was eventually sent out for short periods to various parts of the country helping to install automatic telephone exchanges, meanwhile studying hard and working long hours overtime. Just after my twentieth birthday I was sent for, and asked if I would go to Santiago, to do similar work. I immediately replied "Yes". On the way home that night on my bike, I wondered where Santiago was. When looking the name up in the atlas, I found that there were several. I hoped it would be the one farthest away. So it was to turn out to be — in Chile, South America.

In order for me to obtain a passport, Dad asked Mr. Stuart Low for a reference for me. He did so, and it has survived to this day. Reading it, I wonder if, when Mr. Low wrote it, he had his tongue in his cheek for he must have learned from his nephew Mr. Cook and his great nephew Robin what troublesome boys both Fred and I had been.

To obtain a visa for Chile, I had to do something I had not done before, nor had anybody else done on my behalf since I was born in Mum's bedroom — that was to see a Doctor. It was to be Dr. Cowen, of St. Mark's Road — who charged me 2/6d (12 new pence) for the vaccination certificate.

During the time that I had been working on exchanges away from home I had been receiving a living allowance; also had been working many hours overtime, therefore I was able to save money in addition to buying some good clothes. I was thus well placed to equip myself smartly after receiving the ten pounds kit allowance for my journey. Fred gained a little from it as he was able to take over some of the clothes I did not want, including my breeches. He needed all the money he could save, as he was buying a motor bike on credit.

This photograph of brother Fred in our wintry backyard was taken on the morning of my departure for South America. Fred had come in for his mid-morning hot drink; and to say goodbye. It was the first photo taken with a secondhand vest pocket Kodak I had bought cheaply.
17th Jan. 1929

P.S. The Gramophone is playing "My inspiration is you."

POST CARD

Jan. 18. 1929

Dear Fred.
It is now 9.20pm, and we are still going strong. The sea is still fairly steady and I am still well. I can see the the lighthouses on the coast of France now although it is very dark & windy. It is jolly comfortable in the lounge. Sid.

F.G. Robinson,
Lowe Cottage.
195, Lincoln Rd.
Bush Hill Park.
Enfield.
Middlesex.
England.

A postcard written on the second evening at sea on board the P.S.N.C. vessel 'Oropesa', for it to put into the ship's mail box and to be despatched from La Rochelle Pallice, the French port, where we were due to call next morning. The British stamp is postmarked by the French Sorting Office. The cost of the stamp was 1½d., which, converted into the decimal money today, would be less than 1p. However, the purchasing power of our £ has fallen to one twenty-fourth of the value it was when I posted the postcard some sixty odd years ago.

CHAPTER 33

The month of January had been bitterly cold most days, the temperature rarely rising above freezing all day. On the morning I was to take the boat train to Liverpool, I was awoken as I usually was on a work day, by Dad banging on the banister at the foot of the stairs, and shouting up "Come on, Fred you'll be late again". I reached out my hand to the gap in the curtain, which was only a foot or so away from where I lay, and scratched on the glass. It was still covered with thick ice inside.

In the glimmer of light thrown by the little oil lamp on the mantelshelf I watched Fred for the last time bestir himself, reach for his breeches at the bottom of the bed, pull them over his socks and long underpants, slip the braces over his shoulders, and leave the bedroom, to feel his way down the dark cold staircase to the kitchen. He would there hurriedly put on his boots, leather leggings, jacket, muffler and cap, whilst he ate a chunk of bread and gulped down a mug of hot tea, before going into the Nursery in the dark. There he would labour physically long tiring hours.

Somewhat later that morning I rose from my bed in the gloomy room, removed my shirt and thick underwear and changed them for identical new garments. Pulling on my best Sunday trousers, I stumbled down the stairs into the warm, steamy kitchen, where I finished my dressing. The car to take me to Euston Station for the boat train to Liverpool was due in about an hour. My friend Ken, saddened at my departure, was going to the station with me. Brother Fred came in to say goodbye, and I seized the opportunity of taking a photograph of him in the wintry backyard.

Once on board the ship it was not long before I realised that I had moved into a world of which I had never dreamed. That night, going down to my cabin after a stroll on deck, with my stomach replete with the finest food I had ever tasted, I found the corner of my sheets neatly folded back, and my pyjamas laid out on my bunk bed. The steward asked me if I liked early morning coffee, or tea; and how hot I liked my bath water. I settled into bed, wearing pyjamas for the first time in my life, intending to study my Spanish Grammar before going to sleep; but instead my mind wandered to my family I had left behind.

I knew what Dad would most likely be doing — preparing the hurricane lamp to take out to the outside W.C. to prevent the cistern from freezing overnight — then getting the firewood and paper laid out ready to re-kindle the kitchen fire at 6.00 a.m. Mum would be taking out from the oven the brick to carry upstairs to warm the bed. Fred would be asleep in his winter underwear and shirt, and probably his stockings. Oldest sister Jessie would be last downstairs, pottering about, savouring the rare solitude in the lighted warm kitchen. Then, lighting a candle, she would pull down the chain to extinguish the gas mantle, struggle to shut the kitchen door and mount the stairs with the candle in one hand, and her bag of possessions in the other. She would join her three sisters, Kit, Ivy and Winnie in the bedroom glimly lit by a small oil lamp.

From these harsh conditions, which all my life I had accepted as the natural order of things, I had walked out. But I had not done so deliberately — for I doubt if I had intended to escape anything — in fact, when agreeing instantly to go to Santiago without a moment's hesitation or reflection, I had no idea what I might be letting myself in for. I was behaving exactly as I mostly had done all my life; which was to have disregard for the possible consequences of my actions.

I did not know that this time they would result in a transition from an austere working class life in England to one of comparative luxury at the other end of the world. I was unaware that was being laid the foundations for everything that was to follow into my old age. I was about to embark on an interesting, exciting and rewarding career, during which time I was to meet, work, live and play with people, poor and well-to-do, of many nationalities, in perfect harmony and understanding. It was an opportunity denied to most working class young men of my generation; and I made the most of it. Strangely enough, it came about because I had been an unsatisfactory boy at school, and had been obliged to accept any old job in a factory when I left.

TEL.: ENFIELD 0281.

HOURS OF CONSULTATION
9 TO 10 A.M.
6 TO 7 P.M.
EXCEPT WEDNESDAY
AND BY APPOINTMENT.

BAGSHOT HOUSE,
BUSH HILL PARK,
ENFIELD.

Sydney John Robinson has been recently vaccinated successfully.
His general health is quite good and satisfactory.
Eyes, ears, nose and throat all normal.

W P Covey

Jany 8th 1929

FROM

TELEPHONE: No. 1001, ENFIELD.

STUART LOW CO.,

TELEGRAPHIC ADDRESS: "ORCHIDS, ENFIELD."

Carnation Growers, Fruit and Rose Tree Growers, General Nurserymen,

BUSH HILL PARK, ENFIELD, Middx.

And at JARVISBROOK (CROWBOROUGH), SUSSEX.
(TEL. 20 CROWBOROUGH).

8. Jan 1929

This is to certify that I have known Sydney John Robinson since he was quite young & since had him under my constant observation, & from what I know of him I have every confidence in recommending him a thoroughly steady & trustworthy ... personal character

Widows', Orphans, and Old Age Contributory Pensions Acts. Form O.A.P. 269 (revised).

NOTICE OF AWARD OF A CONTRIBUTORY OLD AGE PENSION.

From :—
MINISTRY OF NATIONAL INSURANCE,
BLACKPOOL,
LANCS.

JAN 46

.........194 .

Pension Number (to be quoted in any further communication).	M 126 39 23 84	PERCIVAL RD ENFIELD MIDDX 0851666
Name and Address of Pensioner.		MR SYDNEY JOHN ROBINSON 195 LINCOLN RD BUSH HILL PARK ENFIELD MIDDX

SIR (or MADAM),

I have to inform you that your title to an Old Age Pension under the above-mentioned Acts at the rate of 10s. a week has been admitted.

The first payment falls due on THURSDAY, the 31-1-46 in respect of the week ending on the following WEDNESDAY and the pension will continue payable until you reach the age of 70, when it will be followed by a similar pension for life under the Old Age Pension Act, 1936, but without enquiries about means, residence or nationality.

A book of Pension Orders in your name will be sent to the Post Office named below, and **you must claim it there,** ~~at once.~~ not more than a week before the date on which payment is due to begin. You should fill up the lower portion of this form, tear it off at the perforation, **and hand it in at the Post Office when you claim the book.** The date on which the pension is payable is shown on each pension order and in general the amount will be forfeited, if not drawn within three months after that date.

Your special attention is called to the circumstances which may disqualify you from receiving payment which are shown overleaf. You must not draw the pension when you are disqualified—see the WARNING below. You should read carefully the instructions given on the inside of the cover of your pension order book.

I am, Sir (or Madam),
Your obedient Servant,

E. G. Bearn

Controller of Health Insurance and Pensions.

N.B.—When title to pension arises on a day other than THURSDAY, no payment is due until the following THURSDAY.

WARNING :

Any person who, for the purpose of obtaining or continuing a pension, either for himself or for any other person, or for the purpose of obtaining or continuing a pension for himself or for any other person at a higher rate than that appropriate to the case, knowingly makes any false statement or false representation, and any person who knowingly obtains payment of, or continues to receive, a pension which he is disqualified from receiving, or which for any reason whatsoever is not payable to him, is liable on summary conviction to imprisonment for a term not exceeding three months.

TEAR HERE.

Dad's Award of ten shillings per week Old Age Pension at the age of sixty five. This was equivalent to about nine pounds per week today.

On the third day of the voyage, after a three course breakfast, and after having been served mid-morning beef tea on deck, I went down to my cabin to remove my winter underwear and change into more suitable garments. The ice cold air of England had been replaced by balmy air of the lower latitudes — for there was a gentle warm breeze blowing in the Bay of Biscay. I searched for my French phrase book, for we were going ashore at La Rochelle Pallice and I was anxious to practise on the natives the only subject at which I had excelled in my last year at school.

I cannot close this account of my boyhood and youth without again referring to our Mum and Dad. We owe everything to them. They really cared for us children from the cradle until we were old enough to fend for ourselves. They made every sacrifice to ensure our well-being, within their limited capabilities and means, Dad working all the hours he could to provide for us. In all my boyhood years Mum was only absent from home for four weeks, during the Great War, when she went with young Ivy to help her mother who had scalded her leg. Apart from this period she was always at home when we came in from play, school or work. She and Dad never had a holiday of any sort from 1902 to 1922 and Dad never had a paid holiday in the fifty seven years he laboured. He did not drink, nor bet, nor smoke — though by 1920 when we were a bit better-off he started to smoke cheap cigarettes, eighteen years after his marriage.

Mum was kind, patient and tolerant with us all in very trying circumstances, not the least Dad's uncertain temper. She had children continually to care for under school age for nineteen years, all of whom had been born in her bedroom, without medical attention except for a visit from Nurse Carnaby, the mid-wife, who, in a bonnet and dressed entirely in dark blue could be seen daily walking round Bush Hill Park with her leather bag. Mum could have done without the many anxious moments Ivy and I gave her.

I wonder if Dad found his children a disappointment. Perhaps he did not have any great expectations for us, but when we left school we all found paid employment and were well-behaved ordinary young adults. As for me, I had been the much wanted son after the prior arrival of two daughters, and in those days a boy with older sisters would not have been expected to help in the daily household chores — I was therefore left much to my own devices. Dad should have bullied me into being more practical and helpful to him — for I could have been. It was a pity that young Fred's talent, of which I was very aware as boys together, was not observed because of his laziness. Later he became very industrious and clever, but lacked the personality to promote himself.

At the age of sixty five in 1946 Dad received a State Pension of ten shillings (50p) a week, but he could not afford to retire on it, so he stayed on at the Nursery until he was seventy. It was fortunate that I was in a position to repay Mum and Dad in a very small way by buying them a house in which they could live, because the Cottage went with the job. He received nothing from his employer after fifty years of service with him.

Then...

...and now

Eight years after Dad gave up work, and the Robinson family moved out of the Cottage, the land on which it stood, and the large area occupied by the Nursery, were sold for office and factory development, and the widening of the A10 road, as shown. Our Cottage stood to the left of the now correctly placed road sign Main Avenue, and my favourite oak tree grew where the Lincoln Road road sign is affixed to the railings of Burleigh House.

POSTSCRIPT

In this book I have ended my boyhood story at the age of twenty, when I left for South America — an immature youth in some respects — but full of self-confidence. However, when I finished the manuscript I realised that in those days adulthood was not reached until twenty one, so I decided to add a postscript intending only to tell what happened to me before I attained my majority; but as will be seen I did not stop there.

Father Neptune preparing me to be thrown into the canvas pool on board the 'SS Oropesa', on crossing the Equatorial Line for the first time. Afterwards I was given a certificate granting me 'Freedom of the Deep'. *February 1929*

A partial view of Santiago showing the lower heights of the Andes with only a little snow remaining in early summer. San Cristobal Hill, prominent, was a delightful picnic site, especially for the less energetic citizens who could use the lift to the top.

Snapped by a street photographer on the way to work Santiago 1930

Chilean boys on their way to school.

Testing the new exchange in Santiago November 1929

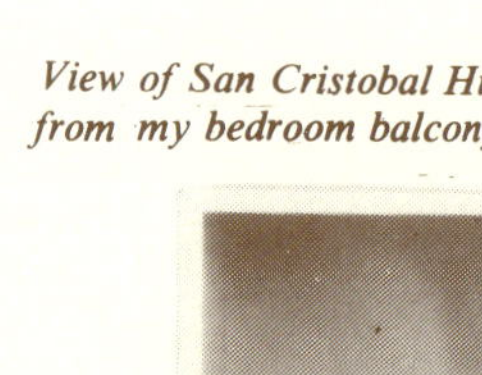

View of San Cristobal Hill from my bedroom balcony.

Aunt Lizzie and Uncle George at the Rio de Janeiro quayside before I left on the R.M.S 'Asturias' 1937

From the window of the Panagra aeroplane when flying over the Andes to Buenos Aires 1938

The sea voyage of five weeks to Valparaiso was sheer delight. We were able to go ashore at La Rochelle, Vigo and Lisbon before crossing the Atlantic where the ship rolled and plunged in the heady seas making some passengers take to their cabins because of sea sickness, but I was at ease and enjoyed it. Due to the unfavourable weather we landed in Bermuda three days behind schedule. After Havana we went through the Panama Canal to the Pacific Ocean.

Travelling down the coast afterwards was not very interesting except for our visit to Lima, Peru. In every port on this long voyage, and at times passing us on the high seas, I saw British merchant vessels, all manned, I knew, by British crews, and flying the Red Ensign. I also saw naval vessels flying the White Ensign of the British Navy. I took this for granted — we had an Empire.

I arrived in Valparaiso in the middle of summer and it was hot and sticky, but when I reached Santiago, the capital, after a two hour train journey, though still hot, the air was dry. The beautiful city nestled at the foot of the vast Andean range. At first I found the weather very uncomfortable in my English tweed suit, but shortly I became accustomed to the heat. I was pleased to find that the clothes I had bought in England were of the type worn by every Chilean urban male, so much so that those men who could afford them bought suits of English or Scottish cloth. The schoolboys wore tweed suits with American knickerbockers. The citizens were very conservative, men not removing their jackets in public, and wearing trilby hats in the streets — some schoolboys wore similar hats. Everybody was courteous and friendly, not seeming to resent so many foreigners in their midst.

For six weeks I stayed at the Cecil Hotel before moving to a boarding house. It was an easy walk to the main building of the Chile Telephone Company where the automatic telephone exchange equipment was being installed. For many months I worked long hours six days a week in order to finish the task on schedule. On the installation team were Chileans, being trained in wiring by a Greek and an Italian sent over from Buenos Aires from an associated Company. On the staff of the Company were two Germans. Our common language was Spanish which I hastened to learn, employing a tutor every late evening. I found it an easy, pleasant language, and I could understand and make myself understood within a short time. I was to use Spanish so much during the many years I lived in Chile that I can speak it today after not doing so for forty seven years.

The installation work took nearly twelve months, and at the end of it I was offered a three year contract with the Chile Telephone Company, together with my passage paid to England and three months leave. I accepted the offer. Bubbling over with energy, enthusiasm and capacity to learn and observe, I made rapid advancement, being made Chief of Exchanges for Santiago.

At the end of the contract I had another pleasant five week voyage back to England, where I stayed at our Cottage with the family. Everything had remained unchanged — I slept in the same bed as I had done as a boy — the room shared with brother Fred who was working in the Nursery. The mice still had their home under the kitchen floorboards. The little oil lamp, probably with a new wick, lighted us when we went to bed. I had chosen Christmas time to come home to England because I wanted to share my affluence with my family. In Chile it was only a one day holiday in midsummer weather — to me not Christmas at all.

I asked the Company if I could return to Chile via Brazil, and then take another boat to Buenos Aires, flying to Santiago by Panagra airplane over the Argentine Pampas and the Andes. It was agreed, so I was able to spend a fortnight with my Uncle George, Auntie Lizzie, my Dad's sister, and my cousin at their lovely house in their Orchid Nursery at Petropolis in the hills above Rio de Janeiro.

On arrival back in Santiago I was appointed General Plant Supervisor, Deputy to the Superintendent of Plant. He was an American, the finest man I was ever to know. The managerial executives were all American; conscientious, skilled, hard working, friendly, gentlemanly and courteous. I still remember with fondness the times I spent with them and I developed a soft spot for America.

The Superintendent was an expert on outside plant construction, and there was a vast pro-

The Chilean Earthquake 1939

Top left: Waiting for the plane to take me down to the affected zone.
Second down, left: The Company's tents.
Left: A crack in a road.
Above: Taking a look at another broken pole.
Below: Looking down the road to grasp the problem facing us in restoring our lines and cables.

gramme of development and replacement of overhead lines running through the length of the country of some one thousand miles. He planned to dedicate his time mostly to this work, needing frequent long absences from Santiago. I had become the expert on the running of exchanges, switchboards and telephone services in general so he was pleased to leave me to get on with it, acting for him in his absence.

At the end of my second three year contract I made another voyage home to England also at Christmas time. I spent the nights in the same bed but alone in the room because Fred had married. I called at Rio again on the way back, taking to Aunty some packets of tea, as well as a tin of Bird's Custard Powder, things she could not buy in Brazil.

One night, when my Superintendent was on leave in the U.S.A., having left me in charge of the Plant Department of eight hundred employees throughout the country, I was awakened by a severe earth tremor. I hurried down the stairs to my telephone, but could not get through to my night engineer, because every other receiver in Santiago had been lifted as well as mine — everybody wanted to talk to somebody simultaneously and our automatic exchanges were overloaded. I took the car to the Office, where I was told that all lines were short circuited south of Santiago — communications were cut off. Our construction and maintenance gangs were alerted; the Supplies Department told to get ready for maximal issue of tents, tools, wire etc., and staff were sent for. The gangs were to head south, not losing contact with the Test Desk and making temporary repairs to the lines as they went, reporting back what they had found. We soon learned that south of Santiago all the overhead lines were twisted and tangled together for a distance of about two hundred miles and it would be slow work. The Ministry of the Interior was informed that we suspected a major disaster further South. We were told that the State Telegraph lines and the Railway signalling were out of order.

Our emergency plans for dealing with the disaster were put into effect. I got a few hours sleep the next night, but no real rest was possible for five days until we knew exactly what had happened, and communications of some kind had been restored. Many people had been killed, houses demolished and parts of our telephone switchboards severely damaged. Poles were down in the towns.

The General Manager had been on a visit to the Head Office in New York; arriving back by plane on the seventh day. He called me in and asked if I could go South, reporting back as I toured the area. Next morning I went along to the Ministry of the Interior and given a written authority to proceed to the devastated zone by any means available. I then went to the airport, given a typhoid injection and vaccination, and told I could leave at once if I was willing to sit on a box in a Panagra plane carrying medical supplies. I went — heading for the devastated town of Chillan 250 miles away.

I toured the area for ten days, sleeping in a Company tent, in my clothes. An employee of the Company who was with me took some splendid photographs all of which have survived. Some of the photos show sailors from H.M.S. Exeter helping in the rescue work in Concepcion. The ship was in port at Talcahuano at the time of the earthquake.

The disaster occurred almost exactly fifty years back from the day I write this. I would have had no difficulty in remembering any incident from 1927 because I have kept a Diary since then.

In the Diary, on the day I returned to Santiago after the tour, there is an entry "Very tired and dirty, but not glad to get back". I wonder why?

The opportunities given to me in Chile to gain experience in all branches of a telephone system in many circumstances were endless, sometimes because the older managers were most willing to delegate tasks to me, especially if they required travelling up and down the long narrow strip which was Chile, extending from deserts in the north to the temperate rainy zone of the south. I journeyed on horseback, by sea, by plane, car and train. There were emergencies caused by political upheavals and revolutions — also major electric power breakdowns in the winters.

My time in Chile was not all work — in fact there seemed to have been lots of time for leisure and

Recovering telephone cables from streets where the offices and houses of subscribers had been destroyed. The cables were to be used elsewhere.

Repairing overhead lines in the Northern desert.

The Linea Aerea National aeroplane re-fuelling in the desert on the trip back from Iquiqui. 1938.

Chilean horses were sure-footed and ideal for the rough countryside.

Top: The four Yeomans' children waiting for a ride in my two seater Chrysler car. It had a dickey at the back in which three children could squeeze (or two of my mates). Neither parent worried that I was taking them about in a vehicle that had a footbrake more or less useless.
There was no M.O.T. or driving test in Chile in 1935.
Yeomans was accountant at the Department Store Gath y Chaves, a branch of Harrods - London.

Climbing mates Dave Torrance, Harold Brown, and a Swiss, Katovski, on the way up in one of our many excursions into the Andes.

With Hopkinson (Hop) on Mount Bonete in the Lake District of South Chile.

In the south of Chile amongst the lakes, virgin forests and volcanos.
In the background is the 'El Tronador' - the 'Thunderer'.

With Harold Brown and a Chilean guide, battling against the wind at about 9,000 feet 1935

Feeling chilly at 12,000 feet, sitting at the base of the Cristo Redentor statue at the frontier between Chile and Argentina 1936

A halt to plan our way up in the early summer 1935

Harold Brown and Dave Torrance exuberant at reaching the San Ramon summit on one of our Sunday climbs.

Waiting for the pilot of the L.A.N. aeroplane at Antofagasta Airport, to return to Santiago 1937

pleasure. Not long after I had arrived first in Chile I moved from the Cecil Hotel to a large house rented by a Scottish descendant who was the wife of a Scot, retired, a man who had driven railway engines supplied from Britain years ago. The lady kept lodgers, six of them including me, on full board and all services of course with a cook and a servant who lived in an outhouse — such labour was plentiful, willing and cheap. The six of us were all young men out on contract from home; full of surplus energy, physical fitness, and a sense of adventure. We made the best of a wonderful country and climate, with absolute freedom of action and free of all responsibilities and duties outside our work.

We mountaineered, we hiked along miles of deserted beaches bordering the Pacific Ocean; we rode horses, we skied in the winter, played golf and tennis. Sometimes in the evenings we played billiards or indoor bowls at the British Club. We had holidays exploring the lakes and virgin forests of Southern Chile, reached after a very long railway journey. There we once went on horseback to the foot of an extinct volcano, and, leaving our horses with our guide, we climbed up over solidified lava to the crater, to take a good look inside it.

The Andean mountains visible from Santiago were so easily accessible that one of them, the San Ramon, was a favourite weekend climb to its peak, 10,000 feet above sea level — I went up it seventeen times with climbers of various nationalities.

I was foolhardy. Galloping ahead of my companions on a mountain track, probably showing off on a horse the others disliked, my mount slipped against a rock and threw me off down a small ravine. When my mates found me I was walking about concussed and unaware of what had happened. I think they were pleased at my downfall.

I was the only one who had a car of sorts. Mine had faulty hydraulic foot brakes for which there were no spares. I drove this, depending mostly on my skill with the hand brake. After several near mishaps my mates who crowded into it cheered me on. Of course there were no driving tests nor road tests in those days. Nor any parking problems — I just left the car anywhere, in the sure knowledge that it and its contents would not be stolen.

Our adventures only brought tragedy once.

This was when a party of us were climbing in the winter. That day I did not like the prevailing conditions and said so, but not wishing to be a spoil-sport, I went. Three of us climbed ahead of the others, an Anglo-Chilean inexperienced chap and his girl friend, a keen climber. I was yards to the left of them picking my way amongst the snow covered rocks when there was a roar from above us. I shouted to the others and moved as quickly as I could further to my left hoping to shelter under a rock before the avalanche struck me. I saw my companions knocked down by a wall of snow and rocks just at the moment that I was caught. The snow, piling on top of me, began to force my neck backwards. Strangely enough I could still breathe, and it was not absolutely dark under the snow. How long I was buried I do not know, though later I was told that it was probably about twenty minutes. Whilst buried I thought it was a soppy way to die — and how upset poor old Mum would be when she got the news.

Then a miracle happened — I felt a terrific jolt, and, with the snow I moved downward, my head hitting something hard. My left arm seemed free of snow. Fear must have lent me strength and I managed to scramble out. There was absolute silence — nothing moved. Low rain or snow clouds made visibility too poor to see much. My face was bleeding. I stumbled down the slope towards the rest of the party. To my dismay my two companions in the avalanche had not returned. Up we went, and because there were several of us we found the girl. She was partly buried and either unconscious or concussed — her face was bleeding. Within a few minutes with some hot coffee from a Thermos flask, she came round. We could not find her boyfriend; and when conditions became perilous because of further movements of snow above us we had to abandon the search. Weather conditions were to become so bad that it was not until the next Saturday that we were allowed by the authorities to search again, when we found his body.

When my closest friend Harold Brown, who would have been with us if he had not been in-

The Empire Day Ball, with Ruth Bown, Santiago 1936

With Chilean maidens

Cheerful little licensed boot-blacks in the main square in Osorno, South Chile. I doubt if they went to school.

Outside the White House, A disconcerting sight for me to see whilst waiting for a berth on a ship to form part of a convoy to the U.K.
The banners were calling for no convoys nor American aid.

June 1941

disposed, saw my injured face, he said he was more convinced than ever that I was destined for a sticky end.

Not many Chileans participated in our outdoor activities, but they were a friendly, happy-go-lucky people who loved parties and dances. The Anglo-Chilean youngsters were even more keen, and celebrated both the Chilean Feast Days and the English, such as Empire Day and the King's Birthday. In fact they were more English than the English. I was invited to so many celebrations that sometimes I had to find excuses, otherwise I would have had five or six late nights every week, and my work would have suffered. The Chilean girls did teach me ballroom dancing, which I enjoyed, especially the tango.

There were many Germans and German-Chileans in the country, and I was friendly with some of them. Hans Rosenfield, an engineer who worked in the Telephone Company was a very good mate, and when he became engaged to be married to a well-to-do daughter of a German business man and a Chilean wife, I spent many enjoyable evenings playing Bridge with them. I have pleasant memories of the sincere friendships we built up over the years. Our common language was Spanish, but both Germans spoke fluent English.

When the Second World War came, our friendship continued. It was surprising how it was possible for us to have lengthy agreeable companionship without ever mentioning the War. In any case I was working with Hans, and we were in an American Company — the U.S.A. was neutral then.

Inflation in Chile was rampant, and being paid in Chilean pesos, I could not have saved much if I had been so disposed; there was also a very severe exchange control. So I borrowed through a mortgage and bought a lovely chalet, letting Hans and his newly-wed wife move into it at a small rent. But after the war had been raging about eighteen months I became unsettled and felt the need to return to England to help my country. I volunteered at the British Embassy and was told that if I paid my own passage home, I could join the ranks. As it was past the end of my current contract the Company paid my passage on a Chilean ship to New York, and made arrangements for our New York Headquarters to pay my passage across to the U.K. after I had found one. My good friend Harold Brown offered to make the necessary arrangements to sell my house to Hans Rosenfeld, who wished to buy it.

When departing Santiago, and saying my last farewells to the Company employees I had worked with harmoniously all those years, and who had become part of my life, Herr Oelerich, the German Chief Janitor of the Company, with whom I had had many a joke over the years, took my hand, and said with emotion "Mr. Robinson, God bless you, and good luck. We have been in touch with our Embassy and requested it to inform Berlin that you may become a member of the British Armed Services, and that, should you be taken prisoner, request that no harm should come to you, for you have been a good friend to many of us in Chile". At the time friend Oelerich said goodbye to me I am quite sure that he, and all Germans living in Chile, thought that we would lose the war, and that I must fall into their hands. At that time I had no more confidence in our victory than they did.

I often wondered if in the event I had been offered preferential treatment in the hands of the Germans, how I would have reacted.

I sailed from Valparaiso to New York on a small Chilean boat, the S.S. Copiapo. In New York I was told that there was no certainty when a berth could be found for me to England. I took full advantage of my enforced stay by visiting all the places within reasonable reach. Whilst in Washington I photographed people marching up and down outside the White House, carrying banners on which in large letters were "No American ships in British Convoys" — "Stay out of this British War". These didn't comfort me much at a time I was awaiting a ship which would be part of a convoy.

In New York I went to see Boris Karloff in "Arsenic and Old Lace". As I had heard he was born in Enfield and had spent his boyhood there, I wrote to him, offering to take anything back to any relatives he had in the U.K. His reply has survived, in which he states that he had nobody he knows

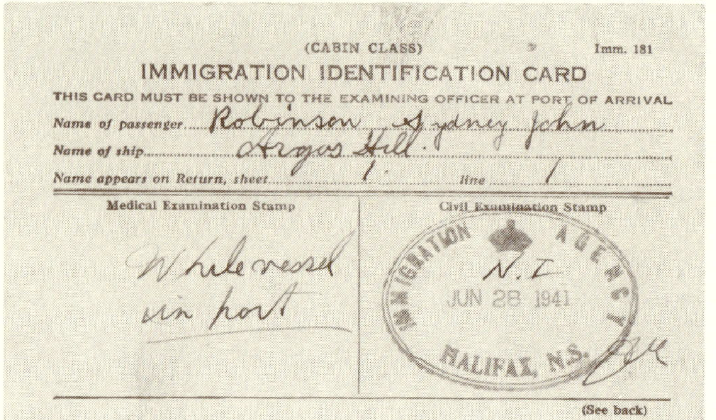
(CABIN CLASS) Imm. 181

IMMIGRATION IDENTIFICATION CARD

THIS CARD MUST BE SHOWN TO THE EXAMINING OFFICER AT PORT OF ARRIVAL

Name of passenger: Robinson Sydney John

Name of ship: Argos Hill.

Name appears on Return, sheet 1 line 1

Medical Examination Stamp	Civil Examination Stamp
While vessel in port	IMMIGRATION AGENCY N.I. JUN 28 1941 HALIFAX, N.S.

(See back)

No. 113 Course at 150 Officer Cadet Training Unit in Catterick

Little German children in a bombed Hamburg street 1946

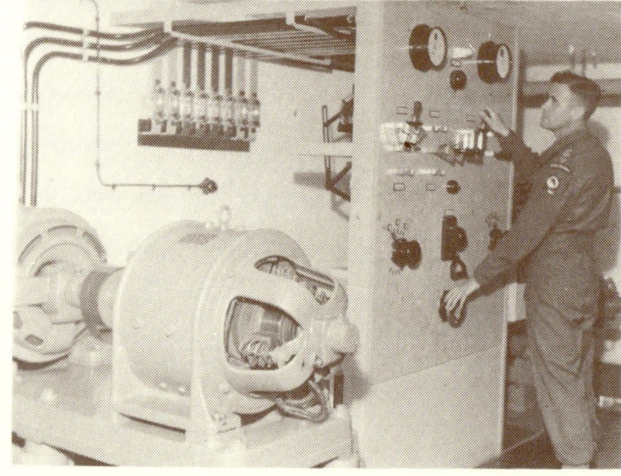
In the power room of the telephone exchange at the Headquarters of 30 Corps in Luneburg, Germany 1946.

in England.

I had a bit of bad luck in New York. Before I left Santiago I had withdrawn from my Savings Account the last of my money, and exchanged it on the Black Market for about seven hundred American dollars. It had not occurred to me to take any particular precautions because I was so used to living amongst people who were extremely trustworthy and honest. I did not therefore think of placing my money in notes in the safe-keeping of the hotel where I was staying. It was very hot indeed in New York, so I carried my jacket on my arm the day I had been walking around Macy's large store, amongst others. That evening I could not find the money — and never did. Its loss cast a bit of a shadow over me during my stay in New York.

After four weeks I was allotted a berth on the S.S. "Argos Hill", an ancient cargo vessel, loaded, I was told by a member of the crew, with ammunition. We sailed up to Halifax, Nova Scotia, where we joined a convoy for our journey across the Atlantic. I shared a cabin with a French soldier who had escaped prisoner-of-war camp, made his way to Lisbon, and worked his passage on a neutral boat to Halifax. He was returning, he hoped, to England to join De Gaulle's Forces. Unfortunately he was not good company because he was scared that we could be sunk and picked up by the Germans. There were no other passengers, so I made friends with the crew. The trip, in lousy weather via Iceland took four weeks in a convoy of eighty four merchant ships and twenty one escorting vessels; the largest convoy, I was told, to cross the Atlantic. We were not attacked, though the previous convoy had been badly mauled. My luck had held, for we had made the crossing at the height of the Battle of the Atlantic.

I joined the Army as a private, and after Infantry training, was posted to the Royal Signals. The Army maintained its reputation of putting square pegs in round holes by trying to send me for training as a morse operator. I protested that I was a telephone engineer, so was put to Line Mechanics training instead. Eventually I was set tests mentally and physically, and asked if I wished to be trained as an officer if found suitable at Pre-Octu. As I was bored, I agreed. I finally went to Officer Cadet Training at Catterick which involved me in a tough six month course, including battle camp, and assault courses.

As Second Lieutenant I was posted to the Cross Channel Communications Section in Northern France — eventually ending up at H.Q. 30 Corps in Germany, based at Luneburg; a Captain, and appointed as Technical Officer. There I was responsible for the installation of military trunk switchboards, automatic telephone exchanges and carrier terminal equipment throughout Northern Germany.

One of my favourite walks when off duty was over Luneburg Heath where Montgomery had accepted the surrender of the German Armed Forces in the West.

I could have made some money in Germany, and some chaps did. The German population was hard pressed for food and cigarettes, and would exchange willingly any of their belongings for such items. Some chaps were able to get supplies from the N.A.A.F.I. and used them to obtain gold and silver jewellery, family heirlooms and collectors' items from the needy inhabitants. I did hear that unscrupulous officers accompanied Army vehicles back across the Channel with all kinds of valuable German property.

When I was released from the Army, I worked on a farm for a while to occupy myself before I made up my mind what I should do. I decided that there was no future in Chile, with its economic problems, so I offered my services to the British subsidiary of the I.T.T. of New York, after I had found farming hard uncomfortable work, requiring skills which should have been learned very early in one's life. I am glad that I did have the opportunity to take part in farming as it had been done for centuries.

I accepted the job of going to Beirut to prepare a specification for a new automatic telephone network for the city, starting from scratch to replace the antiquated magneto switchboard system used during the French mandate which had just ended. Whilst preparing for the task, which required me to make various consultations with the factories and Company engineers, I lived at

German prisoners-of-war pulling on to the shore the repaired Cross-Channel telephone cable 1945

On Luneburg Heath where Montgomery took the surrender of the German forces in the West 1946

Damascus, Syria, 1948. These cheerful little Arab boys were always anxious, as I was at their age, to squeeze themselves into a picture. Without a doubt it was little lads like these who were moving our drums along the road and pushing them over on their sides.

The drum pushed mischievously on to its side was one of many containing cable intended to replace the unsightly wires strung along and across the Damascus streets and bazaars 1947

A luncheon given by the Syrian Government on the occasion of the inauguration of the Damascus automatic telephone exchange in November 1949. It was held in the Omayad Hotel, where I resided when in Damascus for many years.

our Cottage — our family home unchanged since my boyhood. The mice were still around the kitchen.

It had been eighteen years, almost to a day, that on a wintry January morning, at the age of twenty, I had sailed away into warm weather and comparative luxury leaving behind my Mum and Dad, brother and four sisters in the austere conditions I had shared with them. But then, they had had enough money to buy all the fuel and food they needed, and it had been obtainable.

But on this wintry January morning I was flying away, leaving them in more austere conditions than ever. The wartime restrictions were still in force: there was a shortage of fuel; food was severely rationed and in very short supply. Each person was allowed only eight ounces of sugar, one shilling's worth of meat (5 n.p.) and one ounce of bacon. Cheese, chocolate and sweets were almost impossible to buy — oranges, bananas and grapes unavailable.

The plane flew from London Airport at 7.00 a.m. landing at Marseilles for refuelling, stopping at Malta, and arriving in Cairo at midnight, where a room had been reserved for me at the Shepheards Hotel. After being served with an appetising supper of three courses I retired to a splendidly furnished bedroom. For the next two days I was taken around the sights, the Pyramids, the Sphinx and the bazaars, and had tea at the Gezira Club.

By Arab Airline Misr I flew to Beirut on the third day where I was met by our Agent, Sheikh Nagib Alamuddin, who had booked me in at the St. George Hotel positioned at the sea front. It was winter in Lebanon with a temperature something akin to the average English summer. Sheikh Nagib was a fine fellow, who spoke faultless English — he had been educated at Oxford, and was a leader of the Druze Sect. I found that most middle and upper class Lebanese were tri-lingual, at ease with Arabic, English and French, the latter resulting from Lebanon being a French mandate between the two World Wars. When I met a non-English speaking Arab I had to struggle with my rather poor French, but I managed.

I was absolutely amazed at the abundance of food on sale in all the shops and bazaars — there was no shortage of anything. On barrows in the streets there were oranges, bananas, grapes, melons and olives — without queues of people to buy them from the Arab boys.

As soon as I was settled in the office, and given a Lebanese assistant, I made enquiries about sending food parcels home to Enfield. I found a grocer who had a branch in Cyprus, and was willing to arrange for the despatch of parcels from there. I ordered hams, tinned cheese, tinned bacon, tea, sugar, almonds and chocolate to be sent to the Cottage and to my married brother and sisters. These parcels continued to be sent until rationing ceased in England several years later. No parcel was ever lost. I sent nylon stockings in registered envelopes to the ladies — again they all got to Enfield safely.

Although I had been comfortable in semi-tropical climates when younger, I found in Beruit that, as early summer started, it was extremely hot and humid. In those days there was no light-weight clothing, and as my work entailed walking every street, bazaar and alley in the city, I had to don shorts, probably for the first time in my life. Beirut was cosmopolitan, crowded and noisy night and day, with citizens sitting on the sidewalks drinking strong black Turkish coffee and smoking their water-cooled pipes — the barrow boys shouting their wares and ringing their bells. Beirut, with its freedom and abundance of alcohol and night clubs, must have seemed a paradise on earth to the Arab oil-rich men who visited it to enjoy what was prohibited in their own strict Moslem countries.

Towards the end of the Beirut job I was asked to act as co-ordinating engineer for a large contract the Company had entered into with the Syrian Government for the supply of three automatic telephone exchanges, underground cables, broadcasting stations and radio transmitting masts. My headquarters were at our Agent's office in Damascus, and I lived at the Omayad Hotel in the main square. English and Belgian engineers came from Europe and during the installation trained the Syrians. During the years I was in the Middle East Sheikh Nagib was of great assistance, and became a personal friend.

Inspecting the concrete foundations for the 600 feet radio broadcasting mast at Damascus.

The mast erected 1949.

The two Sid Robinsons - Dad at the age of 81, Sid Junior at 54

Sid's Family Robinson in 1934
All the Robinsons gathered in the backyard at Low's Cottage in March 1934 when I was home on leave from Chile.
Left to right seated: Grannie Robinson, Dad and Mum. Standing left to right: Ivy, Sid, Kit, Jess, Fred, Edie about to become a Robinson, and Winnie.

On my office staff were two Palestinian refugees; one, Fahri Abu Gazallah, was my secretary, a fine fellow. He spoke three languages, could take shorthand in all three, and could use both European and Arabic typewriters. He had two fine sons. I am glad that my time in the Middle East was when the Arabs had no animosity towards Britain and the U.S.A. I found the Arabs gifted people and capable of great things.

At the request, mostly telegraphically, of the New York Head Office, I made flights to Addis Ababa, Jeddah, Teheran, Ankara, Jerusalem, Cairo and Amman, when queries or difficulties arose in connection with the Company's contracts. There was no international telephone service at that time.

To cool off, I would sometimes drive down to Beirut and bathe in the Mediterranean, from the private beach in the St. George Hotel. I did not take a great deal of exercise in Syria, except for horse riding, and a walk out to the fringes of Damascus on a Friday, the day in the Arab World which was the equivalent of our Sabbath.

When I retired I vowed I would never go abroad again, nor would I stay in another hotel. I have stuck to this, for since then I have slept in no other bed than my own except for a few days on two occasions when in hospital for minor operations.

During my early retirement I fulfilled one of two ambitions I had as a boy. One was to rear chickens from day-olds to full growth and then send them to market. I did this successfully for some years, until my desire to expend so much physical energy waned. I was then determined to fulfil the other boyhood ambition, and that was to have lots of books of which I felt I had been deprived as a boy, especially childrens' books.

When I started to build up my collection it seemed that most other people weren't interested in what I wanted, the late Victorian and Edwardian books, so I was able to get them. I found that the childrens' books, which had been loved, had been very much read, so that some needed repair. I therefore attended for two years a course of bookbinding and repairs.

For years now books have been my main hobby. Life without them would be dull indeed. My sister Ivy enjoys the same books and is able to share my hobby.

In Ever Loving Memory

of

KATE ROBINSON

Who passed away November 17th, 1928

AGED 44 YEARS

Interred at Enfield Chase Cemetery in Grave No.

In Affectionate and Loving Memory of

ANN ROBINSON

who passed away October 18th, 1941

AGED 86 YEARS

Interred at Enfield (Lavender Hill) Cemetery,
Private Grave No. 1231. C.Gen.

In loving memory

OF

GERTRUDE CHARLOTTE ROBINSON

WHO PASSED AWAY

Wednesday, 17th March, 1954

AGED 75 YEARS

A light is from our household gone,
A voice we loved is stilled;
A place is vacant at our hearth,
Which never can be filled

Interred at Lavender Hill Cemetery
Grave No. 7247 Plot C. Con.

In Loving Memory

OF

EMILY ANTHONY,

Who Died May 27th, 1928,

AGED 80 YEARS.

Interred at Enfield Cemetery.

In Loving Memory

OF

SYDNEY JOHN ROBINSON

WHO PASSED AWAY

Monday, 14th May, 1962

AGED 81 YEARS

"Life's Race Well Run"

Interred at Lavender Hill Cemetery

Grave No. 7247 Plot C Con.

In Loving Memory of

FRANCIS ALLEN ANTHONY,

Who died February 7th, 1919,

Aged 48 Years.

Interred at Great Northern Cemetery, New Southgate,
Section R., No. 1669.

CHASE SIDE
Timber Yard
Chapel
Old Gravel Pit
Allotment Gardens
The Rectory
Fish Ponds
Enfield Court
ENFIELD
Portcullis Lodge
Football Ground
G.N.R. ENFIELD BR. EXTENSION
CHASE GREEN
Band Stand
Hockey Gd.
School
Grave Yard
Vicarage
Grammar School
Church
Bury Farm
Electricity Works
(N. Met. Electric Power Supply Co.)
Enfield Town Station
Station
Free Library
CHURCH STREET
THE TOWN
PALACE GARDENS
Engine Shed
Queen's Hall
Allotment Gardens
Bathing Pond
Aviary
TOWN PARK
QUEEN'S ROAD
SEAFORD ROAD
Moat
Recreation Ground
Cricket Ground
Pavilion
Gravel Pits
Allotment Gardens
Gravel Pit
Riverside
Lodge
Golf Course
Old Park
Camp
Old Gravel Pit
Lodge
Club House
Stones
Old Clock House
Boat Ho.
Pavilion
Tennis Ground
Nursery
Church
Allotment Gardens
St. Mark's Institute
BUSH HILL PARK
Old Gravel Pit
Bush Hill
Lodge
Stone
Bushhill Tower
Metropolitan Water Board
Stone
St. Stephen's Church
Parish Hall
Nursery
QUEEN ANNE'S GARDENS
Station
Gravel Pit
Sand Pit
Nursery
Hallwick
(Cripples' Home &c)
Sluice House
Aqueduct
Hall
ENFIELD BRANCH
G.E.R.
Bush Hill Park